Exposé of the Esoteric

With a healthy dose of humor and skepticism, Lars B. Lindholm examines the most influential people and organizations comprising the Western Esoteric tradition, with special emphasis on the 19th-century order of the Golden Dawn and its 20th-century descendants.

Many magical endeavors and societies are of obscure and hidden origin, which can make it difficult for students of occult techniques to discover the roots of their chosen creeds. *Pilgrims of the Night* will illuminate the dark corners, and place events and ideas into a historical context that will deepen the reader's perspective. If you are a student of the occult, discover how your greatest predecessors rose to incredible levels of attainment, despite their follies and eccentricities … understand the legacy you are carrying forward, so you are able to draw upon the strength and successes of your forerunners, while avoiding their mistakes.

In addition to providing a historical survey of and essay on Western magic, Mr. Lindholm also deals with some basic questions, such as: What is the definition of magic? How does magic actually work? You will be sure to find his observations on these topics and others provocative and entertaining. If you are at all interested in viewing our Western magical tradition in a holistic sense, *Pilgrims of the Night* is the book you need to gain a deeper understanding.

On the cover:

Depicted on the front cover are Heinrich Cornelius Agrippa (upper left), John Dee (center), H. P. Lovecraft* (to the right of Dee), Aleister Crowley (lower left), and Cagliostro (lower right).

*Photo by R. H. Barlow, used by permission of Arkham House.

About the Author

Lars Lindholm was born in 1945 at Limhamn, Sweden. At the age of three months, he left the country with his parents to live abroad. After dropping out of college in the late 60s, he studied art, intending to become a painter. He took up the study of astrology at the same time, and in 1973, he and his Norwegian wife settled in Malmö, Sweden, as astrologers, making horoscopes, giving Tarot readings, and teaching at the local adult night-school circuit. He has spent much of his spare time at the university libraries at Lund and Uppsala studying medieval magic and history. Otherwise, he writes for Scandinavian magazines and recently for the British occult magazine, *Prediction*.

To Write to the Author

If you wish to contact the author or would like more information about this book, please write to the author in care of Llewellyn Worldwide and we will forward your request. Both the author and publisher appreciate hearing from you and learning of your enjoyment of this book and how it has helped you. Llewellyn Worldwide cannot guarantee that every letter written to the author can be answered, but all will be forwarded. Please write to:

Lars Lindholm
c/o Llewellyn Worldwide
P.O. Box 64383-474, St. Paul, MN 55164-0383, U.S.A.

Please enclose an international reply postal coupon for reply.

Free Catalog from Llewellyn

For more than 90 years Llewellyn has brought its readers knowledge in the fields of metaphysics and human potential. Learn about the newest books in spiritual guidance, natural healing, astrology, occult philosophy and more. Enjoy book reviews, new age articles, a calendar of events, plus current advertised products and services. To get your free copy of the *New Worlds of Mind & Spirit*, send your name and address to:

New Worlds of Mind & Spirit
P.O. Box 64383-474, St. Paul, MN 55164-0383, U.S.A.

Llewellyn's Western Magic Historical Series

PILGRIMS OF THE NIGHT

Pathfinders of the Magical Way

by Lars B. Lindholm

1993
Llewellyn Publications
St. Paul, Minnesota 55164-0383, U.S.A.

FIRST EDITION

Cover design by Christopher Wells

Library of Congress Cataloging in Publication Data
Lindholm, Lars B., 1945–
    Pilgrims of the night : pathfinders of the magical way / by Lars B. Lindholm
        p. cm. — (Llewellyn's western magic historical series)
    ISBN 0-87542-474-0 (soft) : $12.00 ($16.00 Can.)
    1. Magic—History.   I. Title.   II. Series: Llewellyn's western magic historical series
BF1589.L55   1993
133.4'3'09—dc20   93-36883
                                                               CIP

Llewellyn Publications
A Division of Llewellyn Worldwide, Ltd.
P.O. Box 64383, St. Paul, MN 55164-0383

Llewellyn's Western Magic Historical Series

Weird shadows flicker over the figure of the Cro-Magnon shaman as he dances around the primitive campfire clad in deerskin and antlers. Sumerian magi study the sky and wonder. Greek nobles sacrifice sheep in attempts to speak with the wise who are no longer living, while their philosophers formulate ideas of mysticism that will dominate Western thought for two thousand years. In the Renaissance, an alchemist works his spiritual advancement through chemical analogs; a magus studies navigation and mechanics along with angelic communication; a member of the old religion, still called "witch" and thought to be evil by the established church, tends her healing herbs. Later, secret fraternities plot the overthrow of oppressive monarchies and succeed in the French and American revolutions. Men and women band together in societies to practice magic or study unknown philosophies. The Age of Aquarius dawns as attention is focused on the deeper realities.

In an unbroken stream from that primordial campfire to the modern magical awakening, a deeper reality continues to assert itself. Historians have tended to ignore magic and the occult as unworthy of serious study, yet how much of world history has been molded by the beliefs and practices of shamans wise men, magi, astrologers, witches, alchemists, and adepts? From its roots in tribal practices, through the stargazing of the Chaldeans and the esoteric mathematics of Pythagoras, the mysteries of the I Ching, and the secrets of yogis and tantrists, magic became one of the noblest of the arts and sciences. Occult thought and philosophy were one and the same. The mystic ideas of the Greek philosophers, mixed with the qabala and other secret traditions, fed the Renaissance revival and led directly to modern scientific thought as well as New Age occultism. Only within the last two centuries has science become the religion of rationalism and sought vainly to divorce itself from its roots—roots that continually appear in new guises such as quantum physics and cosmology.

Llewellyn's Western Magic Historical Series will attempt to trace the myriad pathways that began with shamans and seers before recorded history and that lead in branching but continuous trails to the occult revival of the last decade of our own century. The roots and the realities will not go unrecorded nor be forgotten.

The opinions expressed in this book
are not necessarily those of the publisher.

Dedication

To **Eva Peanberg** for her encouragement above and beyond the call of duty after a hard day with the "I is" Group, and to **Bo Olsson,** proprietor of the now defunct Rainbow Bookshop, for graciously permitting me to regard his premises and stock as my private research library.

Contents

Prehistoric Magic

Writing a history of Western magic presents problems of a more than negligible magnitude. First of all, there is the problem of defining the subject. This can be very difficult: the word "magic" is not really a word. It is a label. The problem is to define its content.

The word "magic" in itself signifies nothing. It's just an umbrella under which such various phenomena as witchcraft, conjuring, and arts and sciences—to mention but a few—seek shelter. To define magic in this context, however, presents problems of yet another kind.

Magic can be defined very loosely; for instance:

> *Magic is anything religious whatever that is declared by religion not to be so.*

Or it can be defined very exactly:

> *Magic is the art or science of making changes in accordance with the will.*

Neither of these definitions, however, is very illuminating. The first definition fails because it would make the history of Western magic equivalent to the general history of the West, merely skipping the paragraphs dealing with religion. The second definition is inadequate because, even though it is certainly more exact and subtle at first glance, it is a fallacy. To accept this definition would entail the same consequences as the first definition, except that all the religious paragraphs would be included as well. All religious accomplishments would be magic, too, but they would be referred to as miracles.

In essence, a miracle is a magical act performed or a manifestation experienced within the framework of an organized religion.

This book emphasizes activities and phenomena that are not accepted by what may be loosely described as organized religion, although it has not been possible to separate the two altogether—especially in the era before Christianity when it was more fashionable to call a spade a spade.

Let us begin with a brief outline of the history of magic proper before its subdivision into Eastern and Western magic.

Anthropologists never seem to tire of explaining that the prehistoric paintings of the Altamira and Lascaux caves were part of the Cro-Magnon or early *Homo sapiens* inheritance, part of their hunting magic. The idea is that the hunters, through meditation, contemplation and identification with the spirits of the animals depicted on the walls of the caves, tried to invoke magical forces that would enable them to succeed in the hunt.

This explanation sounds all right, and it may very well be true, but it is a matter of tradition rather than fact. Quite a different interpretation may be put upon those paintings.

Science tells us that the Cro-Magnon people, because of having a different position of the jawbone or some other physical peculiarity, would probably have been incapable of speaking an articulated language as we know it. Therefore, even though in fact he* had a bigger brain than we do, our ancestor would not have been able to communicate with his fellows to the extent that we do. Accordingly, he had to find another way.

---

*No sexism is intended. In the English language, the word "man," like the German *Mensch* and the Greek *anthropos,* is often used in a generic sense to mean "human," both male and female. Consequently, masculine pronouns are used in indefinite cases where the person involved could be of either sex. In seeking to avoid the perceived sexual bias of this linguistic fact of life, people have resorted to painful awkwardness (he/she, himself/herself, etc.) and unpronounceable orthographic atrocities such as sHe, etc. I refuse to try the reader's patience with such silliness.

I deplore the necessity of such steps, and I must say that it doesn't bode well for the future of man- and womankind to be so fixated about things that have been taken for granted for centuries by people with common sense. It's the worst setback to communication since the Tower of Babel affair and may almost be considered a sequel to it.

When books on magic show an example of a cave painting, it is almost invariably "the sorcerer"—a shaman dressed in a deer skin, complete with antlers. However, we prefer to show this example, from Lascaux, of an early spell failure. Evidently the magician on the left, armed only with a wand in the form of a bird on a stick, was completely unable to stop the charging bison at the right. (Actually, this explanation is facetious, while also being typical. No one has any real idea as to what this scene is supposed to represent.)

In other words, the paintings on the walls could have been made for pedagogical and educational purposes. If, 20,000 years from today, the remainders of our civilization are examined by the Frazers and Campbells of the future, and no coherent history is available, it is my solemn belief that a look at the pictures of any book of our era will drive them to the inevitable conclusion that 20th-century man worked primitive magic. Why else would be bother with pictures of things that were readily available?

Cannibalism is another cultural phenomenon that has long suffered from the same kind of pet theory at the hands of the experts. The theory is another magical explanation, and it goes something like this: If a warrior eats his fallen enemy, he believes that he will be imbued with the prowess and power of his adversary. But what is really the point of eating a fallen enemy? The mere fact that you are capable of doing so clearly demonstrates that you are a better man than he was. What's enviable about a stupid sod that gets himself killed in combat?

Our ancestors probably ate people because they were hungry and because people are the easiest prey in cultures where animal husbandry is nonexistent.

I'm not saying that these prehistoric peoples didn't perform magic. All I'm saying is that we just can't prove it. It's a matter of conjecture and thus belongs to tradition rather than fact.

Tradition also has it that, at some time, in Tibet or somewhere in the Himalayas, the school of magic separated into two different varieties. The one that remained in the surrounding geographical area became known as the Eastern school of magic, and the one that went West, as it were, became the branch that we are going to examine further.

Tradition differs as to how this came about. The first actual historical facts of any substance in the matter are derived from Egyptian pyramid walls. These are the texts upon which are based *The Egyptian Book of the Dead*, which, together with the rather more recent Leyden Papyrus, is probably the best known magical text of ancient Egypt.

The Book of the Dead is a ceremonial guided meditation which, if correctly approached, will enable you to perform advanced astral projection. The Leyden Papyrus is actually a very early grimoire. It contains all the goods to be found in its numberless successors. Of course, it's a different pantheon altogether, but the means and ends are essentially the same as, for instance, *The Sword of Moses* or *Clavicula Salomonis* (perhaps better known under its English name, *The Key of Solomon*).

The Book of the Dead is what one may call "official magic" as practiced by the priests in a legal capacity, whereas the Leyden Papyrus contains magic of an obviously more secular variety: anything from the loftiest and most pure to the crassest and most debased gratification of the sensual and sexual instincts—a feature far from uncommon where magic is concerned.

This dichotomy, which was thus already evident in the days of the ancient Egyptians, still exists and has exerted its influence to this day. It has been described as a manifestation of the dualism between mind and spirit, body and soul. It is also expressed as black and white magic and as high and low magic. These two pairs are by no means identical, although they sometimes overlap.

It may be convenient to deal with this fundamental aspect of magic here:

> *The distinction between black and white magic is an arbitrary matter of convention that differs from one day to the next and that is in practice virtually nonexistent.*

Black magic, then, is a loosely defined term used throughout all times to denounce opponents and adversaries who are more successful than you are. Black magic describes the things that this adversary achieves outside the "rules"; i.e., the fields where you are capable.

Countless crimes have been committed in pursuit of this philosophic beacon, and many pathetic moths have burned their wings in the flickering candleflame of truth. Man's regrettable lack of any sense of proportion has never been able to secure him a harmonious life. History is full of fools who absolutely had to go and die on the barricades for what they thought was the truth.

I do not mean that one should not stand up for his ideals. Of course he should. That's one of the most invigorating things about life—but, as with everything else, it should never be carried to extremes.

It has almost become an axiom that the only way to propagate a novel idea—that is, an unpopular point of view—is by blood. The excellence of a new concept is measured by the number of martyrs it claims.

The prime example is that of Galileo Galilei—who was not even a magician. He was a scientist. This just goes to prove that fanaticism is not limited to people who have no logical or rational capabilities.

For what it's worth, it's a fair assumption that the sun is at the center of the solar system. Galilei made his point with the publication of *Siderius Nuncius* in 1610, and the fact that he supported Copernicus and Kepler should have been sufficient. However, due to a morbid urge to get the last word, he spent the rest of his life under house arrest. Under the circumstances, that penalty must be considered mild. Others weren't so lucky. For instance, Giordano Bruno, who *was* a sort of magician, was burned at the stake.

Personally, I doubt if any cause is worth that kind of endorsement. It's a common belief that a cause is forwarded a hundredfold with every martyrdom that it can claim, but my personal experience is that, the harder you try to put across an unpopular message, the harder will be the opposition that you encounter.

All that's really needed is to release your message with a modicum of diplomacy and cosmic force and rely on the astral grapevine. In this way, the message may travel a bit slower, but it will meet with much less opposition and with fewer obstacles in its way. That's a sign of superior magic, and it doesn't really take any longer. Of course, it's not nearly as melodramatic as a good heretic fire, but great magic is not necessarily self-sacrificial. It can be, but only if no other alternative presents itself in the situation.

This concept illustrates another fallacy concerning magic. There seems to be a notion to the effect that a great magician must be a great man; i.e., a saintlike person. This is not necessarily so. A magician is very much like an artist—and a lot of artists may be geniuses where their art is concerned, but some of them can't even turn a kettle on.

Ancient Magic

While we're discussing prehistoric times, one tradition has it that magic was introduced on this planet by extraterrestrials whose successors settled in Mu, Lemuria, and Atlantis. After the final disaster when Atlantis and/or Lemuria sank into the sea (both did, in the opinion of the majority of scholars on the subject), the survivors trekked across what is now East Asia and the Gobi Desert and settled down somewhere in Tibet or the Himalayas. They were the "Aryan race," and from this base they spread their superior esoteric knowledge.

This is a very brief and general description of a myth which has been mainly derived from H. P. Blavatsky's *Secret Doctrine,* which I hereby recommend to readers who may be interested in these obscure histories.

I think it only fair to point out that this theory by no means represents Blavatsky exclusively. Many pet theories of various occult writers can be interpreted something like this. Of course, we have not a shred of factual evidence for these theories. On the other hand, it can't be denied that lots of esoteric cosmogonies heavily depend upon and adhere more or less to these legends and myths.

All these events are, of course, supposed to have happened thousands of years before the Egyptians; i.e., in a period conveniently lacking in historical facts. It can therefore be justifiably claimed that anything is possible, which, of course, is true in a sense. In addition to this, latecomers on the occult cosmogony scene such as Erich von Daniken (and indeed, many others) have speculated about the origin of these alleged extraterrestrials. Did they come from Venus, or Mars? Apparently it makes a difference

Such theorizing is by no means confined to prehistoric subjects. Countless pseudo-scientists have "revealed" and "proved" the secret of the pyramids. For example, did you know that the height of the

Great Pyramid multiplied by its base length, divided by the number of rocks that went into its construction, and raised to the power of Pharaoh's age will be equal to the year in which it was built? Arguments of this kind are carried to their illogical conclusions in a multitude of books, essays, and articles in various esoteric magazines, which show no signs of becoming saturated with them.

Also, Stonehenge has proved a fruitful source of insane speculation. In the 17th century, John Aubrey wrote about the druids and Stonehenge, and, since then, the "Noble Old Archdruid" has annually presided over the Vernal Equinox ceremony among the rocks.

If we adhere strictly to historical chronology, we find that about 600-500 BC, or perhaps even earlier, Egyptian magic and religion spread to the Greek colonies in Asia Minor, and then, via merchants and soldiers, it made its way to Athens and mingled with the domestic creeds.

The Greek mystery schools absorbed the new impulses, and soon most of them were without doubt able to trace their origins back to the remote past—just like a lot of contemporary orders and lodges.

The Eleusinian, Delphic, and Orphic mysteries all contained some Egyptian influence. The Isis cult is held to have been worked unadulterated and uninhibited in most of the world that was then civilized.

Egypt was not the only inspiration for the Greek magicians. From Persia came the teachings of Zoroaster, as did the Mithras cult. The actual word "magic" is of Persian origin.

Perhaps even greater influence came from Chaldea. The people there had made vast progress in the field of astrology. In Egypt, astrology had been equivalent to Pharaoh's horoscope. The Pharaoh was Egypt. Everything that befell the Egyptians was to be seen in the birth chart of the ruler. There's nothing inconsistent about this. Pharaoh was supreme leader. He disposed of his people 100 per cent as he saw fit. His slightest whim could have far-reaching consequences for even the humblest and most anonymous of his subjects. Otherwise, the astrological and astronomical sciences were mainly employed in forecasting the flooding of the Nile.

Chaldean or Babylonian astrology, however, introduced a novel concept; i.e., the individual birth chart—a very early example of manifested practical individualism. These teachings were readily taken over by the Greeks.

Egyptian Zodiac from Temple at Denderah. Unfortunately for those who would like to believe that this is evidence for the existence of the traditional Zodiac in ancient Egypt, it was created in Roman times.

John Cole, *Treatise on the Circular Zodiac of Tentyra, in Egypt*, London, 1824

Ancient Greek science worked in perfect symbiosis with religion. It tried to explain and not, as is mainly the case today, to explain away. To the ancient Greek, there was no dichotomy between the scientific and the religious mystery schools. Science was simply a religion. Pythagoras, Plato, and Aristotle are the prime examples of the high priests of the new elite.

These men had only one leg in the "ivory tower" and the other firmly planted in local politics, with the consequence that these lofty principles were consistently tried out in at least the theories of government, if not in practice.

In those days, it was not uncommon that politicians knew about things. If a man excelled in a subject, common sense prevailed in his equals (the only people who were allowed to vote), and it was thought that a scholar who mastered a subject was the best suited to make decisions concerning areas in which some knowledge of it was not amiss. Unfortunately, the modern democracies seem to have dispensed with this admirable principle.

One of the most important Greek contributions to the Western tradition of magic is "numerology"—not that numerology as such is a Greek invention. Even inside the Western tradition, it doesn't stand unchallenged. One of the most fundamental principles of the Jewish Qabalah is called *gematria.* It's a very complex and ancient variety, but the "Gematria Pythagorea" goes far beyond the other's more philosophical outlook.

I'm sure that I don't need to elaborate on all the achievements of Pythagoras and his followers. They tried to express the universe in whole numbers, because at that time it was universally acknowledged that it had been created or had evolved that way.

Unlike the Jews, the Greeks had no doctrinal prejudices. Since they were a practical people, the doubtful honor of causing a model of the universe to crash fell to them. Several strange mathematical phenomena were encountered which could not be accounted for. The ratio between the circumference and the diameter of a circle, for example, or the square roots of certain numbers such as 2, 3, 5, and so on, could not, alas, be expressed in whole numbers, and Kronecker* was yet to come. Greek numerology thus suffered a severe blow, but it was never totally subdued. It joined the ranks of the Jewish and other obscure esoteric varieties in the philosophical abyss whence it once originated.

It is still the most popular version today, however, and its popularity is increasing. We do not feel that, because a concept cannot be expressed in whole numbers, it is automatically invalid. It has long since been discovered that mathematics is merely an approximation of nature, a model of the universe or God or whatever, not the thing itself. Of course, an approximation, while not being exact, will in many cases be close enough for a lot of purposes.

---

*Leopold Kronecker (1823–1891) insisted that God made the whole numbers, but everything else is an invention of man.

Until the system crashed, more mathematical formulae expressing natural laws were discovered than ever before. Sometime after the crash, the whole cosmogony was taken over by the Romans, who were in the ascendant.

With the decline and fall of the Roman Empire, the magical tradition degenerated from a counsel solemnly consulted in time of great national crisis (e.g., before going to war or before the election of a new ruler) to a transient transaction performed at the slightest ripple on the cosmic ocean. Eventually it became so bad that, as a Roman writer expressed it, the fine ladies of Rome couldn't go to the "Jane" without first casting a horoscope.

Of course, this didn't exactly promote the concept of high magic, although it certainly did low magic a lot of good. There has never in history existed a niche without some enterprising rascal to exploit it to the limit. Countless swindlers and charlatans popped up all over the Roman Empire, like mushrooms through the floor of a crypt, and sold their (often lethal) potions to gullible fools.

One of the reasons for the survival of magic is the fact that it was not alone in suffering from this degeneration. Everything was debased: administration, economics, general politics, and even religion. The rulers raised themselves and their pet cats and dogs and favorite horses to the level of divinity.

Naturally, the archetypal gods were inevitably overwhelmed by the vast number of colleagues with whom they were suddenly confronted. Of course, reformers and magicians and obscure sects had to move underground, a fact that the rising Christian church would not hesitate to exploit to the limit.

The Emperor Constantine sees the light.

Mackey's History of Freemasonry, 1898

Dark Age Magic

The Age of Christianity can be reckoned from about the time of the ecumenical Council of Nicea in 325. The Roman Empire had been degenerating, declining, and falling for some time, but from the catacombic underground now burst forth the new Christian faith and doctrine.

Constantine, who presided over the Nicean summit, was baptized on his deathbed—an event that lent an air of prominence to an otherwise fairly run-of-the-mill phenomenon, the up-and-coming Christian Church. Ever since the crucifixion of Jesus, the teachings of the Apostles had been gaining proselytes all over the Empire, and in spite of persecution and killings, the number of adherents kept increasing.

It was the age of the great migrations (the Huns, the Westphalians, the Vandals, etc.), and in the breaking down of the old order, the strong and spectacular magic of the Christians caught the eye of many bewildered and rootless people. The time was ripe for a strong leader, and such a one was Constantine.

In 395, the Roman Empire was divided in two: the Eastern Roman Empire based in Constantinople and the Western Roman Empire based in Rome. But in 455, Rome was raped by the Vandals, and that constituted the end of it.

In the vacuum that followed, Christianity gained momentum. In 496, in Reims, Clovis and 3,000 of his vassals were baptized, which meant that the Bishop of Rome (i.e., the Pope) could rely on the support of the Franks. This was an enormous leap forward, the beginning of the Christian avalanche.

In the East, under the Emperor Justinian, was established the Roman civil rights, *Corpus Juris Civilis*, upon which rests the whole law of the West.

In 529, Benedict of Nursia founded the Benedictine monastic

order at Monte Cassino, and in the same year the Academy at Athens was closed. Thus an end was put to the teachings of the ancient masters, and in 596 Pope Gregory I sent missionaries to England and Ireland.

One of the reasons for the quick progress of the Church was of course its superior magic. The representatives of the Pope could be awesome in all their splendor, and they manufactured the most spectacular miracles—all, of course, in the name of God.

Just how much of it was due to magic and how much to conjuring, science, or the placebo effect is hard to ascertain, if not impossible, but the impact that Christianity made on the heathen world was somewhat similar to the impact that Islam made on Christianity some centuries later.

In the year 622, Muhammad marched to Medina with his followers, and when he died 10 years later, he had set a revolution afloat—one of the greatest in history, and with some of the most far-reaching consequences.

In a few hunded years, Islam spread militantly all over the Middle East, North Africa, and even Southern Europe, where it constituted a threat to the Christian Church until it was defeated by the Franks at Poitiers in 732.

From Spain, Islamic culture spread to areas north of the Pyrenees. It was indeed an exotic culture. The Arabs had obviously been more open to the ancient wisdom than had the Christians. The classicial Greek, Zoroastrian, Chaldean, Jewish, and even Indian masterpieces were translated into Arabic, and from the age of Charlemagne (800 AD), the cultural exchange increased enormously. Europeans learned for the first time about the works and thoughts of their ancestors. In addition, the Arabs themselves had made great progress in the fields of astronomy, astrology, mathematics, and alchemy. From our point of view, perhaps the latter, along with the noble art of astrology, is the most important.

In alchemy, the Arabs were practical people. They made many genuine chemical discoveries in their attempt to find the "Philosopher's Stone." In astrology, they introduced the concept of house division; i.e., the division of the zodiac into 12 segments symbolizing the mundane reflection of the zodiacal signs. The "Part of Fortune" and other so-called Arabic parts originated here.

Even if the invention of the "houses" actually is attributed to

Ptolemy c. 100 AD, they were not introduced to European scholars until this time. Ptolemy's was not the only system, but it was the first. Although it was out of fashion for many centuries, it has now once again gained momentum. After World War II, it had a revival in English-speaking countries, mainly due to its simplicity and seniority.*

But perhaps the most important contribution to the Western magical tradition in those years was the Qabalah.

The Qabalah was introduced by the Jews, who had settled under Muslim rule in Spain and Southern France, where they developed centers of learning in places such as Cordoba, Toledo, Salamanca, Toulouse, Albi, Montpellier, and Leon. From Leon came one of the two most famous works dealing with the Qabalah: the *Zohar*, which has been attributed to Moses de Leon about 1250 AD, not as an original work, but rather a compilation of several bits of oral tradition finally set on paper.

The other important Qabalistic work is the *Sepher Yetzirah*, which dates back to approximately 500-800 AD, but it was not written down until after the *Zohar*. These documents are commentaries on the book of Genesis, and as such they are complementary to the Old Testament and the Talmud.

Not until the 17th century were parts of the *Zohar* translated into Latin by Christian Knorr von Rosenroth under the title *Kabbala Denudata*. It is on this work that Samuel Liddell MacGregor Mathers based his masterly translation, *The Kabbalah Unveiled*. This work preceded the foundation of the Hermetic Order of the Golden Dawn, which must be considered Mathers' pièce de résistance.

Europe was different in those early days. The national states as we know them today were yet to come. These were days of dissolution and upheavel. In the great migrations, people moved from place to place, marauding as they went, until they finally settled down somewhere or another.

Not until Charlemagne (800 AD) do we see the beginning of a structure, although that structure was still nothing even remotely resembling the Europe of today. In short, it was the beginning of

---

*For sorting out the intricacies of house division, the reader is referred to *Casting the Horoscope* by Alan Leo (Inner Traditions, 1979) and *The Elements of House Division* by Ralph William Holden (Fowler, 1977).

the age of feudalism, which developed into the age of chivalry.

In those days, there were no attachments to the land in terms of "patriotism." The principle of serfdom efficiently saw to that. In fact, most of the serfs and minor peasants whose livelihood depended on agriculture actually hated it. In most cases, only the "Word of God," as provided by the Church and backed up by the armed henchmen of the local squire, kept the "rabble" in its place.

As always, the bottom layers of society suffered the most, in war as in peace. In war, they had their land ravished, their wives and daughters raped, their sons killed, their fields and houses burned down, and their supplies stolen or requisitioned (if the reader is able to distinguish between the two). In times of peace, on the other hand, they had their land ravished, their wives and daughters raped, and their supplies stolen or requisitioned. They had to harvest for the squire before they could harvest their own part. Sometimes they just had time to get his harvest in before the bad weather came, and when their own crops rotted in the fields, they either died of starvation or got even more deeply indebted to the squire than before.

It should be obvious that this kind of social and political system failed to promote any feelings of patriotism. In fact, there was a law in force during the whole of this age decreeing that whoever managed to escape his squire and get into a town or a city and remain there working and paying his taxes for a year and a day became a free man. It is very doubtful whether the landowners subscribed to or endorsed this practice, but the fact is that it worked. As the Middle Ages progressed, it was promoted from common practice to common law. This was possible because of the tension between the authorities; i.e., in the relationship between Church and state, land and town, priest, squire, or merchant. They all had their axes to grind.

This state of affairs gave the magical practitioners somewhat better conditions to work under beginning around 1000 AD. As the opposition to Church and state grew, it became possible for the magician to take advantage of the situation. If he was persecuted or excommunicated by the Church, he was likely to find a protector within the opposition. A magician was always welcome by the gentry. He was generally a learned man, a gentleman, and a scholar. In many cases, he was a fugitive monk from one of the orders, and the

orders were respected for their high ideals and compassionate practices—sometimes even more so than Rome itself.

A squire would always welcome such men. They had many
uses. They took care of the sick. They tutored the squire's children.
They helped develop and cultivate the land. The monasteries were
far advanced in agriculture because they were self-governing entities with no greedy landlords to rob them of their means. Furthermore, they were not compelled to depend on agriculture. They had
other sources of income, such as donations, legacies, inheritances,
and tithes. That gave them freedom to experiment, and great
things happened in a creative environment like that and had a
tremendously beneficial impact upon the whole age. Of course,
learned people from such an environment could not be turned
away. The squire's guest may have been excommunicated by the
Holy Father in Rome for practicing the Arts, but what difference
did that make? It was a more than public secret that the Pope himself dabbled in the occult. Most of the gentry in those days never
had ample funds, and many of them never gave up on the dream
of reorganizing the finances of their estates with a few loads of
scrap iron in the alchemical crucible.

The squire himself would not suffer from patriotic sentiments
any more than would his serf. To him, it was a matter of convenience and allegiance—in short, politics. A ruler sat on his land for
the power, glory, and cash that it entailed. If he could gain more by
accepting the vassalship of another ruler, he wouldn't be likely to let
any sloppy sentiment get in his way. He would gladly stab his feu-
dal lord and master in the back if he could do so without losing face.

Many filthy political deals have been enacted under the guise
of "keeping the world free for Christianity" or some similar worthy cause. Count of Aix one day, Duke of Champagne the next—
what's the difference, except the increased money and power? All
this reached its first peak in 1077 at Canossa.

Two years before, Pope Gregory VII had interfered in the
attempt of the German ruler Henry IV to control the appointment
of bishops and abbots. Henry was a young man who had recently
succeeded his father as king. He was hot tempered and arrogant
and determined not to let anybody interfere with what he considered to be his private affairs. When he received a message from the
Pope to the effect that he should abstain from matters concerning

Church investiture. he told the pontiff what he could do with it.

Henry gathered the support of the local bishops and suggested that Gregory had better retire. Gregory replied by excommunicating him. This provided Henry's brave and loyal vassals with an excuse to eliminate him. They sent word to Gregory that they were willing to support him and invited him to visit them in order to elect Henry's successor. Gregory accepted and began his journey north. Henry realized that he was in hot water and decided to eat humble pie. He arrived on foot at Canossa where Gregory had retired, and after having waited barefooted in the snow for three days, he accomplished his desire: Gregory nullified the excommunication.

This might look like an unadulterated victory for the Church, but it was not so. The German vassals refused to take Henry back. It was therefore evident that they had only acted in accordance with Gregory's ban because it suited their current policy.

On the other hand, Henry gathered some new vassals together and, in 1084, occupied Rome, kicked Gregory out, and installed a "new" Pope who paid Henry back in kind by crowning him emperor. It was all to no avail, however. The original vassals never accepted Henry again, and he died in exiled obscurity.

Nor did the Church recover from this Pyrrhic victory. Gregory was so shocked that he died a few weeks later. That was rather unfortunate, as he was one of the few ardent idealists and true Christians that history can claim. His demise paved the way for the crass materialism and vile decadence that culminated in the Borgia Popes and the Reformation. However, nobody but the prophets and seers knew that at the time.

Like the worm hidden in the fruit, this harbinger of agnosticism permeated the whole time to come in the most inconspicuous of disguises, that of education—an aspect that we shall go into more deeply in the next chapter.

Medieval Magic

Until now I have kept myself to generalities, with a few names thrown in for good measure. It's not because the people before 1000 AD were in any way less interesting than those who succeeded them, but simply because we don't know enough about them to associate them definitely with the various techniques and works ascribed to them, let alone any attempt at gathering biographical material. Most of the references to the classical masters and their names on various works, or second-hand information about them, was mostly written several centuries after their deaths by people who gracefully dispensed with the habit of leaving clues to their sources. Sometimes in cases where a bibliography is present, the works quoted are inaccessible because no copies are known to exist anymore.

Conditions improve tremendously at the approach of the "High Middle Ages" (i.e., 1200–1500) because of the increase in the number of surviving records. Several reasons for this can be found, one of which was the change in the "balance of power."

Feudalism was beginning to creak. With the introduction of the monetary system, the towns and cities grew more and more independent of the land. Wealth was measured in more abstract attributes; e.g., potentials and possibilities. The merchants became the new elite, and with currencies of somewhat more indestructible materials than vegetables and chickens, the concept of hoarding became more agreeable. Gold and silver coins could be accumulated without any danger of rotting. In addition to that when, later on, "letters of credit" hit the world of finance, many people preferred those to holding land, which, indeed, looks clumsy by comparison, and as long as I.O.U.s are cashed in, who can tell the difference?

With the emergence of the new estate (the merchants), habits changed. It became imperative that a tradesman could read and write. Only that way could he make money; i.e., draw up contracts, write invoices, calculate prices, and generally swindle his fellow man. Besides, these people wanted to educate their sons in the fashion of the gentry and the clergy.

This created a demand for concentrated education on a scale never experienced before.

Professional teachers settled in various places where the demands of their skills were greatest. A good teacher would draw a lot of students, sometimes too many for one, and that might attract other teachers. The places where good teachers congregated survived, while less good places disappeared. The surviving units became the first universities.

These universities spread during the 12th and 13th centuries all over Europe, and such an accumulation of creativity and knowledge led, of course, to experiment for experiment's sake.

In the beginning, the Church's attitude was one of benevolent patronizing, but as the political implications of the new teachings and discoveries became obvious, and as they kept coming faster and faster, the religious leaders realized that they had to lay their principles on the line again. In order not to face a situation like Canossa once more, they assigned Thomas Aquinas to assemble a revised doctrine, so broadly defined that it could be accepted by anyone (of importance).

This was a shrewd move, but, alas, to no avail. The thirst for knowledge that had been aroused was quenchless. It was not altogether unlike the opening of the lid of Pandora's box. When first opened, it was impossible to close it again.*

Thomas's final work, *Summa Theologica*, was the masterpiece of

---

*This has continued to the present day: the eternal struggle of the spirit of adventure versus the bounds of ethics, a battle that ethics will always lose because of its elusive nature. The modern example is the question of genetic engineering. Should man be allowed to manipulate the creation of God? Some say he should, whatever the consequences. If he was not meant to, he would not be able to. He was not able to before now. That means that this is the auspicious moment. To forbid him would be equivalent to having forbidden the fishes to go on land after they had developed lungs. Every generation must accept the responsibility of carrying out any measures needed, or they will be subdued and become extinct.

scholastic philosophy. It almost put the lid on again, or so it seemed for a while, and he eventually wangled a sainthood on the strength of it.

Let us now look at some of the great names and exponents of the magical arts from the "High Middle Ages" and onwards. A more or less chronological list of names, persons, and organizations, all of whom are in some way connected with the subject of this book, is given in appendix A. The list is long but by no means exhaustive, and we are not going to study every item in detail, but we will pluck here and there and see what emerges. The actual purpose of the list is to furnish the reader with some material for his own edification and further studies, if he so desires.

I have arbitrarily drawn the line between the Middle Ages and the Renaissance at the year 1400. Of course, this is a matter of convenience with no relation to history. In my opinion, Roger Bacon was a Renaissance magus *avant la lettre,* but the first "real" Renaissance magician within the meaning of the act was Johann Trithemius, or possibly his teacher Johann Reuchlin—but let's begin at the beginning.

Roger Bacon was a Franciscan friar born—in all probability—somewhere in England. Most modern scholars put his birth at approximately 1215. However, in *The Magus* (1801), Francis Barrett claims that Bacon was a fellow at "Brazen-Nose" College at Oxford in the year 1226 and "his cell is shewn at Oxford to this day."

Several things speak against this; e.g., Brasenose College officially dates back no earlier than June 1, 1509, when William Smyth, Bishop of Lincoln, laid the foundation stone on the site where it's located today. Another objection is that, if modern scholars are

---

Perhaps it will be necessary one day to alter the human biology by genetic engineering to render man more resistant to environmental poisons on the increase, and remove the threat of total extinction. Another case is terrorism. Either we crush and subdue the terrorists, or there'll be a new order, and whichever prevails must be the best solution to our global problems. This may sound cruel, but it's only the law of karma compensating for man's inability to prevent himself from destroying our planet, and, of course, all other considerations are, at the most, modifying and regulating factors of a secondary nature, and should be regarded as such. Others are more fatalistically inclined and believe that God's wonderful work is perfect the way it is and shouldn't be tampered with.

right about his birth, then Bacon would have been a fellow of his college at the age of 11. Although unlikely, this is not altogether impossible. There is ample evidence of people having been bishops and generals at the age of 14 or 15—but only by name. Some guardian would carry out the actual duties until the boy himself came of age. But then again—a fellow of a college by proxy? Not very likely, even allowing for Bacon to have been a child prodigy. If, on the other hand, he actually was a fellow of a college in 1226, I would be obliged to set his birth to about as early as 1190.

Another problem is, which college? The first colleges that we know of at Oxford are University (1249), Balliol (1263), and Merton (1265). (The years in parentheses are the years of foundation or, if before that, the year of its first appearance in any written source.)

It is known that these first colleges were active before their official connection with any building or charter, and that there has been a holy school at Oxford since the ninth century. It's even conceivable that Bacon was a student and later a fellow at one of them, but certainly not of the modern Brasenose. I have never heard of any Brasenose College operating in the Oxford area from approximately 1200 to 1509 with no premises of their own. The only alternative is that an ancient hall or college of the same name was active until approximately 1240, then lay dormant for several centuries and then revived. Or simply a new college was founded, by coincidence bearing the same name—another not very likely possibility.

Although there are certain doubts about his alma mater and his academic status, there are fewer doubts about his actual person. It is well established by now that he rose and was favored under Pope Clement IV (1265–1268), but after his death Bacon was charged with heresy and imprisoned.

A Greek version of *Clavicula Salomonis* in the British Museum has been dated to the 12th or 13th century, and Roger Bacon knew of books which described in detail rituals of intercourse with demons and demoniacal sacrifices, ascribed to Solomon. A *Livre de Solomon* with instructions concerning the evo- and invocation of demons was burned around 1350 by order of Innocent VI.

Knowledge of such books as these contributed to Bacon's arrest. After glancing through works such as *Specula Mathematic & Perspectiva, Speculum Alchymia, De Mirabili Potestate Artis & Natura, Epistolæ, Cum Notis, Of the Secret Works of Nature*, etc., it's clearly discernible that the good Roger Bacon had other strings to his bow than the invention of gunpowder (for which he has been known by generations of schoolchildren).

As opposed to the scholastics, Bacon favored personal experience over logical proof. In some ways, he was somewhat of a Galileo long before Galileo himself. In public, however, he was forced to place belief higher than knowledge in order not to loose his head.

No one can doubt his religious convictions. The problem was only that he didn't see any opposition between belief and knowledge. Unfortunately, the Church did.

Roger Bacon's greatest contribution to Western magic is not his treatises concerning the personal experience *per se*, but his wonderful individualism in his approach to living. He displayed his theses and propositions with the freshness that characterizes personal knowledge and conviction and a charming disregard for any authority no matter how awesome.

When he contradicted, he didn't mince words, but made it perfectly clear that the other fellow's opinion was sheer rubbish— sometimes in an arrogant way, but just as often by suggesting that the reader investigate the controversial issue himself.

Even today, with our superior technology, his works are wonderfully lucid, and his approach impeccably modern. Some of his results may be in need of correction due to better conditions and a wider range of knowledge based on centuries of accumulated experimental results, but these instances are far fewer than one would expect. Any student of spiritual advancement will greatly benefit from reading Roger Bacon. He would constantly be reminded that he has no responsibility toward anything but the truth, himself, and his god, whatever that might be.

So, the modern magician is encouraged to explore and investigate for himself, and himself only, in order to excel.

Apart from that, he left an impact upon such magic disciplines as judicial (horary) astrology, alchemy, and the magical philosophy.

That Bacon had great contemporaries cannot be denied. Albertus Magnus and his pupil Thomas Aquinas must be mentioned for the impact they had on their times, especially the latter. Be it known that they both practiced the arts and contributed to, first and foremost, alchemy, as did the rest of the medieval magicians listed in the appendix. But the greatest of them all, so atypical of the time in which he lived, was in my opinion Roger Bacon. He can be compared to Leonardo da Vinci, who was so far ahead of the Renaissance that he is almost never referred to in connection with that epoch alone. Among scholars there is a tendency to set him apart from the mere times he lived in and consider him a universal genius, atypical of any period. While this attitude generally leaves a lot to be desired, it is hard to see how it can be avoided in certain cases. I wholeheartedly agree that Roger Bacon and Leonardo are two of the most significant. There's no other way if one wishes to obtain a full perspective of these people.

Who were Bacon's teachers? No one, it seems. Of course, he read all the classics of the day. A lot of his work consisted, it would seem, of verifying the ancient masters, Aristotle in particular. But not without a purpose.—among other things, it was for the sake of building a point of departure for his flights of fancy. His experiments and theses concern phenomena of such diverse natures as gunpowder, glass lenses for improving failing eyesight, and the telescopic effect of two lenses on a distant object. He also had some theories concerning the living spirit of all things. All in all, he was an experimental soul with no preference for one thing over another and with ideas derived from nowhere in particular.

The works of Bacon that we know of probably don't represent his total knowledge. He must have held back a lot of things. In those days magic—that is, "high magic"—was termed "natural philosophy." By the nature of things, the natural philosophers had to be cautious about what they said and did, because the line between natural philosophy and black magic was negligible and, what was worse, it moved constantly. The philosophy of today was the heresy of tomorrow, and to add insult to injury the laws of heresy were retroactive.

More typical of the medieval magicians were the two already mentioned, Albertus Magnus and Thomas Aquinas, of whom the first was the master and the latter the pupil.

Albertus Magnus was born 1193 at Lauingen. His parents were wealthy and gave him the best teachers that money could buy, but he showed no particular aptitude for the life of the scholar. As a matter of fact, he was about to leave the cloister in which he studied

Albertus Magnus. In English, his name means "Big Al."

The Occult Review, March 1911

when, suddenly, the inexplicable and miraculous change occurred. We don't know exactly what happened, but according to legend he had a vision of the Holy Virgin, who asked him in what subject he wished to excel, divinity or philosophy. He chose the latter and his wish was granted. However, the Virgin was angry with Albertus for not having chosen the former subject and informed him that, as punishment for this ungodly attitude, he would return to his original state of (blessed?) ignorance in his old age.

This unlikely story probably originated shortly after Albertus' death. It does account for the facts, but as the good maestro lived till the ripe old age of 87 it is just as likely that we are dealing with a straightforward case of senile dementia or the consequence of some kind of stroke, because it is supposed to have happened three years before his death in 1280.

However, sometime after his vision, he was inducted into the Order of Dominicans, and he showed such promise in his studies that the order granted him substantial dispensations from the rules; e.g., he was allowed to keep his worldly fortune, which made him financially independent, in order to pursue his studies. This was no less than an unheard of revolution in a time when no man of the Church was supposed to own money himself. This being the age of true "communism," all the Church's wealth was God's wealth, to be administered by the high dignitaries. That's true at least in theory, and I suppose that in practice every expense was for the glory of Heaven. Every penny spent by the popes and bishops on whores, assassinations, luxuries, bribery, corruption, and so forth was basically for the purpose of promoting God's kingdom on earth.

In 1245 Albertus left Cologne for Paris where he taught at the Sorbonne. The year before he had received his most famous pupil, Thomas Aquinas, who must also be reckoned as one of the great medievals.

Aquinas' contribution to the magic of the West is indicative of a compiling rather than an innovating nature. He wrote treatises on alchemy, and you don't have to go far to find examples. In his magnum opus, *Summa Theologica*, he argues the case of "hermetic" versus "ordinary" gold and arrives at the conclusion that one is as good as the other. More detailed is the *Aurora Consurgens*, which deals with alchemy on the strict personal level. He died in 1274 while his master was still going strong.

Back to Albertus. There's another story going around concerning him: From Paris, he returned to Cologne. Recent investigations, which have been conducted into local records in the Cologne area where the incident took place, show that many people who experienced the said "miracle" have left consistent and correlating accounts of it. We are talking about sober citizens who depended upon honesty in their daily lives. Thus it is indeed hard to see the reason for such elaborate accounts if the people involved were not convinced personally that what they related was the truth.

Albertus had retired to a place near Cologne. He wished to found an abbey, and for that purpose he wanted to acquire a piece of land belonging to William, Duke of Holland. The duke refused to sell, and Albertus had to employ unorthodox methods, which he did. When the duke went to Cologne, he was invited to dinner by the master. He graciously accepted the invitation and arrived at the scholar's home with his court. It was in the middle of winter, and the chill was so heavy that the Rhine was frozen. Therefore the duke and his followers were surprised to see that Albertus had set the tables in the garden. He was about to leave, but Albertus suggested that he should join him at the table. After some hesitation the duke did so. As he sat down, the sky turned clear, the sun began to shine warmly, and the north wind, which had been blowing in gusts, suddenly ceased. After a while the snow began to melt, and there were even those who said that flowers burst forth from the ground and the trees started to bud. The duke was so impressed with this display of wonder that he agreed to sell the land that Albertus coveted. On a word from the maestro, at the end of the meal, the sky again turned gray, the snow began to fall, and the chill destroyed the prematurely budding flowers.

Whether Master Albertus used mass hypnosis or some other kind of legerdemain is impossible to ascertain. Several persons in the duke's company, citizens of Cologne, and peasants from Albertus' estate, related this story coherently and separately, so it is hard not to accept their *bona fides*.

In 1259 he became bishop of Rattisbon (Regensburg), but he was soon compelled to resign on account of his inability to deal with administrative and representative matters and go back to lecturing. He continued to do this until, just like the prophecy had said, one day, some say in the middle of a lecture, he had some kind of stroke and lost his faculties. Three years later, in 1280, he died. Apart from this, and the fact that he was a very small man physically, nothing much is known about him. He was later canonized. Thomas Aquinas was also, as already mentioned.

Of the rest of the medievals I will mention only Peter de Abano, not because he was bigger or better than his contemporaries, but because we meet him again in the writings of Agrippa— or rather in a controversial work generally ascribed to him under the title of *Agrippa's Fourth Book of Occult Philosophy*.

Renaissance Magic

From the Renaissance (1400–1600) we will consider two magicians in detail: Agrippa and Dee.

The reason for this choice is not obvious. It's for their contributions to modern magic. In Dee's case, it's all right. No question. He was unique, and his contribution is in every way original. On the other hand, some readers may justly claim that Agrippa's teacher and teacher's teacher were greater adepts than he, and that he was a bit vulgar in his ways. I suppose that is correct. Both Johann Reuchlin and Johann Trithemius were greater magicians. Agrippa's works derive from theirs to such an extent that a more accurate term for them would be a *compilation*. The first book of his *Three Books of Occult Philosophy* reads like a Readers Digest condensed version of Pliny's *Natural History*. So why not go to the sources? Because Agrippa turned all previous occultism into the first real modern philosophical system of magic, and thus collected not only Reuchlin and Trithemius but also the ancients and the medievals, the lot. So, by dealing with Agrippa, we also deal with his predecessors.

Heinrich Cornelius Agrippa von Nettesheim was born at Cologne* September 14, 1486, into a noble family of Belgian descent. He served the Emperor Maximilian, first as a secretary and later, for seven years, as a soldier in the emperor's Italian army.

He was knighted for bravery in the field, but soon tired of soldiering and turned his attention toward an academic career, in which he quickly excelled. A regular "jack-of-all-trades."

He was a contemporary of the legendary Dr. Faustus, and I dare

---

*A city well known in magical circles for harboring, at some time or another, people such as Albertus Magnus, the Cosmopolite, and many others.

say that Christopher Marlowe and Johann Wolfgang von Goethe both drew heavily on the character of Agrippa when they created their hero. The original Faustus was a rather inferior magus. He was born at Knittingen, Württemberg, in 1480, Agrippa's senior by six years, and he died at Staufen in the Black Forest in 1540. He had a dubious reputation. Even Martin Luther called him a bad hat. He was a swindler and confidence trickster who infested towns, cities, and markets with home-brewed patent medicines, remedies, and miraculous cures, working on the assumption that it's easier to find a new public than to produce something that can be sold more than once. At times he worked as a teacher, reportedly having sleazy affairs with his students, but he never seems to have kept a job very long—one thing that he had in common with Agrippa. No wonder that, when the poets later expounded their ideas, they borrowed from the latter; from his philosophy as well as his personal characteristics.

Why pick Faustus in the first place? One might wonder. For a very good reason. Faustus was already a household word signifying black magic when Marlowe was looking for a hero, whereas Agrippa was known only among the cognoscenti or, at least, the educated. Since 1587, the ripping tales of Dr. Johann Faustus had been published by Johann Spies of Frankfurt am Main, and the lurid and edifying story of how the ungodly and learned doctor "made a pact with the Evil One and thus sold his everlasting Soul to eternal perdition in his vain arrogance" was known to every man, woman, child, and dog. It was promoted by the professional storytellers ("Don't miss next week's gripping episode of this grand drama of sex and sadism!"), so when Marlowe was looking for a plot to make the bestseller list, the title and the name of the hero were self-evident. But as Marlowe was one of the greatest artists of his day, or any other for that matter, he couldn't help borrowing from Agrippa to put the subject matter up where it belonged. On the astral level, so to speak.

Back to Agrippa. He soon absorbed the learning of his day, and became a doctor of "laws and physic." He was a pupil of the great Trithemius, who "wrote upon the nature, ministry, and offices of intelligences and spirits."

Agrippa was a bit like Roger Bacon and Galileo in temper. Always this fatal urge to get the final word. In this way he lost a lot of positions and goodwill, and what was worse, he aroused the

Agrippa—the last word?

J. Scheible, *Das Kloster*, Stuttgart, 1846

attention and suspicion of the Church. His writings didn't go down awfully well with the papal court.

By 1507 he had spent some time in France and the following year he went to Spain, where he settled as a lecturer for a while until 1509.

He lectured on Johann Reuchlin, and gained a mixed reputation. He was popular with the students, but, alas, not with the local monks, after a public debate with their leader, the Cordelier Catilinet, from whom Agrippa plucked all the feathers of learning before the eyes of the spectators, to their mutual detriment. The Cordelier's because it displayed his regrettable lack of erudition, and Agrippa's because he yet again had to leave a good position in a hurry, at night, with the Church's condescending glances and a lot of unpaid bills in his wake.

He then tried to suck up to Margaret of Austria with a treatise on *The Excellence of Women*, but the long arm of petty revenge pulled the carpet of opportunism from under his feet, and the publication was prevented.

The next time we hear of him. he's in England writing on *St. Paul's Epistles*. Then off to Cologne giving lectures again, and again off. This time to Italy to fight in Maximilian's army again until he was called to Pisa by Cardinal de Sainte Croix. With his views he would, no doubt, have been termed persona absolutely non grata with the papal authorities had he joined the Council Assembly there as he had been offered, but he had already moved on to Pavia and Turin, where again he lectured on divinity. While in Pavia he lectured on Hermes Trismegistos as well. This was during 1515.

Three years later, by intervention of his friends, he was appointed "Advocate Syndic and Orator" to the Lord of Metz, but he had to leave in 1519 or 20. The monks were after him again for having protected and defended a woman accused of being a witch. The woman was acquitted and her tormentors were fined, for which they blamed Agrippa.

In 1520 he went back to Cologne, where his wife died the following year, after which he again felt compelled to leave. This time he tried Geneva without much success. The year 1523 found him working as a doctor in Friburg, and in another year he had moved to Lyons in the hope of getting a pension from the mother of Francis I. But, as usual, something got in the way. The daughter had asked him to search the planets for indications of the fate of

France. He gave her an impolite answer and told her she had better take an interest in her soul rather than meddle in things that were none of her business anyway. In addition to that, he perversely went and predicted success to the party opposing the one that paid him. This was no wise policy, and he again found himself without employment.

After this he tried Antwerp. This was in July 1528. He had married again and had four children, one by his first wife and three by his new wife. Again he had trouble, this time with the Duke of Vendôme. But the following year he received a kind invitation from the King of England. Even an Italian marquis and Margaret of Austria, who ruled the Netherlands, invited him. This last offer he accepted, and he was appointed historiographer to the emperor.

In 1530 he published *The Vanity of the Sciences*, which set the whole establishment against him, but it was not until the following year with *De Occulta Philosophia* that the lid of Pandora's box blew off. He was imprisoned at Brussels but, thanks to support from the Cardinals Campegius and de la Mark, a pope's legate, and the Bishop of Liége, he was soon released—but, alas, with no chance of a pension.

After this he went back to Cologne to pay a visit to the archbishop to whom *De Occulta Philosophia* had been dedicated. By now he was having trouble again with his creditors. His salary had been withdrawn, and the Inquisition had stopped the printing of his book just as he was working on a second and enlarged edition. But even this was overcome with the aid of his protectors and, in 1535, when the publishing was over, he left for Bonn, whence he soon went on to Lyons once more.

In France he was arrested again and charged with insulting the mother of Francis I. He was released by the intervention of some protector and went to Grenoble, where he died the same year.

All possible stories of his magical exploits were told after his death; e.g., how he had paid his inn debts with stones and pieces of horn that were bewitched so that the innkeepers took them for real currency. Another story about the master relates how, in Louvain, in his absence, a boarder went into his room and raised the devil, whereupon he died on the spot. Agrippa then came home and found the body lying on his floor while demons and spirits were dancing a *valse macabre* on top of the house. He thereby commanded one of them to enter the dead body and then sent it away. It obligingly left, only to drop down in the middle of the market-place, to the consternation of the good citizens.

These kinds of stories are told about all magicians of any repute. This is only to be expected. It's very hard to say what lies behind them, or if anything at all, but one mystery remains in this case.

About 40 years after his death, a *Fourth Book of Occult Philosophy* was published under Agrippa's name, containing treatises by Georg Pictorius Villinganus (c. 1500–1569), Gerard Cremonensis (1114–1487), Agrippa himself, and especially the famous *Heptameron* or *Magical Elements* by the medieval magus Peter d'Abano.

Where the book came from is a mystery to this day. Most likely it was compiled and published by Johann Wierus, who was an apprentice of the master. He might have obtained the papers from Agrippa with orders not to publish until after his death, in view of the troubles he had had with his previous work—although Agrippa hadn't published *De Occulta Philosophia* until 1531; i.e., four years before his death. It had, however, circulated in manuscript a long time before that. It is known, from letters, that his teacher Trithemius had read it and found it very good before April 8, 1510. He never intended to publish, but in the end so many pirated and misconstrued copies were circulating that he decided to publish in order not to be associated with ideas that were not his, let alone ideas which he could not or would not endorse.

Agrippa's importance lies in his knowledge of those occult phenomena that were not analyzed and investigated until this century. He mentions telekinesis, transmission of thoughts (telepathy), trance, hypnosis, and other sides of the occult, and he even offers a theory for their explanation.

The second and perhaps the most original magus of all time was John Dee, born in or near London in 1527. A child prodigy who, at the early age of 15 went to Cambridge, Dee worked regularly 18 hours a day. In 1548 he attained to the degree of Master of Arts, after which he left Cambridge to study abroad.*

---

*It has been said that he, like Aleister Crowley some centuries later, was "found out" by the university authorities, who notified him that his presence was no longer required, and that he was to continue his "abominable practices" elsewhere.

He went to Louvain, where he encountered people who had known the great Agrippa personally. The fact that *De Occulta Philosophia* was topping to local bestseller chart contributed to Dee's drinking his fill from the tantalizing tankard of hermetic knowledge.

At the age of 24, in 1551, he returned to England, where he was received by King Edward VI, for whom he performed an important task, in consequence of which he received a pension.

The nature of this task was never specified in the royal budget, hence the fact that it has become an object of ardent speculation. It is very likely that it was a task of magical nature, since only payments to whores, spies, assassins, and sorcerers were conspicuous by their absence from the accounts.

Alas, Edward died and was succeeded by Mary, who suppressed her "enemies" wholesale and earned the epithet "Bloody." Dee was accused of having attempted to murder or harm the queen by means of casting her horoscope. This was impossible to prove, so the charge was altered to heresy, and he was imprisoned. He managed to get acquitted, and his reputation as a sorcerer soared to new heights. No one save the devil himself could have twisted the poor victim out of the bloody but eager hands of the prosecutor, the notorious Edmund Bonner, Bishop of London, who—except in this one instance—"always got his man."

Eventually, "Bloody Mary" left this "vale of tears" (1558), her half-sister Elizabeth ascended the throne, and John Dee's troubles were over. He became advisor to the queen, who even visited him at his home, in Mortlake outside London, several times without ruining him or emptying his wine cellar.

Dee's titles of Astrologer Royal and Magical Advisor to the Crown were not entirely sinecures. He erected the queen's chart to find the most auspicious moment for her coronation, and later, when her picture was found stabbed and molested in Lincoln's Inn Fields, Dee was called in to exorcise the spirits involved and neutralize the astral effects of this desecration.

He was a prolific writer and a creative scholar. His lectures on Euclid's *Elements* at the Sorbonne were tremendously popular and helped to popularize mathematics at the various universities. However, he had many other interests in life, one of which resulted in a meeting of the utmost importance to modern occultism.

Probably on March 10, 1582, he met his future assistant and partner, Edward Kelly, sometimes spelled Kelley, and together they made magic. They belong together like Gilbert and Sullivan, or Rodgers and Hammerstein, so a biographical outline is indicated.

Edward Kelly, whose real name was probably Talbot, was born at Worcester August 1, 1555. He was a dropout from Oxford who settled down as a lawyer's clerk and scrivener. The story goes that he was pilloried at Lancaster and had his ears cut off for forgery or counterfeiting, causing him to wear a special hat with earflaps for the rest of his life—a not very likely story. However, that he was a man with more than one dubious string to his bow is indisputable. He may even have been a confidence trickster, but his occult talents and his part in his and Dee's joint venture are above suspicion.

The story leading up to their meeting may be true or not. I don't know. I believe the general outline as it fits the facts, but I won't vouch for all the details because one of my sources is inexact on many points. However, it would be a pity to deprive the readers of a good story, so here it is for what it's worth.

After getting out of jail or in order to evade justice, it's not clear which, Kelly went into voluntary exile in Wales. There, at a lonely inn, on a dark evening, he was chatting with the innkeeper over a tankard of ale before a blazing fire. During the course of the conversation he confessed to a knowledge of foreign languages and old manuscripts. The innkeeper then produced an old document, which no one in the neighborhood had been able to decipher, and he asked Kelly if he could do anything with it. When asked how he had come by it, the innkeeper told him a strange story. Some time before he had been offered the paper and two small balls of red and white powder as payment for food and drink by a stranger at the inn. Naturally he asked the stranger where the things came from, and he was told that they had been found at Glastonbury Abbey where the stranger had robbed the old abbot's grave. As the innkeeper was a protestant, and Henry VIII's parliament had declared Catholic holdings property of the crown nearly 50 years before, there could be no question of sacrilege by merely digging in the ground. The innkeeper accepted it as payment of the debt, and the stranger went on, and that was the end of it.

A brief investigation of the paper and the balls of powder told Kelly that this had to do with alchemy. He had never seen the philosopher's stone, but he knew instinctively that this was it. Since he was no fool, he saw at once that the manuscript was infinitely more valuable than the powder if it contained the recipe

John Dee—Alchemist, Astrologer, and Confidante of the Angels

British Museum/*The Occult Review*, May 1908

of the elixir. He had no trouble in translating the paper, although his knowledge of practical alchemy left a lot to be desired. He wasn't discouraged for he knew whom to turn to. Naturally he told the innkeeper that it was difficult to translate and that it would probably take a long time, and, unfortunately, he couldn't stay that long. However, as he was interested in that sort of thing, he was willing to buy the stuff from the innkeeper for say, one guinea? (A considerable sum in those days.) The innkeeper probably thought him insane. He accepted immediately, and Kelly left the inn the very next morning for London. He had decided to pay a visit to the renowned scholar Dr. John Dee at Mortlake.

This was a truly karmic meeting. As I mentioned before it was probably on March 10, 1582, that it took place. As at any karmic meeting, cosmic sparks began to fly right away.

After a quick glance at the manuscript Dee decided that they should test the powder. They went to one of his friends who was a goldsmith and made a successful transmutation.

They decided, then and there, to become partners, and Dee also had a secret of his own to let Kelly into.

For some years he had, aided by different scryers (mediums, or rather, media) tried to established contact with discarnate spirits. Lately, he and his current medium, Barnabas Saul, had received messages from an entity calling itself the angel Uriel. Dee promised Kelly that he could participate in a seance.

It turned out that Kelly was a much better medium than either Dee or Saul. He moved into Dee's house, and Saul was dismissed. Thus many years of cooperation began, in which Kelly would communicate with the spirits and Dee would write down the revelations.

After the successful attempt at transmutation* Dee decided that they should try to reproduce the process outlined in the

---

*There are more than ample records of these transmutations and all those that followed, both in England and on the continent, and several pieces of transmuted metals are kept here and there. Of course, we have no way of knowing exactly what transpired on these occasions. Those who discount any theories concerning the Philosopher's Stone have to explain how two men, constantly in need of money, could give away gold on the scale that Dee and Kelly did. Why were they constantly broke if they could turn mercury or lead into gold? That answer is that it all went back into their futile attempts to produce the Stone.

manuscript. However, alchemy is a costly affair. Since neither Dee nor Kelly had any money, they agreed to look for a sponsor. He turned up in the guise of a Polish nobleman Albert Laski, Count of Siradz. On a visit to London he was introduced to Dee, who showed him enough to make him interested in the project. As a result, the two alchemists traveled to Poland with him, where he built them a laboratory close to his castle near Cracow. There they set to work.

It has been well established by the aficionados of the Art that, unless the alchemist makes progress on the spiritual plane as well as in the physical process, he has no chance of succeeding. Apparently Dee didn't know that, or thought that he knew better, or he wouldn't have exploited the Pole. Kelly might or might not have known, but as he was something of a rogue he would probably have ripped off the count under any circumstances. The fact remains. The count lost a considerable fortune and threw in the towel. He suggested that they should pay a visit to Emperor Rudolph of Bohemia in Prague. He supplied them with letters of introduction, and off they went.

In order to stimulate sponsorship and to prove that they were different from all the other alchemists and "get-rich-quick" hustlers who victimized the gullible populations of medieval and Renaissance Europe, Edward Kelly, against the advice of the doctor, used part of the powder in some public transmutations.

Kelly was by now taking over command of the partnership. There were two reasons for this. Partly because it was his doing that they had obtained the powder in the first place, but there was even a deeper reason. Under normal conditions Dee would probably have washed his hands of the whole affair. The association with a man like Kelly didn't do his academic status any good, nor was it an easy relationship, and now, to top it all, a disturbing development in the scrying business had occurred. All communication with Uriel was now limited to Kelly, and Dee was totally dependent on him for further messages. It is obvious that Dee took these seances very seriously, and he put up with a lot of inconvenience from Kelly for science's sake. Let there be no doubt, Dee was an eminent scholar.

One of the more dubious demands from the angel Uriel was that they should swap wives—at least, a very popular misconception to that effect has been going around for centuries. This story has sometimes been the basis of theories supporting the point of view that what Dee and Kelly were doing was nothing but low and debased debauchery, excuses for perverse group sex and sodomy.

It has been pointed out that Dee never would have consented to such a thing, had he been a serious scholar. He should have known that such an idea could not have come from an angel, and that he must have been stupid to believe Kelly's nonsense.

Thus Dee was either dishonest or stupid, and he should not, therefore, be taken seriously in either case. This is not a very good argument, partly because the logic fails and partly because the premises are wrong. Even if Dee had doubted Kelly, he had no option but to consent since, by now, Uriel only communicated through Kelly. This shows how serious Dee was, that he was willing to put up with Kelly's demands for the sake of not risking his closing down on him. The other thing is the misconception that it was a matter of wife swapping. This is not exactly true. It was a recommendation from the angel to institute a joint family community; i.e., living in common, which of course meant the men having their wives in common, as women had no rights in those days (hence the misconception). Of course, even this may be an elaborate hoax, perpetrated by Kelly, and it is well documented that Dee wasn't very keen on the idea. In no way does it invalidate the theory that Dee accepted in the name of science.

Back to the narrative. The transmutations that Kelly performed in public, fake or genuine, made an impact on the people. To clinch the matter, he gave a performance before the imperial surgeon Thaddeus von Hayek, in which he transmuted one pound of mercury into the same amount of solid gold.

He was now invited to the court of the German Emperor, Maximilian II, where he again transmuted publicly. Again he succeeded to such a degree that the emperor made him Marshal of Bohemia. This went to his head and resulted in his increasing his performances. What was worse, he forgot to stress the fact that he was not an adept himself. On the contrary, he let people understand that when his supply of "gold powder" was exhausted, he would "again" produce the "philosopher's stone" himself.

This contributed to his fall. He was arrested and ordered to make power for the "economy of the reich," which of course he couldn't. He was placed in custody in the castle Zobeslau.

Even at that point Dee tried to save his scryer. He suggested to Maximilian that he and Kelly together should try to produce the powder that he demanded, and the two friends were taken to a laboratory in Prague where they worked under surveillance. Needless to say, no stone unturned, no stone produced. Even the angel Uriel refused to serve the god Mammon. Kelly then got panicky and killed a guard in an attempt to escape, which resulted in his being transferred to the castle Zerner.

It would appear that Dee then went back to England and persuaded the queen to interfere, which she apparently did, but to no avail. The emperor answered that Kelly had broken the law of the country and therefore could not be released.

Finally Kelly attempted to escape. He tied some sheets together and tried to climb down the wall beneath his window, but, alas, he was too fat and the "rope" broke and he fell to the ground, breaking his legs and some ribs. He also received internal injuries, from which he died in 1597.

Dee had been kindly received by the queen, but in his absence tragedy had befallen him. His library, which was one of the largest in the world in his day, larger than Oxford's and Cambridge's put together, containing about 4,000 volumes of which approximately 150 were rare manuscripts, was partly destroyed in 1583, in his absence, by an ignorant mob.

Accordingly he decided to hide his valuable private diaries and manuscripts, magical and otherwise, in safe places, and how some of these came to light again many years after his death is a fascinating story, or rather are fascinating stories, since several works came out of limbo, directed by the law of karma, in different and strange ways. I won't go into that here. It will have to wait until we deal with the various works' reappearance before an unsuspecting world.

Dee himself retired to Mortlake where he lived his remaining years in relative obscurity. Queen Bess died in 1603 and her successor James I was vehemently against the "black arts." Dee was once again a controversial subject in both meanings of the word. However, the fact that he was an old man and the king was terribly superstitious caused him not to revoke the pension that Elizabeth had granted Dee. He died in 1609, 81 years of age.

Giordano Bruno. He was right. A crater of the moon was named after him. He doesn't care. He was burned at the stake in 1600.

Apart from his mathematical preface to Euclid's *Elements* (1570), and his famous *Monas Hieroglyphica* (1564) and several other writings, his most important esoteric and magical works remained, on the whole, unpublished until long after his death, but a lot of his handwritten manuscripts found their way to the British Museum Library.

In 1659 the diaries containing Dee's and Kelly's scrying sessions, covering the period from May 28, 1583, to Kelly's death and, from then on, occasional notes by Dee until September 7, 1607, were published. In 1983, the *Heptarchia Mystica* which covers the period before 1583, was published at Edinburgh.

A bizarre combination brought the Renaissance magician before the spiritual world and the magical fraternity again in 1978, but we'll return to that later.

Agrippa and Dee were not the only Renaissance magicians. The age can boast of such names as Paracelsus, Nostradamus, Giordano Bruno (who should have boasted less), Francis Bacon, and Robert Fludd, none of whom, with the possible exception of Nostradamus, have had any impact upon modern magic and occultism, so we will leave the rest of the age to itself and proceed to the period of the Reformation, or the Age of the Orders.

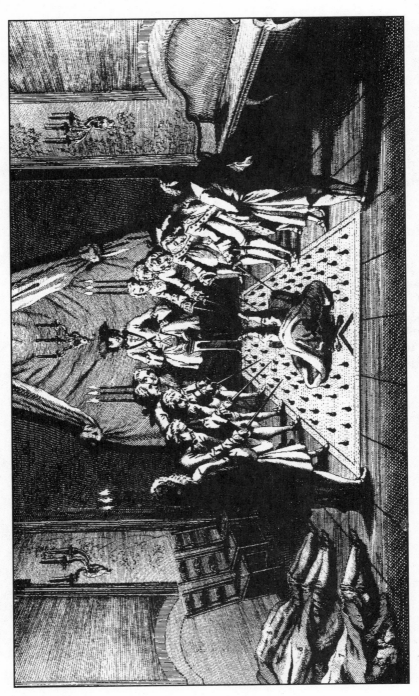

18th-century French Freemasons

Print, c. 1750

The Age of the Orders

We have seen how knowledge of magic and science increased and spread from around 1000–1100 and onwards with the growth of the universities. This, of course, was due to the fact that various manuscripts started to circulate. Most of these were copied, and the copies were copied again, and so on. This led to more and more copies circulating and getting copied again on an exponential scale.

The art of copying was not a new one. From the very beginning, the Christian Church had seen it as its duty to preserve the noble thoughts of man. One of the basic activities of the various abbeys and convents was that of copying the masters, but until the beginning of this millennium this activity was carried out under the strictest control.

The works copied by the monks and nuns remained in the monastery or convent libraries, and only the most trusted scholars had access to some of the treasures. Even they could not pick and choose. They were only permitted to handle works that related to their own line of research—an attitude that still existed far into this century at Oxford and Cambridge, at least as far as works on erotica and pornography were concerned.

With the rise of the universities, the proliferation of manuscript material was a fact—not only the old masters, which worried the Church enough, but also brand new and contemporary ideas, which worried the papal dignitaries much more.

All through the Middle Ages, the Church tried in vain to control this dissemination of ideas, mainly by burning the controversial manuscripts. Sometimes even the people who had written or merely possessed them were burned.

Around 1440 as far as can be ascertained, Johann Gutenberg

of Mainz solved the problem of printing with movable type. He was not the only one. Everything exploded in those years. Before, even if the number of manuscripts had increased, it had still taken about a year or so to copy a book such as the Bible. This still limited the number of available works on the market. Bestsellers such as the Bible were printed long before 1440, but they were reproduced using block type; i.e., each page was cut out in wood and used as a stamp. It was therefore not subject to changes. But now, with small metal type, you could dismantle the whole thing and set up a new page with the same type, over and over again, and very fast.

As prices fell, more people could afford to buy books, and more people began learning to read and write, and thus the "evil" circle began.

It also became more difficult for the Church to prevent works of heresy from proliferating; e.g., when Agrippa published his *De occulta philosophia*, the Inquisition tried to prevent it. Agrippa was arrested, but the whole edition had been sold out, and this was not yet 100 years after Gutenberg.

The Church was facing serious problems. In 1517 Luther had nailed his 96 theses to the door of the Wittenberg Church. They didn't remain there. They were turned into pamphlets and distributed to all and sundry, and soon, just as the mother Church had feared, people were sitting around in their little homes contemplating apostasy.

They might have stopped at the mere thought had it not been for a number of reasons. The secular powers no longer considered the Church an asset. The short reigns of the various popes were too unstable for any long-term planning. Furthermore, the Kingdom of God was quickly becoming the biggest property holder on earth. There was a general understanding among the nobility to the effect that this wouldn't do. With Luther, then, came the first legitimate excuse for breaking with Rome. Soon the kings, dukes, and their vassals were jumping from the Holy See like fleas from a dead dog. More and more left as the number of excuses increased. Of course, it was primarily the doctrine that they objected to, but also the personal lives of some of the popes had doubts cast upon them. It was felt that, with men such as

Alexander Borgia as God's representative on earth, hell couldn't be all that bad.*

A minor flaw in this premeditated desertion was the masses. Even they had gained from this proliferation of knowledge. Although they couldn't read or write, they had had their Bible and other books read aloud to them for their edification. It turned out to be a deplorable and inconsistent idea. They now got the impression that all this freedom and independence should benefit them to some degree, and as the results failed to appear, they decided not to procrastinate their hour of liberty and called to arms. The rebellion was mercilessly and brutally suppressed, and even the privileges they had were taken from them after the bloody slaughter of their leaders.

The Church of Rome tried some measures of rehabilitation: a general Counter Reformation. The most corrupt were thrown out, and a few rules were changed, but it was too late. The far-off regions of what used to be the Roman Empire were lost.

Even Henry VIII of England broke with the Pope.** Although he wasn't exactly in league with the continental kings, he was certainly not long in getting inspired by them.

The Church could do nothing about this until the execution of Mary, Queen of Scots, by Elizabeth in 1587. This provided Phillip II of Spain with an excuse to invade England, rid Britain of the Protestant pest, and batter her into submission under the "One True Church." Alas, the impressive "invincible" armada was destroyed, partly by the British fleet and partly by bad weather north of Scotland. Thus the day of reckoning was yet to come. With the tense relations between the One True Faith (they were both called that) and the eruption of novel ideas, promoted and endorsed by the greatest minds of the day, it was evident around 1600 that sooner or later things would explode again.

In 1610, Galileo Galilei published his *Siderius Nuncius*, which drove another nail in the coffin. Not only were the Church's

---

*Alexander was the father of the notorious cardinal, Cesare Borgia. These two specimens together, along with the indulgence business, were mainly responsible for paving the way for Luther.

**I sincerely hope that it was for the sake of confiscating the Church funds; I'd hate to think that he did it for "a bit of crumpet."

ethics challenged, but now also its scientific foundation.

Into the middle of all this confusion and corruption, Cosmic Lightning suddenly struck. This flash of lightning has exerted its influence to this day, insofar as its symbolism is concerned.

In 1614 a small manifesto was published at Kassel entitled *Fama Fraternitatis; oder, Des Löblichen Ordens des Rosenkreutzes.*

This was not altogether new. It had been circulating in manuscript for some time, but now it was down in print, and it spread like mushrooms. So did a sort of sequel, printed in the same place the following year, entitled *Confessio Fraternitatis,* and what you could consider the third volume of a trilogy, *Chymische Hochzeit des Christian Rosenkreutz anno 1459,* at Strasbourg in 1616.

Although these three works were published anonymously, they have sometimes been attributed, together with the *Allgemeine Reformation,* another work along similar lines, to a priest from Tübingen; one Johann Valentin Andreae. Indeed, most modern scholars tend to regard Andreae as the author of *Chymishe Hochzeit* (Chemical wedding), but the styles and structures seem to indicate different authors, and even Andreae's contribution is far from ascertained.

The works, at least the *Fama* and *Confessio,* postulated the existence of a secret fraternity, which, for centuries or millennia, had worked as a regulating factor on the development of mankind, a kind of concentrated power that manipulated the collective karma of the earth, an order attributed with the loftiest virtues, which, of course, it would have had to possess, if it existed at all the way these manifestoes claimed. Most scholars doubt this.

One must admit that historical evidence of these original Rosicrucians (for that was the name they made themselves known under) is rather scant. Not to put too fine a point on it, there is not much more than the three manifestoes and, as I have mentioned, they were anonymous.

In addition to these, there is the famous (or infamous) call to the citizens of Paris in 1623. This constituted yet another manifesto from the R.C. brethren of the "5 minutes to 12" variety.

It is at this point in history that we hear about them for the first time, but the brethren of the Rosy Cross claim, even today, a long tradition. Briefly it is said that this fraternity has roots dating back

Johann Valentin Andreae—the original Rosicrucian?

17th-century German engraving

to before the written word. Since then it has, in all secrecy, been working behind stage in Atlantis, Lemuria and Mu, etc. until the emergence of the high cultures of the historical period, Egypt and Greece.

After that, there is not an incident in history that the mysterious R.C. brethren have not been behind.

As we have seen, in 1614, they finally admitted their existence. Conditions were by then so deplorable, that the Supreme Council of the R.C. decided that it was now time for direct appeal.

In *Fama Fraternitatis* , it is related how the founder of the order, one Christian Rosenkreutz, was born in 1378. At the age of 16 he traveled around Europe and the Orient. On his return to Germany, he reunited with three fellow monastic brothers, and together they founded the Order of the Rosy Cross. Another five brothers joined them, and together they traveled all over the world collecting lore and gaining knowledge. Every second year they assembled and exchanged experiences.

In 1484, at the age of 106, Christian Rosenkreutz died and was buried in a seven-sided vault, which is very significant in view of the later teachings of the Hermetic Order of the Golden Dawn. It was prophesied that the grave would be forgotten, but also that it would be discovered again 120 years later, and this would be the sign for the order to step out into the public light. Thus, the grave would have been found in 1604. Just how long the *Fama* had been circulating is not known, but at least as early as 1608–10 has been suggested. This is mainly based on contemporary letters.

These works bemoaned the general condition of mankind and intimated that the members of the order had access to all knowledge concerning the philosopher's stone and the elixir of life and other wonderful phenomena, and all this would be given to every true postulant who would take up the cross and turn his back on the corrupt morals of the day. Serious seekers were encouraged to join the order. It was said that nobody had to look for the order. The brethren would know them and contact them in due course.

All esoteric orders of any standing perform some kind of astral investigation of prospective neophytes, and it's a comparatively safe way of excluding the *persona non grata.* This was badly

needed now, as suddenly the world was full of worthy true seekers who would more than willingly take up the cross—and the
secret of how to make gold out of lead along with it.

The fourth manifesto appeared in 1623 as posters on the walls
of Paris, and it said:

> We, the deputies of our Head college of the Rosy Cross,
> now sojourning, visible and invisible, in this town, by
> grace of the Most High, towards Whom the hearts of
> sages turn, do teach, without the help of books or signs,
> how to speak the language of every country wherein
> we elect to stay, in order that we may rescue our fellow
> men from the terror of death.

Most historians are of the opinion that many of the great contemporaries were interested in joining the brotherhood, but no
one was found worthy of admission, or else it didn't exist at all.
This conclusion is based upon the alleged failed attempts of
Descartes and Leibniz to make contact with the brethren but, as
the Rosicrucians were a secret order, one would suppose that
these people would deny any knowledge of it, at least in public,
even if they had been associated with it.

I see no reason why these two shouldn't have gained admission, whereas I would like to comment on the theory that Sir
Francis Bacon was Supreme Magus, Ipsissimus, or Imperator as
several sources claim.

Personally, I find it very unlikely. There has been a lot of
insane speculation about Bacon. Heaven knows why, but he
seems to have been a person capable of exerting an eccentric fas-
cination on people with a limited sense of reality. Several pseu-
doscientific theories have "proved" that Bacon was the author of
Shakespeare's plays. One of the most blatant works to that effect
is *Bacon, Shakespeare and the Rosicrucians* (1888) by F. W. C.
Wigston, who, in this and other works, claims this, and adds that
Shakespeare's plays are Rosicrucian rituals in disguise. Some
enthusiastic players of this fascinating game maintain, according
to Christopher McIntosh*, that:

The Rosicrucians. Crucible (Aquarian Press), 1987.

. . . Bacon and Andreae, the author of the *Chemical Wedding*, were one and the same person. Bacon, it is held, did not die when catching cold on Highgate Hill, but subsequently went to Germany and began to write under the name of Andreae. Although engravings of Bacon and Andreae show a certain similarity it is difficult to square this theory with the fact that if it were true Bacon would have been 133 years old when he died—a remarkable age, even if he had possessed the Rosicrucian elixir of life.

Common sense, and a reading of *The New Atlantis* by Bacon, published posthumously, will make clear that he knew of and had read the *Fama* and *Confessio*. But at the same time it is obvious, if one studies Bacon's personal career, that he was definitely not a person of the kind that one would expect to find among the Rosicrucians. Personally, he followed a code of ethics normally associated with the Mafia. He was a ruthless opportunist, who, by hook or by crook and various intrigues, managed to rise to the peerage as Lord Verulam, and later on as Viscount St. Albans. He was Lord Chancellor when he was convicted of taking bribes and subsequently had to retire. It is true that he was made the scapegoat for what was in those days common practice, but to do illegal things because everybody else does is not true Rosicrucianism. In short, he was an Elizabethan entrepreneur in the same category as Francis Drake and Walter Raleigh.*

The next time we hear of the Rosicrucians is in 1630, with the publication of *Arcana Totius Naturae Secretissima*, in Leyden, this time not anonymous, the author being one Peter Mormius. He claimed to be a representative of the "Collegium Rosanium." Eventually he admitted that he had never himself been a member of the order. He had merely been the servant of an old man by the name of Rose, who had been a true adept. This man, whom

---

*No doubt theories to the effect that Bacon wasn't Bacon, but another man named Bacon, will in due time appear. After all, such has been the case with Homer, and various people and groups have invested more in Francis Bacon than their sense of reality will be able to rectify. It is hard to give up any illusion, let alone a philosophical or religious raison d'etre.

Mormius had met in 1620, was one of a triad of men, who at that time made up the whole of the "Auriæ Rosæ Crucis."

This is very interesting, because this is the earliest example known of the word "Rosicrucian" not being used alone, and also the first time that the concept of the triad is introduced. As we shall see, the order structure with a leading triumvirate, as it were, is a recurring phenomenon within secret orders.

Apart from Mormius, people associated with the R.C. were reluctant to step forward, and not without reason. They had received a mixed bag of criticism, mainly from the secular authorities. The Church was rather reticent in the matter. Of course, by now, the Thirty Years War was in full swing, and although it really wasn't a religious war at all (no war ever is), the religious authorities were waiting to see which way the cat would jump. Not that they didn't comment upon and criticize the order; they did, but not to the extent that one would expect. It never amounted to anything that looked like persecution.

About this time, 1640, we also hear the first about the "speculative Freemasons."

The freemasons as such have been known to exist since the building of the great Gothic cathedrals, but only as a sort of ordinary guild. From the 17th century, the speculative element enters the craft. The earliest reference we have to this effect is from 1641 and concerns the circle of men who gathered around Elias Ashmole (1617–92), men such as Thomas Vaughan (1622–66), Kenelm Digby (1603–65), William Lilly (1602–68), John Aubrey (1626–97), and others.

It was Ashmole who received some of John Dee's works—works no one had heard of, together with other things that had disappeared at Dee's death. It is a very interesting story, which will be dealt with later.

There was even a growing interest in druidism in those years. In a book called *Polyolbion,* as early as 1612, Michael Drayton expounded on the virtues of the magi of the ancient Celts, and in 1649 John Aubrey connected them with the prehistoric Stonehenge monument.

It's very difficult to distinguish among the various organizations that sprang up during the rest of that century, partly because all these orders had more or less the same ideals, purposes, and goals; partly because of the scant material that exists of these early days; and finally because it was generally the same people who were involved in all of them. It's hard to tell from a document whether the writer speaks on behalf of one or the other or is merely expressing his personal opinion.

In 1710, in Breslau, *Die wahrhafte und volkommene Bereitung des philosophischen Steins der Brüderschafft aus dem Orden des Gulden und Rosen Kreutzes* was published by Sincerus Renatus, the pseudonym of one Sigmund or Samuel Richter. In this work the rules and the constitution of the Rosicrucians appear in print for the very first time. It's strongly influenced by the writers of the previous century. Especially where alchemy is concerned, one can feel the ghost of Michael Maier. But that's not all. The rules and regulations have much in common with a pre-Rosicrucian order by the name of "Orden der Unzertrennlichen," or sometimes "Indissolubilisten." This order was founded in 1577 and later merged with a pan-Germanic brotherhood, founded in 1617 by Prince Ludwig of Anhalt; i.e., at the height of the debate on the R.C. order. As a matter of fact, Andreae himself was a member of this fraternity, which went under the name of "Fruchtbringende Gesellschaft." As I said, these two orders merged, and from 1680 and onwards it thrived.

A lodge of the order was founded in the town of Halle that year, and a lot of prominent people joined. It did not officially employ the symbols of the rose and cross, but, in view of Richter's book, it is very possible that it is the same. Many organizations have one doctrine to show the world and another, more esoteric one for the true initiates.

In 1717, in London, the first grand lodge of the Freemasons was founded under Anthony Sayer. As previously mentioned, Freemasons were not a new phenomenon in the modern sense; i.e., the "speculative masons." They date back as early as 1641 when they are first mentioned in writing, among Elias Ashmole's circle in London, but they are probably older. Of course they themselves claim an ancient heritage, as do the Rosicrucians and the druids.

This is the true "age of the orders." A lot of them were founded locally and never went beyond the area. Others flared up like supernovas only to burn themselves out in a couple of years. Others again were modeled directly on one of the more established and famous ones. Many of these copy-cat orders were and are totally devoid of any spirituality, let alone esoteric practices; e.g., the Moose, Rotary, Elks, and so on.

A great many of these orders are strictly business and pleasure—an excuse to get plastered in the absence of the wife and to make dubious deals which, if not directly against the letter of the law, then at least against the purpose of it, defying all ethics of modern society. The Italian lodge P.2 is the archetype of this kind of Masonry.

The order with the most influence on the modern magical philosophy is the Rosicrucian, but alas, even this admirable institution has degenerated to a certain extent.*

Twenty-five years later, in another publication, the number of Rosicrucian brethren had increased to 77. This is a gain of 14 since Mormius's day. A lot of stress was still laid on alchemy.

---

*One needs only to look to the fringes of the occult scene and magazines to spot the strange and vulgar way that some of these self-styled esoteric orders promote their money-grabbing schemes, while, at the same time, denouncing any other organization of the more or less same persuasion, and with no more particular right to use the name than any of the others. They can even be heard on local radio stations with feeble enlistment offers, somewhat late at night among programs like "Young Conservatives Disc Jockey Spin," or the local computer club's download program. I defy anyone to make sense of any of them.

I'm not saying that these modern esoteric orders are totally without merit. On the contrary, the traditional teachings of some of them are very profound, even if no one in the order has any idea of what it's all about anymore. To some, the rituals are merely empty ceremonies that one has to go through before one can go in and eat like a hog. This was the chief reason that Israel Regardie decided to publish all the secret order material of the Golden Dawn. It can be very hard to get the essence out of a ritual performed by an assembly of ignorant people who don't even bother to learn it by heart. Their running about the temple reading aloud from a stack of papers in their hands, which crackles each time they turn a leaf, can be an abominable disturbance of the proceedings, not to mention the danger of having your eye struck out by some frater who is waving a sword in one hand while looking at this lines at the same time. It's much cheaper and safer to buy the rituals from the bookshop and perform them in the privacy of your own sanctum.

Although the subject is not touched directly, it seems as if the "masters" had returned from India, whence they had departed, according to Richter.

From 1750 and onwards R.C. flourished. New orders appeared, old ones merged with Masonic ones and changed names; e.g., "The Knights of the Shooting Star." It was also about this time that the celebrated *supérieurs inconnus** appeared. In 1764 we find them in Baron Carl Gotthelf von Hund's order, the "Strikte Observanz" (Strict Observance).

Even Masonry proliferated at that time. Lodges popped up everywhere, especially in France. Not content with the two or three traditional degrees, the continentals began to multiply rites and degrees to an alarming extent. The initial impetus came from a man named Andrew Michael Ramsay (1686–1743), from Ayr, Scotland. Knighted in France and a devotee of the Jacobite cause, Ramsay got things rolling with "Ramsay's oration" in 1737, an address he made to a lodge in Paris. In this Pandora's box of a speech, Ramsay claimed that the Freemasons did not originate in a guild of common laborers, but rather represented the survival of the Knights Templar. If Masons were essentially knights, then membership might be a feather in the cap of a nobleman.

Of course, a noble could not be limited to the same three degrees held by common stonecutters, so advanced degrees had to be invented. It would fill many pages just to list the rites that arose at this time like mushrooms on cow manure on a rainy

---

*In some orders in the mid-1700s we find, for the first time, what would later become the *bête noire* of many mystery orders—the so-called *supérieurs inconnus*, "mahatmas," or "Secret Chiefs," teachers who, from their caves and temples on the astral plane, lead the misguided world back to the straight and narrow through the work of the orders. They very seldom manifest themselves in Malkuth (the physical world), and then only to the highest initiates, the grandmasters, the supreme magi, the imperators (many mystics have a weakness for pompous and fancy titles), and so on. Apart from the romantic element in these tales, the mahatmas have served purely practical purposes. Many a Ruler of the Universe, Defender of the Faith, and Son of the Morning Star has weathered the storm by crediting unpopular decisions to the whim of the Secret Chiefs. ("We are but dust beneath the chariot wheels of the Lord. Who are we, that we should doubt the orders of the astral chiefs?")

morning, but I'll name just a few: The Rite of Memphis, the Rite of Mizraim (these two later combined), Beneficent Knights of the Holy City, the Blazing Star, the Elected Cohens, the Emperors of the East and West, Fessler's Rite, Swedenborg Rite, and even Cagliostro's Egyptian Rite, which he made up entirely on his own. As for degrees, no man could live long enough to take them all. Some of the rites contained as many as 95 degrees.

It was from the rites of the Emperors of the East and West, which was established in Paris in 1758 and included 25 degrees, that the American organization known as the Ancient and Accepted Scottish Rite took its origin in Charleston, South Carolina, in 1801, with a fake charter supposedly from Frederick the Great. In the mid-19th century, the 33 degrees of the Scottish Rite were rewritten and revised by a Confederate general and frontiersman, Albert Pike (1809–1891). The Scottish Rite retains the good fellowship and pompous-sounding degrees of its predecessors, but is most notable for its extensive charity work.

There is a statue of Gen. Pike in Washington, D.C. Recently, there has been a campaign to tear it down, like the statues of Lenin in Eastern Europe, on the grounds that Pike was a leading figure in the Ku Klux Klan. Since there is not the tiniest shred of evidence to suggest that Pike was even so much as an ordinary member of the Klan at any time, one wonders about the true motives of these people.

Pike has been in trouble before. Even during the war, his rivals accused him of letting his Indian troops scalp the Yankees. Later, a novelist and prankster named Leo Taxil wrote a little speech and atrributed it to Pike. This speech was supposed to have been made by Pike in his capacity as a fictitious officer in an international Masonic organization in Paris that never existed. In Taxil's forgery, which is to the Masons as the Protocols of the Elders of Zion is to the Jews, Pike calls upon Masons to inform new initiates of the higher degrees that Lucifer is God and Adonai is evil.

In recent years, many television and radio evangelists have been stubbornly and repeatedly violating the ninth commandment by making free and frequent use of this forgery in their anti-Masonic campaigns. They do it for the greater good, no doubt. There can be no question that they are trying to alarm people in order to drum up more and fatter contributions. Men of

God would not resort to such tactics. Meanwhile, these attacks all proceed upon the assumption that Pike was some sort of Masonic Pope whose word is binding to this day upon all Freemasons. Even in the Scottish Rite, however, most men consider whatever Pike had to say as interesting at best and, at worst, the tiresome and irrelevant pronouncements of an inveterate windbag.

Be that as it may, many people for a variety of reasons seem to think that Albert Pike belongs right up there with Aleister Crowley as a prime candidate for "the wickedest man in the world." Someone with more ingenuity than I have can probably get his name to add up to 666.

Many of the old French rites represented the decadent variety of Freemasonry, with lots of exotic rituals, pompous titles, and incense galore, the experimental stage of occultism, indescribably vulgar, and an abomination to the eye of every decent traditional Mason. The attitude of most modern Masons toward some of these rites as they were at that time and place is roughly equivalent to the lack of desire of the modern Californian Rosicrucians to be associated with the O.T.O., one of the more colorful orders at the beginning of this century that was involved with Aleister Crowley and sex magic—and which had its beginnings in Freemasonry.

The Strict Observance borrowed a lot from other contemporary groups: the Scottish Freemasons, the Templars, etc. Von Hund (1722–1776) pilfered from them all, and then to top it all, the magi dived headlong into politics.

With the emergence of Adam Weishaupt's "Ordo Illuminati Bavariensis" (Order of the Bavarian Illuminati), the step was taken fully. It was a quaint mixture of all the occult lore of the day, and it inclined strongly towards something which can possibly be described as the predecessor of the political anarchism that we know from the 1880s.

Weishaupt's order has been accused of all foul deeds—among other things, the American and French revolutions. According to Roberts and Gilbertson*, an English pamphlet from 1786 entitled *The Original Writings of the Order and Sect of the Illuminati*, author

---

The Dark Gods by Anthony Roberts and Geoff Gilbertson. London: Rider/Hutchinson, 1980.

Albert Pike. The wickedest man in the world?

Mackey's History of Freemasonry, 1898

unknown, states that a stranger on horseback was struck by lightning in Rattisbon (Regensburg) in 1785. Both the stranger (an evangelical priest named Lanze) and the horse were burnt to ashes, but, as if by a miracle, and of course it *is* a miracle, the horseman's courier pouch remained intact. In the bag was found a book entitled *Einige Original Schriften*. The book was not the manifesto of Weishaupt's order, but its secret plans for taking over the world. These plans included, among other things, riots and uprisings in the Western states, organized by the Illuminati; viz., the revolutions in America and France. The Illuminati recruited their members from the highest economic, political, and military circles, and there are actually scholars who maintain that it was the activities of the Bavarian Illuminati that caused the unrest in the world to break out at that time. This is perhaps somewhat exaggerated, but there is no doubt that the kinds of ideas held by members of such orders influence those members responsible for the actual political decisions that are taken at any time. Otherwise, they are bizarre sets of circumstances, and it must justifiably be pointed out that history is made up of just that kind of bizarre circumstances.

Even on the other side of the border, in France, there was hectic activity. Several rites became attached to the Jacobite cause through people attached to the exiled court of the heir presumptive. They were later associated with notorious people such as the Count St. Germain, Cagliostro, Franz Anton Mesmer, and other characters I'd consider dubious.

Martinez de Pasqually (1727–79) founded an order called "The Elect Cohens" (sounds like a vaudeville act). It was taken over at his death by Louis Claude de St-Martin (1743–1803) and later on re-established as the Martinist Order.

The most spectacular of all these odd orders was no doubt the one run by Count Cagliostro, probably an alias for the Italian entrepreneur Giuseppe Balsamo. It was the "Egyptian Masonic Rite." He had been initiated into the Esperance Lodge of Freemasons in London on April 12, 1777, and in a few years he had introduced "Egyptian Masonry"—the "Mithras and Ephraim Rite"—and proclaimed himself Grand Master. His wife, whom he married when she was 14, was the incarnated Queen of Sheba to his own Solomon, or some such nonsense. Together, they made

Cagliostro—He knew the wrong cardinal.

Paul Christian, *Histoire de la Magie*

magic and became fashionable overnight. Their star continued to rise as they infested the continent, ending up in Paris, pets of the decadent classes—and friends of Cardinal Rohan, which turned out to be their fall. When the cardinal got entangled in a fraudulent jewel purchase, he dragged Cagliostro down with him. The scandal involved her majesty, the Queen of France, Marie Antoinette herself. Some swindlers had persuaded the cardinal to buy, secretly, a diamond necklace worth approximately £100,000 in today's currency. When the jeweler demanded the first payment from the cardinal, he was informed that the Queen was the buyer. When confronted with the jeweler, Marie Antoinette denied any knowledge of the purchase and vehemently denounced the cardinal and Cagliostro as well. The latter's only crime seems to have been his mere acquaintance with the cardinal. Nevertheless, he was thrown into the Bastille, where he languished for a while. This is said to have broken the magus completely. At the trial, he cut a pathetic figure in the dock and became the laughing stock of Paris—even though both he and the cardinal were acquitted and the guilty adventuress captured, tried, flogged, and branded.

Even for the queen it meant another nail in the coffin. As one will remember, she received her punishment five years later on the scaffold, but it was this particular incident that brought her popularity to new depths.

Cagliostro was a broken man. He moved back and forth through Europe for a couple of years and finally decided to force a showdown with the Catholic Church. He went to Rome and opened a temple of the Egyptian Lodge. He was immediately imprisoned by the Inquisition. He died in captivity in 1795.

The year before saw the colorful initiation of Dr. Sigismund Bachstrom on the island of Mauritius by Louis, Comte de Chazal. Perhaps they even used dodo bones in the ceremony. (It was on Mauritius that these birds lived until they became extinct about 1600).

Of course, there were other orders with fascinating histories; e.g., the Knight Templars, the Jesuits, and other monastic orders, but as they were religious rather than magical they fall outside the scope of this book. That does not mean that they didn't perform magic. They did, but magic in itself was never their *raison d'être*. Futhermore, their influence on modern magic is rather negligible. They are at best mystical orders.

So now, around 1800, the esoteric orders, Rosicrucian or Masonic, included a wide variety of magic—Christian, ancient Babylonian, Greek, Egyptian, and even Hebrew, introduced in the 1600s to the Gold and Rosy Cross by Knorr von Rosenroth, who had translated parts of the *Zohar*, a Qabalistic classic, into Latin under the title *Kabbala Denudata*. Occultism was synthesized in just a little under a century. However, how this came about will be dealt with in the next couple of chapters.

The Occult Revival

In 1801, in London, Francis Barrett's book, *The Magus,* was published. It was a comprehensive work that not only systematized the occultism of the day, but also drew heavily on knowledge derived from the Renaissance magicians that had long been forgotten. Barrett is therefore considered the first great name of the new era. It actually looks as if he stepped out directly from limbo, ready and able, into the great book of history. No one seems to have heard of him before the publication of his magnum opus, and to my knowledge no other works from his hand exist. But *The Magus* exists, and that means that Barrett may have been comparatively wealthy. Yet nothing indicates that he was. As a matter of fact, more than ample evidence can be found to the contrary. The alternative is that the vibrations were in the air at the time, awaiting his genius.

In the book, Barrett recommends himself and announces that he gives lectures "in the Magical Arts." Interested persons might inquire at 99 Norton St., St. Mary le Bone.

As a matter of fact, most of *The Magus* was more or less plagiarized word for word from the 17th-century English translation of Agrippa's *De Occulta Philosophia* and from the *Heptameron* of Peter d'Abano. Barrett therefore may have been one of the first to make money giving lessons out of somebody else's published book, presenting the material as his own.

It would be interesting to see a list of Barrett's pupils, if such a thing existed, because one of the transition figures in the Hermetic Order of the Golden Dawn in the latter part of the 19th century, Frederick Hockley, is held to have been a pupil of a pupil of Barrett's. Just as interesting as finding such future connections is, of course, to find out about Barrett's background. *The Magus* hasn't much autobiographical material to offer, although it is crowded with biographies of various occult philosophers. This part of the book was added later, and it is very doubtful that it was written by Barrett. After all, he wasn't able to copy such material from Agrippa.

On the title page, Barrett has blown himself up to something as splendid as:

FRANCIS BARRETT F.R.C.
Professor of Chemistry, Natural and Occult
Philosophy, the Cabala, etc., etc.

Perhaps a bushel to put the light under would not be amiss here!

A year later, Barrett turned out to be not only a magus, but a balloonist. He announced the ascent of a hydrogen balloon at Greenwich with himself as pilot and passenger. Unfortunately, he was unable to inflate the balloon, although he spent all day trying. This rather displeased the crowd. The next day, with troops there to keep the increasingly unruly audience in line, Barrett did get his balloon off the launching pad, with no passengers. It drifted limply for three miles and came down in a marsh. After a couple of months, the persistent Barrett tried yet again. This time he succeeded in getting the balloon a few feet off the ground with himself in it. His weight almost exactly matched the lifting power of the balloon, so he hopped from field to field for six miles before the balloon gave up. At least he had succeeded in distancing himself a little from the unhappy mob. If Barrett had only saved all his hot air for the balloon, the space age might have arrived about 160 years earlier than it did.

In his excellent book about the Golden Dawn,* R. A. Gilbert doubted if there were any Rosicrucians at all in England at that time. He maintains that Barrett must have had knowledge of the fraternity had it existed in the country. F.R.C. after Barrett's name on the title page cannot mean anything but Frater Rosae Crucis—it's not F.R.C.S. (Fellow of the Royal College of Surgeons) or F.R.G.S. (Fellow of the Royal Geographical Society) after all, but just F.R.C. Anybody can call himself that for advertising purposes,

*R. A. Gilbert. *The Golden Dawn: Twilight of the Magicians.* Aquarian Press, 1983.

Francis Barrett—FRC and Balloonist

The Magus, 1801

of course. On the other hand, Gilbert is not necessarily correct. A secret order is a secret order. It doesn't exactly advertise in the media if it's the real thing.

Personally, I consider it very likely that Barrett was a member of some contemporary R.C. organization, perhaps an order run by the no less mystical Dr. Sigismund Bachstrom, mentioned in the last chapter.

We must, then, register some uncertainty regarding the development of Rosicrucianism in England prior to 1865. In that year, an organization called the Red Cross of Constantine was founded in London by a Freemason, Robert Wentworth Little, and two years later its name was changed to Societas Rosicruciana in Anglia, otherwise known as the SRIA, or Soc. Ros.

There's been a lot of disagreement among scholars as to how this order came about. The longest lived and most romantic version has much in common with another story concerning the founding of the Golden Dawn (or GD*). It seems that Little, who was a clerk employed at Mark Masons Hall in London, during some tidying up, discovered a bunch of old papers containing some ancient rituals, upon which he built the SRIA. However, lately discovered facts suggest that Little, together with a fellow Mason, William James Hughan, was initiated into a Scottish Rosi-

---

*I see no need to cater to the quasi-Masonic pretensions of many if not most occult orders by resorting to the mystification of using three periods in the shape of a triangle to indicate an abbreviation, thus: G.∴D.∴. Nobody seems to be very clear about what it means, anyway.

I've heard it said that they refer to the Supernal Sephiroth of the Kabbalistic Tree of Life, though why Kether, Chokmah, and Binah should be used to indicate the abbreviated form of some pompous name or title, I cannot tell you. Perhaps it means that the individual or organization concerned is the embodiment of the Father, Son, and Holy Ghost.

In his *Encyclopædia of Freemasonry* (1884), Albert G. Mackey says:

> Frequently, among English and always among French authors, a Masonic abbreviation is distinguished by three points, ∴, in a triangular form following the letter, which peculiar mark was first used, according to Ragon, on the 12th of August, 1774, by the Grand Orient of France, in an address to its subordinates. No authoritative explanation of the meaning of these points has been given, but they may be supposed to refer to the three lights around the altar, or perhaps more generally to the number three, and to the triangle, both important symbols in the Masonic system.

crucian order, working in Edinburgh under Anthony O'Neal Haye, editor of *The Scottish Freemason*. Not much is known about this organization except that later, influenced by mutual feedback, it became the Societas Rosicruciana in Scotia.

Little and Hughan were initiated on December 31, 1866, and subsequently went through all the grades during the next six months. And so the first meeting of the SRIA took place in London on June 1, 1867.

Some scholars are of the opinion that another of Little's fellow Masons, Kenneth R. H. Mackenzie, author of a contemporary giant classic *Royal Masonic Cyclopædia*, supplied most of the order material for the SRIA, but now it seems more likely that it originated in Scotland. Besides, occultists of all times have been notorious for unscrupulously pilfering from each other with no regards to copyright, let alone any ethical considerations about academic honors or credit. This adds to the scholar's difficulties in tracing the various teachings. For instance, the above mentioned *Royal Masonic Cyclopædia*, published as the work of Mackenzie, is said to be almost entirely made up of material collected by a certain A. F. A. Woodford, of whom we will hear more later.

Little didn't live very long (1840–78), but he managed to found the order from which the Golden Dawn descended. All of the members of the SRIA of any standing were occultists. Apart from Little himself can be mentioned not only such names as Hockley and Mackenzie, of whom we have already heard, but also so advanced a spirit as Edward Bulwer, Lord Lytton, numbered among the members of the SRIA and best remembered today for his classic *Last Days of Pompeii*, but said to be a real adept. He also wrote several so-called Rosicrucian novels; viz., *Zanoni, A Strange Story, The Coming Race*, and others.

It is possible that the French magus, Eliphas Levi, was an honorary member. In any case, he was considered the greatest occultist of his time, and, by some, the first of the moderns—but both statements are very doubtful. Mircea Eliade was moved to comment, "His books . . . met with a success difficult to understand today, for they are a mass of pretentious jumble."* He was born in Paris in

---

Occultism, Witchcraft, and Cultural Fashion. University of Chicago Press, 1976.

1810 and lived in dire poverty his entire life. For years, he was on the edge of the law, being occasionally imprisoned for subversive political activities. He was a personal friend of Bulwer-Lytton, and it was probably as his guest, during one of his rare visits to London in 1851 or '52 that he, on a commission from a wealthy woman, attempted to invoke the spirit of Apollonius of Tyana to visible appearance, with a highly remarkable result. The apparition manifesting itself in the triangle was a different entity altogether, something that scared the living daylights out of the master—but then again, Levi (or Alphonse Louis Constant, to mention his real name) was always a theoretical occultist rather than a practical one.

In 1854 came his *Le Dogme de la Haute Magie,* followed two years later by *Le Rituel de la Haute Magie.* These two works, most often printed together, make up his masterpiece, one of the all-time classics of the genre. Levi's originality manifested itself in the fact that he was the first to get the ingenious idea of connecting the trumps (or Major Arcana, as they are sometimes called) of the Tarot cards with the 22 letters of the Hebrew alphabet and the 22 paths of the Tree of Life. Aficionados of the Qabalah have been fascinated by this attribution ever since.

Other members of the SRIA relevant to our investigation are Messrs. William Wynn Westcott, Samuel Liddell "MacGregor" Mathers, and Dr. William Robert Woodman, of whom both Westcott and Woodman were Supreme Magus (the big cheese) of the SRIA Woodman succeeded Little, and Westcott succeeded Woodman.

Frederick Hockley was perhaps the greatest scryer since John Dee. He used a modus operandi strongly resembling Dee's, and, like Dee, he had no particular aptitude for receiving messages from beyond. Like his great predecessor, he employed various mediums (media), for many years his wife, but, after her death sometime in the 1850s, a young girl about the age of 13, Emma Louisa Leigh, daughter of a retired excise officer, with whom he explored the astral plane. This was a rather remarkable pursuit for a modest stockbroker, although he had in his youth been employed by an occult bookseller, John Denley of Catherine Street, Covent Garden.*

A lot of things happened at this time. London was the center of

---

*John Hamill, ed. *The Rosicrucian Seer: Magical Writings of Frederick Hockley.* The Aquarian Press, 1986.

Eliphas Levi, author of "a mass of pretentious jumble."

James Hyatt/*The Occult Review*, Feb. 1913

the universe, the costly pearl of the mightiest empire the world had ever seen. An empire where the sun never set, Britannia ruled the waves. The Industrial Revolution had enabled her to do so. The fangs of Whitehall reached the remotest spots of the planet and brought home religions, philosophies, and rites, as well as treasures, spices, and curios. It was the time of Dickens and Thackeray as well as Marx and Engels. In 1851, the first Great Exhibition of the world's marvels was held in Joseph Paxton's eighth wonder of the world, the newly built Crystal Palace in Hyde Park, the heart of the metropolis, the heart of the empire. And all this and much more was covered by the gentlemen of Fleet Street.

It was the heyday of the penny press, a sudden awakening of the masses, mainly as a result of the idealism of the middle classes. As more and more people learned to read and write, the insatiable craving for news, manufactured and otherwise, went berserk. Organizations were formed to promote all kinds of new phenomena and causes, worthy or not. A lot of these were modeled after the Freemasons and Rosicrucians. Even the working classes formed organizations, though most of them were trade unions.

Not that there weren't problems. The giant empire creaked. It had its rivals. In Europe, France and Germany were constantly creating trouble, and out in the colonies it often came to military showdowns. So far Britain had managed to control the situation apart from the sad debacle which constituted the United States of America. In 1776, the American people had, with help from France, thrown the British out of the U.S., and, as recently as 1812, the Brits had tried again, without success, to subdue those blasted cousins who talked funny. Apart from that, the Crimean Campaign and the Sepoy Rebellion (for "Campaign" and "Rebellion," read "War") and other local uprisings were just around the corner.

All kinds of new and strange things were assembled to provide a freak's holiday for the new bored and blasé middle classes. As far as the elite upper classes were concerned, they had been bored and blasé for centuries.

One of the new concepts was spiritualism—the final proof of the existence of God, or so its devotees thought. It was a novelty introduced by those cousins from across the pond who talked funny, dating back only a few years, to the karmic year 1848. Apart from spiritualism, which may be considered a manifestation on the spiri-

tual plane, hence the name, one can say that, on the mental or intel-
lectual plane, the analogous manifestation was *The Communist Manifesto* by Marx and Engels. Finally, on the physical level, the
corresponding realization was the discovery* of gold in California.**

Spiritualism, then, began in Hydesville, New York, in the house
of the Fox sisters. For some time they had heard strange sounds in
their new home. They started to knock back in code, with the result
that the knocking changed, adapting to the code. It turned out that
the knocking was made by a discarnate entity—the spirit of a former owner of the house, who had been murdered by burglars and
buried in the cellar. Some time later, a skeleton was found there,
and another field day for the pre-yellow press. After the exposition
in the media, spirit knocking soon became the latest scream, infest-
ing the parlors of the cultured.

That Frederick Hockley had been doing this stuff for years
meant nothing. He was just an ordinary stockbroker, and stockbro-
kers are not the stuff that dreams are made on—certainly not as
opposed to three beautiful (sexy) sisters from a former colony. In
those days, anything from the colonies was preferable to the
domestic brand.

What was Hockley compared to, for instance, a man such as
Paschal Beverly Randolph? Even though he wasn't a spiritualist, he
had other attractions. He was born in 1815, of doubtful parentage
(although he claimed to be the illegitimate son of the governor of
Virginia). As a boy, he went to sea and in Europe became the dar-
ling of the fashionable salons of Paris. How could it be otherwise?
He had the looks of a bodybuilder and the sexual philosophy of a
goat—an unbeatable combination in the beds of the women of
Paris. On his travels all over the world, he had encountered many a
novelty, and all this he willingly demonstrated to the fair daughters

---

*Actually, the word "discovery" is a misnomer, as gold had been known
to exist in California for at least a century. The gold fields of "Eldorado"
are mentioned in a paper named *La Gazette de Hollande* (1737) and in a
book, *Histoire naturelle et civile de las Californie* by Buriell Paris (1767).
**All these phenomena are ruled astrologically by Neptune, which was
discovered in those years by John Couch Adams and Urbain-Jean-Joseph
Le Verrier from perturbations in the orbit of Uranus.

of "La Belle France." Around 1840, he had been initiated into the Hermetic Brotherhood of Light, a.k.a. the Fraternitas Hermetica Luxor. Under the influence of Eliphas Levi, he founded his own order in 1868, the Brotherhood of Eulis. It practiced unadulterated tantric (sexual) magic as outlined in the order's bible, *Magia Sexualis,** written by the Master. Randolph can be reckoned the Cagliostro of the 19th century, as Aleister Crowley no doubt holds the title in our own.

Another "strange genius" was Hargrave Jennings (1817–90). He was employed by the Italian Opera in London. In 1870, he published *The Rosicrucians: Their Rites and Mysteries*—another sensational (sexational) bucket of sod exploiting people's lower instincts. This, his magnum opus, has not only inspired mystics and pornographers, but it is also blatantly obvious that Sigmund Freud built his new theories on this work, conveniently forgetting the quotation marks. So when Freud shocked the citizens of Vienna at the turn of the century, he was merely popularizing anothers man's 30-year-old ideas. As Richard Cavendish so rightly observes:

> Jennings was obsessed with sex, believed that worship of the sex organs was the root of all religions and saw genital emblems nodding and winking at him wherever he looked.

The year 1875 has been described as a milestone in the history of occultism, and not without reason. That year saw the deaths of P.E.M. Vintras, Paschal Beverly Randolph, and Eliphas Levi, as well as the birth of the legendary Aleister Crowley. Crowley always claimed later to be an incarnation of Levi, whereas others, who knew Crowley, were sometimes tempted to believe that it was a case of mistaken identity and that he meant Vintras instead.

Vintras was a contemporary of Levi and leader of a French religious sect. A Norman peasant born in 1839, he evidently became quite mad after getting involved in the effort to restore the French monarchy under Louis XVII (who had died, but who was rumored

---

*The title was in Latin no doubt to conceal the subject matter, or at least to lend it a scientific or medical air. It was all right to talk about sex if you were a physician.

to be still alive). Vintras was considered by his followers to be a new Christ. He had several mystical experiences, produced many magical ("miraculous") religious effects, and formed an order that ended up being condemned by the pope—whereupon Vintras appointed *himself* pope. At some point he was charged with sodomy and sentenced to five years in prison for fraud. Some say that it was a gross miscarriage of justice and that he was a victim of religious persecution by the establishment; i.e., the Catholic Church. Others maintain that no smoke is possible without a fire—the fire in this case represented by the notorious Abbé Boullan.*

Unfortunately for Crowley's adversaries, this theory can't pass muster, as "the Beast" had already been born by the time Vintras died.

Another event of the first magnitude this year was the foundation of the Theosophical Society in New York by Helena Petrovna Blavatsky. Overnight, occultism became organized, serious, and *au fait*. It would later be the victim of scandal, but this was its first real breakthrough.

Before 1875, esoteric occultism mainly consisted of little private seances in spiritualistic groups who were generally ignorant of one another's existence. The phenomenon was only 27 years old, and already it was a dubious project, thanks to a multitude of itinerant confidence tricksters posing as mediums and parting gullible fools with their money. Of course, there were also genuine mediums, but their conditions were not the best and they were far outnumbered by the swindlers. The notoriety that arose about the spiritualists, and the vagrancy act, finally forced the mediums to "perform" in traveling fun fairs and side shows among other con men and horse thieves. Naturally, this image did nothing to promote the business to the level of a serious science. For many years, the serious mediums were therefore compelled to work more or less underground, and their income derived mainly from the pockets of the solid middle classes. The very same people who officially condemned that

---

*Boullan was another unfrocked priest who took over Vintras's sect after his death and turned it into an organization for the promotion of original sexual creativity; i.e., a gang of perverts. For the whole sad story, the reader is referred to *Les Maitres Spirituels Contemporains* by Patrick Ravaignant (Paris: Culture Art, Loisire, 1972), or *The Occult* by Colin Wilson (Colin Wilson [Publications] Ltd., 1971).

sort of superstition during the day would try, night after night, to establish contact with their late husbands and wives, uncles and aunts, dogs, cats, and canaries, and these fat bourgeois were just as eager as the mediums to keep the activities under cover. It's obvious that such an attitude does not exactly stimulate basic research. There's no truth in the ancient adage that, if standards are good, double standards are twice as good.

The Theosophical Society, with the motto "There is no religion higher than the truth," changed all this. This was something entirely new. It was perhaps not so different from spiritualism; indeed, some said that it was hard to distinguish one from the other and that it probably was the same thing, but in curry, another example of the exciting and exotic air possessed by anything from the colonies—the teachings of the Theosophists were full of incense and Indian philosophy.

Only two years later, Disraeli persuaded Queen Victoria to let herself be crowned Empress of India. After that, everything went. Famous or at least well-known scientists and men of letters joined the Theosophical Society, and in 1882 the Society for Psychical Research (SPR) was formed—the first organization that tried to use scientific methods to gather information and knowledge about phenomena outside the normal.

Madame Blavatsky, or H.P.B., as she was called by her devotees, published two mammoth works: I*sis Unveiled* and *The Secret Doctrine*, two of the classics of occultism. Each of these works contains roughly 1200–1500 pages and is filled with obscure facts about comparative religions, occult lore, and so on. An admirable feat, but, as Aleister Crowley once pointed out:

> The best of the serious attempts to systematise the results
> of comparative religion is made by Blavatsky, but though
> she had an immense genius for acquiring facts, she had
> none whatever for sorting and selecting the essentials.

Now this is typically Crowley, but it's not far off the mark. The two giant works are interesting indeed, but it's hard to see the forest for the trees.

Of course, all this didn't go off in silence. When H.P.B. moved her headquarters to London, and she, as founder of the T.S., took over the most active and controversial lodge at the time, the Church

Helena Petrovna Blavatsky—"an immense genius for acquiring facts"
The Secret Doctrine, 1888

of England declared war. It just so happened that the clergy in particular found the Hindu and Buddhist aspects stimulating, with the result that several good men of the cloth received word from the Archbishop of Canterbury to the effect that they could either resign from the T.S. or be excommunicated by the C. of E.

The Theosophical Society now had several thousand members. In order to separate the wheat from the chaff, HPB organized a smaller, esoteric circle made up of her most devoted supporters. Only among these were the theosophists with connection to the Secret Chiefs, or the Mahatmas, as they were called. These were the actual leaders of the T.S. They existed only on the astral plane but once in a while manifested themselves before HPB and others of the elect.

Most of the people whom we later find in the Golden Dawn were also connected with HPB and the inner circle. Both Westcott and Mathers gave lectures on the Qabalah at the T.S. on several occasions. Westcott was a member of the inner group and acted as a sort of liaison between Blavatsky and the Golden Dawn, once he'd founded it. It was with the blessing of "Ms. Theosophy" that he translated the *Sepher Yetzirah*, in fact.

Although there existed a close connection between the two groups, the direct cause for the foundation of the Golden Dawn is rather to be found in the SRIA. This was basically a Masonic organization, preserving the esoteric tradition—at least in theory. It resented all the controversy and publicity that hung over spiritualism and theosophy, but neither group was totally without influence.

It is fairly obvious that the actual founder of the GD, W. Wynn Westcott, used Blavatsky's organization as an example of how his own brainchild should absolutely *not* be constructed. Point one: he was a Freemason and a Rosicrucian. Accordingly, he wasn't apt to throw the Christian and Western esoteric tradition in the garbage for the sake of a mixed bag of oriental symbols and philosophies suiting a way of life with no chances of ever being integrated into the customs and lifestyles of Europe and the rest of the West. He didn't intend to let in anybody right off the street, either. He belonged to the British upper middle class. He was a doctor of medicine and coroner for the North London district and, in addition to that, a man with great and original learning, with a love of tradition and his fellow man. That doesn't mean that he was an archetypal reactionary bourgeois. The mere fact that he thought of founding a new order was partly caused by his knowledge of the limitations of the Masons and the SRIA.

Both were organizations with prejudice and mixed traditions. At the same time he was leading the SRIA, he had plans about founding a new group which would be more open and creative. Most others would surely have taken advantage of their position of leadership to introduce novel ideas. The fact that he didn't proves that his ideas were so revolutionary and radical that such a procedure would have been impossible. This was his way of rebellion. He wanted to achieve two things above all: He wouldn't limit the membership to Master Masons, and he wanted women to be admitted to the new organization. This was a tall order in the England of the 1880s. Above all, he was a diplomat, and there is no doubt that the foundation of the Golden Dawn was due to Wynn Westcott alone, whatever happened afterwards. It is possible, though, that he would have let it stop at the dream, had karma not interfered.

There are several different versions as to how the founding came about, and it has provided ample reasons for disagreement. A lot of scholars even feel that all these stories are sheer rubbish and nonsense and that Westcott and Mathers probably founded the Golden Dawn over a mug of beer one mild spring night in 1888. But the order's archives and various members' private letters and notes indicate different possibilities, of which we will examine the most generally accepted in the next chapter.

MacGregor Mathers of Golden Dawn fame. Here, he is taking part in a public performance of his idea of the mysteries of Isis—another attempt to bolster scanty funds.

The Birth of the Golden Dawn

The most elaborate and criticized version of the foundation of the Hermetic Order of the Golden Dawn is the one that follows. Of course, it hasn't been allowed to stand unchallenged. There are many other versions. Even among adherents to this theory, there seems to be little agreement about even minor details. Some say that a bundle of papers belonging to Kenneth MacKenzie's estate found its way to W. Wynn Westcott and MacGregor Mathers, who accepted it as genuine, and that they improvised from there. The most quoted story, however, goes somewhat like this.

Around 1887, A.F.A. Woodford, a Master Mason and a member of SRIA, bought a second-hand book at a bookstall in Farringdon Road. On further perusal of his new treasure, he discovered some papers among the leaves of the book. These papers turned out to be written in an unknown cipher, or rather alphabet, which he couldn't understand. He therefore turned to Westcott, whom he knew to be an expert on that sort of thing. Westcott recognized the style as being that of the 15th century, and he possessed the key to the language. It was actually a secret alphabet described in the *Polygraphia* of Abbot Johann Trithemius.

The papers were found to be the loose structure of some rituals after Rosicrucian and Qabalistic models, and the letter was written by a female Rosicrucian adept by the name of Anna Sprengel, with an address in Germany—Nuremberg or Stuttgart. Her magical name was Sapiens Dominabitur Astris, or Soror SDA. Westcott wrote to the address and received in answer a charter that authorized him to establish, with two fellow chiefs, a temple in London. This temple, Isis-Urania, was to function more or less independently of the mother lodge in Germany, which called itself Die Goldene Dämmerung.

Since Westcott was a busy man, he needed help with the project. He approached a brother in the prodigious assembly which constituted the Freemasons: a comparatively young man, 34 years of age, by name of Samuel Liddell Mathers, of Scottish descent. It was no coincidence that he chose this person. For one thing, he was a fellow Mason. For another thing, his knowledge of these arcane things was, if possible, even greater than that of Westcott himself. Finally, he was destitute. He spent all of his time in the British Museum Library, studying old grimoires and the history, strategy, and tactics of war. He had no other interests, no occupation, and consequently no income. He was born in the East End of London in 1854 and later moved to the provinces, where he finally settled in Bournemouth with his mother until her death on January 27, 1885, from pneumonia. Subsequently, he moved to London, where he lived in modest rooms in Great Percy Street in the King's Cross district near the museum.

It was thanks to Westcott's generosity that Mathers was able to move to the metropolis. He was the one who actually fixed him up with the rooms and paid the rent for several years. Mathers had become a Mason in the provinces, and one may assume that Westcott, as a consequence of the order's ideals, considered it his duty to help a brother in distress.

He had previously successfully sponsored Mathers' research. It resulted in the publication of the latter's book, *The Kabbalah Unveiled*, in 1887. It was an English translation of Knorr von Rosenroth's Latin edition of *Kabbala Denudata*, which, in its turn, was a translation of parts of the Hebrew *Zohar*, a Qabalistic masterpiece believed to have been written by Moses de Leon in the 11th century. Mathers' translation is generally agreed to be one of the greatest masterpieces in the field of the occult, and it's not strange that Westcott approached his protege again with this new project. It must be said to Mathers' credit that, although there can be no doubt that the GD was created on Westcott's initiative, it was due entirely to Mathers' work that the order developed into what it did—something absolutely unique, a milestone in the history of occultism and the foundation of all modern Western magic.

Mathers put meat on the ceremonial bones, and he soon had a set of really effective rituals ready. In order to maintain the holy principle of the triad, Westcott and Mathers invited the Supreme

Magus of the SRIA, Dr. Robert Woodman, to become fellow founder and chief, and, from about the spring equinox of 1888, they started to recruit members from their closest circle of friends and acquaintances.

The first time that the Golden Dawn encountered the public, even if modestly and inconspicuously, was December 8, 1888. It was in connection with an ostensibly innocent inquiry by one Gustave Mommesen, of whom nothing is known.* The inquiry could be read in an issue of the magazine *Notes and Queries*, and it went as follows:

> Johann F. Falk succeeded to the Directorate of a secret society of students of the Kabbalah about 1810, in London I believe. Its name was Chabrah Zereh Aur Bokher as nearly as Hebrew can be put into English. The late Eliphaz Levi, of Paris, was concerned in it later on. Is this society still in existence?

The answer came with the February issue the following year:

> The order of mystics which gave Eliphaz Lévi (Abbé Constant) his occult knowledge and of which Johann Falk was at one time the lecturer on the Kabbalah in London, is still at work in England. It is not a Masonic order, and there is no distinction between men and women students.
>
> The greatest privacy is maintained and some knowledge of Hebrew is essential, but the whole course of study and experiment is so abstruse and complex that the membership is very limited as to numbers, and the proceedings have no public interest. Its true name is only told to initiates, and the few outsiders who have heard of its existence only know the society as The Hermetic Students of the G.·.D.·.
>
> W. Wynn Westcott
369 Camden Rd.
London N.

---

*It has been suggested that Mommesen is a pseudonym for Westcott or Mathers or both.

R. A. Gilbert is of the opinion that it was an advertising stunt perpetrated in order to increase the number of members, and something seems to bear this out, although new members had already begun to enlist during the summer of 1888. We will look more closely at some of these members. Who were they, and what brought them to the GD?

The official inauguration of the Isis-Urania temple was at the equinox of March 20, 1888, and that was also when the first new members were initiated. On the original parchment roll that holds the names of the members, we find Mathers, Westcott, and Woodman as the first three listed, along with their respective magical mottos.* Next we find no less than Fräulein Anna Sprengel, Sapiens Dominabitur Astris. Why she is listed as a member of Isis-Urania is a mystery. She belonged to the alleged mother lodge No. 1, Licht, Liebe, Leben, of which only two other members are known, and only by their magical names at that. They were Ex Uno Disce Omnes and In Utroque Fidelis. The former informed Westcott about the death of Anna Sprengel, and the latter functioned as her secretary on several occasions. He or she had personally written one or two of the existing letters addressed to Westcott.

Isis-Urania was not even the second temple, but only No. 3. About Hermanubis Temple, No. 2, even less is known than about the mother lodge. SDA mentions in a letter that a charter was given to some Englishmen some years before, and she adds that she never heard if they succeeded in organizing a temple. Other sources claim that it possibly was a temple in Bristol, not to be mistaken for the temple of the same name, same place, which descended from the Hermes Lodge. Dr. R. W. Felkin, whom we shall meet later on, opened the Hermes, together with several others, in 1916. That year was busy for Dr. Felkin, and it was also this tireless man who was behind a third lodge of this name around 1930. However, the first of its kind, GD No. 2, possibly could have been a temple which had Kenneth MacKenzie, Frederick Hockley, and Edward Bulwer-Lytton as members. This is pure speculation, however. Nothing directly indicates that these people belonged to

---

*Mathers and his two colleagues appear again on the list under different mottos. They acted as Secret Chiefs as well. This can cause some confusion in trying to get a picture of the membership situation.

an early pre-GD, perhaps with the exception of the latter. Bulwer-Lytton was a personal friend of Eliphas Levi, and there are quite a lot of hints in the early GD papers as to the predecessors of this order, but serious reservations can be raised. Levi didn't speak any English and, as far as can be ascertained, only visited England a couple of times.

On the other hand, it seems as if a Dr. Thyssen or Thiessen, Lux et Tenebris of Liege, was connected with Hermanubis No. 2. I haven't been able to confirm or discount this assertion, but I am working on it. Mathers claims that he received all the Second Order material from Thyssen, who may be identical, in Paris in 1891. It's just possible, although not very likely.

Next is the name of the first actual member apart from the three leaders. It was a woman, Mina Bergson, of French/English/Jewish descent, sister of the world-famous philosopher Henri Bergson. She was a beautiful student at the Slade School of Art near the British Museum, and she met Mathers while studying Egyptian art around 1887. They became engaged and later married. As stated, she became the first neophyte. She was initiated at the equinox.

Her importance to the GD can only be compared to that of Mathers and Westcott and should not be underestimated. She was Mathers' medium, scryer, and inspiration through a long and laborious life, but that's not all. Her artistic training was greatly to the benefit of the Order for years to come. She designed the decorations and costumes in the temples, especially the famous and very important color compositions in the Vault of the Adepti, which was the *pièce de résistance* of the whole Adeptus Minor ritual. Apart from her artistic talents she was also an accomplished leader. After Mathers' death in 1918, she ran the Ahathoor Temple in Paris, and later on the AO (Alpha et Omega) in London until her own death 10 years later.

When she and Mathers became engaged, she changed her name from Mina to Moina which undeniably has a more Celtic ring to it. Mathers had developed a Jacobean fixation. He was possessed by an idea to the effect that he was a descendant of the Scottish clan of MacGregor, and since the 1870s he had been calling himself nothing less than Samuel Liddell MacGregor Mathers, Comte de Glenstrae. Like Crowley later on, he believed himself to be the reincarnation of various famous people. Later critics have accused him of snobbery, but the fact is that his claims cannot utterly be dismissed. It is conceivable that an ancestor had received the sword stroke and with it the title Comte de Glenstrae from the fugitive Scottish pretender in the 17th century during his exile in France, and under those circumstances the title could be genuine without being registered in the Heraldic Colleges of Arms for England, Scotland, or Ireland.

The next member was Theresa Jane O'Connell, with the motto Ciall Agus Neart. She was a pupil of the Slade School of Art like Moina, and was initiated the same day, together with Eugene E. Street (Certus et Constans) and William George Lemon (Via Crucis Via Lucis), of whom we know nothing. They later resigned, and Miss O'Connell was later expelled from the Order.

Others initiated in March were more important: Benjamin Cox (Crux Dat Salutem) and Thomas Henry Pattinson (Vota Vita Mea), both of whom founded lodges under the Isis-Urania supervision. We will return to this in a moment. John Collinson (Servabo Fidem), who also later resigned, was among the day's initiates, but his name was added later on in July, when another batch was initiated.

For a first initiation it might be said to be a modest affair. It took place in a set of rooms in Gower Street, and afterward the assembly dispersed and everybody went about their business, most of them to the nearby British Museum. There was not as much pomp and circumstance about it as there would be later on such occasions.

The three chiefs had, as I have mentioned earlier, double identities, and also double magical names. Mathers was 'S Rioghail Mo Dhream, Celtic for "royal is my tribe." In addition to this, he was an anonymous chief of the Second Order under the *nom de guerre* Deo Duce Comite Ferro (God is my master and my companion is the sword), usually abbreviated DDCF. Westcott's aliases were Sapere Aude (dare to be wise) and Non Omni Moriar (not everything dies), and finally, Woodman's were Magna est Veritas (truth is great) and Vincit Omnia Veritas (truth conquers all).

The GD's structure was an hierarchical one, according to the following grades:

0 = 0 Neophyte
1 = 10 Zelator
2 = 9 Theoricus
3 = 8 Practicus
4 = 7 Philosophus
5 = 6 Adeptus Minor

These were the only degrees mentioned in the original cipher. In addition to these, the following grades were established:

6 = 5 Adeptus Major
7 = 4 Adeptus Exemptus

And finally the Third Order:

8 = 3 Magister Temple
9 = 2 Magus
10 = 1 Ipsissimus

The Third Order was made up of the astral chiefs with whom only Mathers was able to communicate.

In the beginning, only the first five grades were actually being worked, and nobody apart from the three leaders was aware of what was going on above the grade of Philosophus. One can't say that they were missing much, as nothing really *was* going on there until 1892. For all that the members of the lower grades knew, any activity above this grade might have been taking place on the astral level. This was not so, however. Mathers was working busily to compile a curriculum for what was to become the Second Order. The Third Order (i.e., the grades above 7 = 4 Adeptus Exemptus) would be the domain of the astral world exclusively until Crowley penetrated it years later, according to himself, but all this was yet to come.

If activities were scant along the inner lines, then the same could certainly not be said for the physical world, the world of Malkuth.

During the first year, two more temples were erected. One was Osiris, in as unlikely a place as Weston-super-Mare. Its charter is dated April 17, 1888. Its Imperator and driving force was a devoted Soc. Ros. member, Benjamin Cox, who happened to live in that seaside resort. It was never a big temple. It only had about a dozen members at its peak. Cox died in December 1895, and after his death the temple slowly dispersed.

The other temple started during 1888 was the Horus Temple in Bradford, inaugurated on Oct. 9 or 19 (dates differ). This was a very active lodge, and it increased its membership very quickly. Thomas Henry Pattinson, a Yorkshire watchmaker, was its Imperator.

Two more temples were later opened in the original Golden Dawn; i.e., before 1900: the Amen-Ra in Edinburgh and the Ahathoor in Paris.

Amen-Ra received its charter on June 8, 1893, and the temple opened on December 19 of the same year. John William Brodie-Innes (Sub Spe), one of the really accomplished magicians, became imperator. He had been initiated into Isis-Urania in 1890.

The Ahathoor in *fin de siècle* Paris was the smallest of the original temples. It started out as a subbranch, but opened on a regular basis on January 6, 1894. It was more of a prank. In 1892, the Matherses moved to Paris. Mathers, of course, couldn't be expected to go to London every now and again, as he expected other members to do (from Edinburgh, for example, before the Amen-Ra Temple was established), and as magic was his *raison d'être*, he wanted a temple of his own to play in. He continued as chief of both Isis-Urania and Ahathoor, appointing Florence Farr (Sapientia Sapienti Dono Data), the actress who later contributed to the fall of the original Order, to act in his place. There can be little doubt that Mathers' voluntary exile helped undermine his position as leader, and when the break came, he wasn't there to suppress the insurrection.

In July, he who was going to be the grand old man of the GD, William Alexander Aytoun (or Ayton), was initiated. Born in London April 8, 1816, he was at the ripe old age of 72 when he joined the Isis-Urania. He has been described as "a clergyman with an alchemical laboratory in the cellar, hidden from the bishop's penetrating glance."

He told William Butler Yeats that he once succeeded in producing the Philosopher's Stone, but he didn't dare drink the fluid he composed from it until, in his old age, when he didn't have so much to lose, he went to get the bottle of Elixir only to find that it had evaporated. Bad luck. His magical name was Virtute Orta Occident Rarius.*

Further down on the membership roll is the name of Dr. Edmund William Berridge (Resurgam). Apparently he had misgivings about signing the pledge in April 1888, but eventually he seems to have reconciled himself to the rules, for he was admitted on May 10 of the following year. His unorthodox medical philosophy was a contributing factor to the final breach between Mathers and Annie Horniman, but more about this later.

Two of the most important members were Annie Horniman and William Butler Yeats. Annie Horniman (Fortiter et Recte) was the daughter of the tea king, Frederick Horniman, the owner of Horniman's Tea. She was a highly emotional lady with more money than she knew what to do with. Soror FER could be kind and gentle, or she could be a bitch. She subsidized Mathers and Moina for years, but her intolerance of other members caused Mathers to expel her. She was later reinstated, but, in the end, she finally resigned after another disagreement with someone in the Order.

W. B. Yeats (Demon est Deus Inversus) is by far the greatest celebrity of which the GD can boast—poet, playwright, and Nobel Prize winner for literature in 1923.** Taking into consideration the year and the fact that he was Irish, one would suppose that it was for political reasons. He later took over the leadership of the Order, and he was an accomplished magician. Not that that had anything to do with it. At that time it was all sharp elbows and club politics.

Another member was Constance Mary Wilde, the wife of Oscar (Qui Partitur Vincit). Interesting, but of no special importance to the Western Esoteric Tradition.

Another celebrity was Mrs. Florence Beatrice Emery, otherwise known as Florence Farr, the actress. Supposed mistress of Yeats.

---

*Some of Ayton's letters have been published as *The Alchemist of the Golden Dawn: The Letters of the Revd W. A. Ayton to F. L. Gardner and Others 1886–1905*, edited by Ellic Howe. The Aquarian Press, 1985.

**I am aware that the Swedish Academy and the Nobel Prize Committee deny any political affiliations or motives, but it seems to me the only way to explain why, for the last 20 years or so, prizes have been given to obscure third-world writers of third-rate material. If I'm entitled to an opinion, that's it.

Acknowledged mistress of G. B. Shaw. Some rumors even say that she had an affair with Aleister Crowley. In spite of her social standing she was also a gifted magician and writer on the occult.*

And the roster of early joiners goes on and on, with many names ranging from the most famous magicians and occultists of the day to totally obscure shopkeepers:

Arthur Edward Waite's motto was nothing less than Sacramentum Regis. He was a mystic with no aptitude whatever for magic. After the schism, he took over the Order by a coup. After the takeover, he dispensed with most of Mathers' original material, and one can say that that constituted the death of the Golden Dawn, as far as the Isis-Urania is concerned. There's no need to comment further on Waite. Crowley has already done so. Suffice it to say that I agree with Crowley's assessment up to the point of slander and libel.

Maud Gonne's magical name, Per Ignem ad Lucem, was very apt. She played with fire most of her life. Another one of Yeats's unfortunate affairs, she was *the* beauty queen of her day, freedom fighter for the Irish cause. She married a drunken sod of an officer in the I.R.A. or something, a rebel who beat her up properly before the went to the pub to conspire and fight for freedom. In short, a fast lady.

Allan Bennett (Voco, and later Iehi Aur). A very skilled magician; in fact, Aleister Crowley's teacher in the Order. He later turned to Buddhism and moved to Ceylon. He lived and died in extreme poverty in London in 1923.

Brodie-Innes was another good all round magician who at least knew what the Order owed Mathers. His writings on various occult subjects are not bad, even if the influence of DDCF peeks through quite a lot.

Another active member, rather prominent in his day, was Percy William Bullock (Levavi Oculos)

Frederick Leigh Gardner (Experto Crede, and later De Profundis ad Lucem) was insignificant as such, but he turned out to be a mine of information. His private papers and letters give a rare insight in certain aspects of the Order, its teachings, and so on.**

Egyptian Magic by Florence Farr. The Aquarian Press, 1982.

**The Magicians of the Golden Dawn: A Documentary History of a Magical Order 1887–1923* by Ellic Howe. Routledge & Kegan Paul, 1972.

Julian Baker (Causa Scientia) was also one of Crowley's teachers. Yet another Crowleyite was George Cecil Jones (Volo Noscere). Baker or Jones put Crowley up for admission.

Marcus Worsley Blackden (Ma Wahanu Thesi) was another of the big ones.

After 1896–7 others joined, but for the time being we will stop at these.

Annie Horniman was a bosom friend of Mina Bergson and very interested in her promising artistic career. I gather that it actually *was* promising. Naturally FER resented Mathers' attentions towards her protégée, but in the end she accepted the fact that Mina was determined to go through with the marriage. Horniman's attachment must have been rather serious, as she continued to subsidize her friend, even to the point of persuading her father to employ Mathers as custodian of his private museum at Forest Hill in 1890. The prospect and the income from this situation finally enabled him and Mina to marry.

It was not any ordinary match. They were both vegetarians. Both of them abhorred the sexual act, and the union was never consummated. Moina's devotion to him was second to none. Over the years she never for one moment questioned the fact that Mathers' egocentric demands on her killed any chance she may have had of becoming a successful artist. On the contrary, she more than willingly administered to his genius and defended him against any criticism of his tyrannical ways of running the Order.

Annie Horniman put up with all this from her protégée's new husband, and even inceased the amount of their annual allowance, as Mathers had been unable to keep his job. In less than a year, he had fallen out with his employer. As unable as he was to suffer the least objection from the members of the GD, he himself was just as unable to take orders from his own superiors.

For a year or so, he had been in contact with several discarnate entities, the true chiefs of the Order, and they had instructed him to institute a new Second Order within the existing framework.

From 5°=6□ Adeptus Minor to 7°=4□ Adeptus Exemptus, the new inner Order was to be known as Ordo Roseae Rubeae et Aureae Crucis, or R.R. et A.C. Mathers busily worked on the new material and rituals, hoping to get everything ready by the beginning of 1892. How this went will be described in the next chapter.

The Decline and Fall of the G∴D∴

On December 7, 1891, a strange ceremony took place at Thavies Inn, Holborn Circus, London. An initiate was led into the seven-sided Vault of the Adepti to be tied to the Cross of Suffering, after which the lid was removed from the coffin and laid across the altar to reveal the corpse of Christian Rosenkreutz (that is, Mathers), who slowly rose, to the relief of the candidates, and chanted in a barbarous language that resounded to every corner of the temple.

This was the very first Adeptus Minor ritual ever performed and the first one to go through it was Annie Horniman—probably in recognition of her great work for the Order; i.e., the financial support of Mathers and his wife. Later on, she was again specially invited to consecrate the Ahathoor Temple in Paris. Relations were strained again, and in the end it came to a break after all. More about that later.

Now, this was new and exiting. Not only was the ritual ingeniously conceived and very effective, but a whole special curriculum of nothing less than practical magic had been devised for the members of the Golden Dawn. We shall examine the syllabus in Appendix B, as it is the foundation of most modern magic.

Only a handful of members were initiated at Thavies Inn. Already in August 1892, the Vault had been dismantled and moved to new premises at 24–25 Clipstone Street, near Regent's Park. This was to be the first of many such moves over the years, from one dingy place to another, deteriorating as they moved step by step away from central London. A lot can be read into the changing of addresses every now and again. They finally ended up in Blythe Road, Hammersmith, where a notorious confrontation ended the life of the original Order.

At their own premises, the members could come and go at their own convenience—not that the Second Order ever gained as many members as the GD in the outer. From the foundation of the Order until late 1893, only some 30 people went through the Adeptus Minor ceremony. One may therefore wonder why they needed their own quarters. Well, first of all, there was the matter of the "Vault" itself. Until the Second Order was started, the GD met at the Mark Mason's Hall or the Freemason's Hall, and it would have been impossible to keep the Vault erected there from one meeting to the next. In addition to that, there was the difficulty of not always being able to arrange the meetings at convenient times, as the Masons saw to themselves first. This resulted sometimes in double bookings and the undesirable situation of members arriving from the provinces only to find that the meeting had been postponed. This circumstance was especially unfortunate, because excuses along the lines of not being able to attend under such circumstances didn't go down too well with Mathers. However, with rooms of their own, there were lots of things to do apart from meetings.

As a matter of fact, members of the GD continued as before. Only the Second Order had access to the "Vault of the Adepti." In addition to the Second Order meetings, there were hours of meditation, group gatherings, and private work. Everybody was free to use the temple for magical purposes; i.e., consecrating equipment and, above all, private magic rituals and operations. There was a fairly heavy traffic to and fro.

Two years later, in August 1894, the temple moved again to new premises at 62 Oakley Square, still in the vicinity of Regent's Park, where it remained for a brief period.

It was also about this time that the first early seeds of destruction were sown. Mathers' growing commitments to the Jacobite cause led gradually to more and more illusions of grandeur. It caused increasing distress to Annie Horniman, as Moina's pleas for more money tended to arrive more and more frequently. She had granted the couple an annual allowance of £200 for their work for the Order, and she was particularly annoyed at Mathers when he installed himself and Moina in an expensive house in 16th arrondissement, near the Bois de Boulogne, when a modest flat in Montmartre would more suitably have fitted the bill, Moina being an "artiste" and all. On the other hand, living among rats, artists, and other undesirable specimens was not befitting for "la Comte de Glenstrae"; nothing short of the best would do, even if it meant traveling across the whole of Paris by means of a bicycle to get to the Bibliotheque Nationale and l'Arsenal, where he spent most of his time collating old manuscripts.

He also operated on the fringes of the Paris stockmarket, peddling "hot tips" to all and sundry. Like so many "geniuses," he preferred anything to regular work.* Aside from that, Annie Horniman became more and more annoyed with Mathers' "neglect" of the Order for the benefit of "theatrical politics" or "political theatrics."

Of course, it didn't really begin with the "first seed." The seed was already contaminated with poison before the planting. The death of the organization was in fact caused by the actual birth of the Second Order. Its nature being magical, it naturally involved meditation and mental practices, releasing the terrifying powers of the human ego. This "ego trip," for in essence that's what it is, is indispensable to the art of magic.** Without control over and access to the ego, no willpower, and without willpower, no magic. But to release these powers means carrying your strong passions and your nerves on your lapels, and when too many "antsy" people congregate, sparks usually fly.

And sparks did indeed fly. A.H. was a weak link in the chain.

---

*Hitler, Crowley, Lovecraft, and Modigliani are just a few other examples of this constitutional phobia against ordinary employment lest it detract even a jot from their no doubt unique karmas. Their time was apparently otherwise spent daydreaming, totally absent from the world.

It is interesting to note that, of the four people here mentioned, including Mathers, only Modigliani seems to have had a normal sex life, as far as can be ascertained. Perhaps Mathers loved to dress in Highland fashion because of a transvestite urge; i.e., the only legitimate way to wear women's clothing (the kilt). In that case, his whole Jacobite craze would be a sophisticated sublimation. Of course, it may not be so, but such a fixation on martial symbols as Mathers suffered from should be regarded with a certain amount of suspicion.

**That's the reason a magic circle should never be too big; hence the traditional custom of forming a new coven when the mother organization exceeds 13 members.

As she didn't get anywhere with her attitude towards Mathers, she started to look for faults closer to home; i.e., the Isis-Urania Temple and other British branches.

Documents exist proving that, as early as September 1892, Horniman reported some Horus members' bad behavior to Mathers, resulting in the said members' expulsions or resignations.

Mathers was well aware of this deplorable situation and would probably have done best in expelling Annie Horniman but, dependent upon her financial support, he postponed it until it was too late. However, he did throw a bone to her by asking her to consecrate his new Ahathoor Temple in January 1894, probably hoping that this honor would make her keep up the payments and keep her out of mischief in the Order. It didn't have any lasting effects. When she got back to London, she found other things to upset her.

A new rising star in the GD was Florence Farr. Deputized by Mathers to run the Isis-Urania in his absence, she was the ideal object for Horniman's attention. She was certainly to be envied. She was extroverted, beautiful, and famous, a successful actress in her own right, moving in the right circles, with two such admirers as William Butler Yeats and George Bernard Shaw (who, with the possible exception of Oscar Wilde, was the greatest British dramatist of the period). With a view to Annie Horniman's later engagement in the Abbey Theatre in Dublin, it is quite understandable that she would sooner or later find fault with Florence Farr, who was everything that she herself wasn't. A.H.'s involvement in the Abbey Theatre shows her to be a generous and unselfish soul in many ways, but one can understand her reaction to the other woman. She wouldn't have been human if she hadn't been jealous of her under these circumstances, and as she was watching for her to slip, she soon found grounds for criticism. But before anything could come of it, another moral, or rather, im- or amoral problem had occurred.

Dr. Berridge (Resurgam), a health freak and homeopathic practitioner, was a true disciple of a man called Thomas Lake Harris, the founder of an obscure political-religious sect called "The Brotherhood of the New Life." The fraternity moved to the wild West and settled in what they hoped would be small, self-supporting communities after the fashion of Robert Owen. Like Owen's brand of "communism," Harris's scheme failed, but here the resemblance ends. The former had been strictly sociopolitical in its ideology, but the latter had other strings to its banjo. The Brotherhood of the New Life initiated its members into strange sexual practices; i.e. group-marriages, Karezza, etc.* Needless to say, the brotherhood became the subject of fierce antagonism from the establishment, and as Harris's political theories were unassailable, at least in theory (all political theories are), his adversaries, true to the principles of Darwinism, whether they liked it or not, played the man instead of the ball.

As Dr. Berridge was an advocate of Harris's ideas, it can hardly come as any surprise that Fortiter et Recte (Horniman) had found another cause to promote, namely the expulsion of the abominable sodomite. However, two things worked against her. One, Berridge was a staunch supporter of Mathers, and two, she had herself fallen out with the Imperator. For some time she had been dissatisfied with the fact that Mathers spent the money she sent the couple for Order work on political claptrap. Lately he had given a banquet in honor of a Royal Personage for the purpose of promoting the Jacobite cause. A.H. notified him and Moina that no more checks would be forthcoming.

One must realize that, at that time, she had increased their annual allowance to £300, a considerable sum in those days when a housemaid's wages were about £20 a year. At the same time, she resigned from her office as Sub-Praemonstratrix of Isis-Urania.

Mathers wrote her a rude answer in September 1896, but as he had been absent from the London lodge for so long, and as the Second Order members had grown in number—and there were a lot of them who hardly knew Mathers, let alone owed him any allegiance—he felt compelled to take action. This resulted in the famous manifesto of October 29, 1896, in which he made clear who was boss.

I'm not including the manifesto here, partly because it's too

---

*Karezza is a Western adaptation of the Indian Tantra Yoga; i.e., sexual yoga. One of its practical aspects is prolonged intercourse with no movements and no ejaculation with the orgasm, thus keeping the Kundalini power intact and channeled to the astral level. It obviously takes years to master, and, equally obviously, it is rather difficult to understand for a bunch of straitlaced, God-fearing farmers in the sticks.

long and partly because it has been quoted in a multitude of other works.*

The manifesto included an order to the effect that all who wished to remain in the RR et AC or join it in the future were to sign a pledge of total submission to Mathers personally.

Even though Annie Horniman signed the pledge, it didn't satisfy Mathers, as she gave no sign of resuming the annual allowance. He sent her a critical letter, bemoaning the lack of fraternal feelings in the Order. Still no check arrived, and he had to eat humble pie. In November Moina wrote and asked for money in a direct manner. A.H. was away at the time, but it is very doubtful whether she would have given them any had she been at home. She answered the letter, but never sent any cash. Mathers expelled her immediately in anger.

The Imperator had been falling out with several members for some time now. He had, by issuing his manifesto, taken over the authority of the Order completely. He didn't even bother to tell his fellow founder Wynn Westcott that A.H. had been expelled. Sapere Aude (Westcott) could do nothing about it, as he found himself in a situation similar to that of John Dee with Edward Kelly a few centuries before. It was Mathers who was in contact with the Secret Chiefs, and accordingly, it was he who called the tune.

A petition for the reinstatement of A.H. was drafted and signed by about 30 members, but it was never submitted.

Westcott had been unable to support her, as we have seen. He had his own problems. Somehow, his activities in the Order had come to the attention of the authorities, and he was informed that his occult pursuits were incompatible with his position as Her Majesty's Coroner for the district of North London. He was always convinced that somebody had blown the whistle on him—a theory that Crowley confirmed later on, even giving a name to the whistle blower. He claimed that Mathers dropped

---

*The manifesto has been quoted in its entire length in *The Magicians of the Golden Dawn* by Ellic Howe (Routledge & Kegan Paul, 1972), and an excerpt concerning the nature of the Secret Chiefs can be found in *The Sword of Wisdom* by Ithell Colquhoun (Neville Spearman, 1975), *The Golden Dawn* by R. A. Gilbert (Aquarian Press, 1983), and *The Morning of the Magicians* by Louis Pauwels and Jacques Bergier (Granada, 1960).

the hint to the authorities by conveniently "losing" some compromising Order material bearing Westcott's name in a hansom cab, in order to eliminate Westcott from the scene. This is quite possible in view of Mathers' later letter to Florence Farr, which contains the accusations against Westcott which led to the final schism of the original Order.

Mathers was having lots of problems. Since the break with A.H., he had been obliged to raise funds elsewhere. He obtained a £55 advance payment on a project from another member of the Order, Frederick Leigh Gardner. It concerned a translation of a manuscript in the Bibliotheque l'Arsenal that Mathers had first suggested should be financed by the publisher of occult lore, George Redway. Unfortunately, he had fallen out with Redway; he persuaded Gardner to take over his liabilities. He probably thought he could eventually wriggle himself out of the deal, but he soon discovered that Gardner was no Annie Horniman. He was a businessman, and he wanted his money back with interest, as soon as possible. He wrote Mathers in Paris to that effect, with no beating about the bush.

Deo Duce Comite Ferro wrote an arrogant and insulting letter along the same lines as the one he'd sent to A.H., but was told that, if he was dissatisfied with the deal, he could pay back the £55 that he owed Gardner and sell his manuscript elsewhere. Gardner thereby resigned from the Order.

Again the Order had been compelled to move. The new address was 36 Blythe Rd., Hammersmith. It was consecrated September 21, 1897, and things moved towards the final confrontation with karmic inevitability. In less than a year, a new neophyte would join the brethren. It was like letting the cat in among the pigeons. This neophyte would drive the final nail into the coffin and rise from the ashes as a dark and sinister phoenix. He was a 23-year-old man by the name of Edward Alexander Crowley, better known as the "Beast 666," the greatest, the most famous, and the most notorious magician of the 20th century. We will deal with him *in extenso* later.

After his official resignation from all his offices in the GD, Westcott ran a small private circle within Isis-Urania, which included even Annie Horniman. They met in a house in the Kensington district. Westcott must still have felt himself betrayed and attacked, probably by Mathers himself, because it was about this time that Westcott obtained written affidavits from some employees of the Sanitary Wood Wool Company Ltd., in which he had financial interests,* stating that the employee in question had helped Westcott write letters in German addressed to a Fraulein Anna Sprengel of Nuremberg or Stuttgart, and also translate letters signed by the same lady—a remarkable example of foresight, because he soon would be in a position where such documents were badly needed.

Meanwhile Mathers had written A.H. a letter in which he suggested that they let bygones be bygones. I suppose that he needed money more badly than ever. She replied by telegram that she no longer considered Mathers necessary for the advancement of the Order, as she was confident that the Secret Chiefs in the future would deal directly with the leaders in London. Mathers must have felt himself extremely threatened, because he replied by telegram the very same day, October 19, 1899. In the reply, he claimed that it was no use for her to look to Westcott for guidance, because he (Mathers) could prove that Westcott never had any connection with the Secret Chiefs whatsoever. Westcott admitted as much, but Mathers must now have looked upon his former fellow founder with a suspicion not unlike the one with which Stalin regarded Trotsky after Lenin's death, especially as A.H. didn't go for the bait. So Mathers, in spite of his previous bad experiences, tried F. L. Gardner again, but was reminded that he still owed him money. The result of this encounter was that Mathers expelled Gardner, who in his turn threatened to publish some Order papers that he had copied as a member—which he in fact did in spite of Mather's threats of legal action.**

As his economic situation was rapidly deteriorating, Mathers was now forced to unorthodox financial operations and measures. For some time, he and Moina had been experimenting with the Egyptian rite of Isis, and one of the French members of Ahathoor,

---

*The Sanitary Wood Wool Company Ltd. was located at Thavies Inn, and it was there that the first Vault of the Adepti had been erected.

**Gardner had previously resigned, but Mathers had never acknowledged it officially, presumably because he wanted to keep all prospective financial channels open.

Jules Bois,* a journalist, suggested that they should perform said rite in public, before a paying audience.** The performance was given at Théâtre Bodinière in the Rue Saint-Lazaire in March 1899. It received mixed criticism, but, from this spectacle, we have one of the only two existing photographs of Mathers. He is in toga and leopard-skin stole, holding a flower wand as if he were an Egyptian high priest under the pharaohs delivering a spring offering. One can almost hear Stravinsky in the background. The show was performed once a week for a few months, but *les hommes de vivres* and their *petite grisettes*† soon lost interest. And so, as the new year 1900 approached, it again became necessary for Mathers to find some means of existence.

One thing that can usually be done in such circumstances is to increase the number of members, and thus the membership fees.

After the public performance of the Isis rite and until February 1900, nine new applicants were admitted. Most of them were sensation seekers, no doubt, but it is understandable that, with his eternal need for money, the trouble in the Order, his Jacobite commitments, his translations of manuscripts before deadline, and his general paranoia, Mathers was apt to be a trifle careless with the new people he encountered.

This partly explains why he wasn't up to dealing with he Horos couple when they presented themselves.

Sometime in January 1900, he received three visitors who had lately arrived in Europe from Capetown: Mr. and Mrs. Horos and Dr. Rose Adams.

---

*Another French member, and apart from Mathers the greatest occultist in the Ahathoor Temple, was Dr. Gerard Encausse, known better under his pseudonym "Papus," author of *Le Tarot des Bohemians, Le Qabalah,* etc.

**Even Crowley took up this strange idea some years later in 1910 when he rented Caxton Hall in London on seven consecutive Wednesdays, performing the rites of Eleusis. The charge of admission of £5 was enormous, even if a mescaline trip is said to have been included in the price.

†A rather brilliant account of this time, and even the theatrical event itself, can be found in a couple of French comic books by Tardi and Wininger. They are set in and cover the period from the *fin de siecle* until the end of the First World War. The titles are *Les Onbres de Nulle Part* by Vininger and *Le Demon de la Tour Eiffel* by Tardi.

Mrs. Horos called herself Swami Vive Ananda. In some way or another she convinced Mathers that she was none other than Sapiens Dominabitur Astris—the late Fraulein Anna Sprengel* of the mother lodge, Licht Liebe Leben. She had come to help him in his hour of need, to help him spread the Rite of Isis. It still remains a mystery how she had obtained knowledge of the grade lectures and rituals. She told Mathers that her companions had been initiated in America, whether in a temple chartered by Mathers or by the mother lodge, I don't know,** but the fact is that she convinced Mathers that she belonged to the Ihme Temple No. 8 in Boston, and she persuaded him to part with copies of all the First-Order rituals and lectures. The trio then disappeared from Paris, leaving a lot of unpaid bills behind.

The Horoses were the direct cause of the final collapse of the Order. In January 1900, Mathers received a letter from his deputy in

---

*After Westcott had received the charter in the first letter, Anna Sprengel sent him another four or five letters attending to Order business. Her last letter is dated December 12, 1889, but the mother lodge did send one final letter after this. It is dated August 23, 1890, and is signed by Ex Uno Disce Omnes, regrettably informing the GD about the death of SDA, which would have taken place on July 20, 1890. The letter also announced that they were now on their own, as not everybody had sanctioned SDA's initiative.

**Since the first temple in exile, Ahathoor in Paris in 1894, the GD had become international. Compared to Paris, London was the back of beyond, culturally as well as socially. Everybody went there. Especially the Americans. Even they found their way to the astral plane, and even that was brought back by the tourists. It's likely that Mathers issued charters to no less than three different American temples around 1895. They included Temple No. 8, Ihme, probably in Boston, and No. 9, Themis, most likely in Philadelphia. Nothing much is known about them. They probably dispersed around the turn of the century.

The third, however, is different. No. 10 Thoth-Hermes was erected in Chicago and run by a Mrs. Lockwood. It had such members as Michael Whitty and Paul Foster Case, who eventually took over the leadership. From about 1920 the temple changed name to the School of Ageless Wisdom and, after the Second World War, it reorganized again, this time under the name of the Builders of the Adytum. Ann Davies, Case's widow, ran it after his death, and it is still working today as one of the very few lodges still in existence.

London, SSDD (Florence Farr). We don't know what it contained, but it must have reinforced Mather's galloping paranoia about Westcott, because on February 16, 1900, he sent the explosive letter to Farr in which he put forward a new and disturbing statement (perhaps suggested by Mrs. Horos posing as Fraulein Sprengel).

In the letter, he says that Westcott ...

> ... has never been at any time either in personal or in written communication with the Secret Chiefs of the Order, he having either himself forged or procured to be forged the professed correspondence between him and them ...

Mathers swore that he could prove every word to the hilt, and it was only because of an oath of secrecy that he had let it pass all these years.

It is perhaps at this point that Mathers' conduct is most open to censure. He really cuts a bad figure here. If he was bound by an oath of secrecy, he should have continued to keep his mouth shut. (He never seems to have been bothered by a guilty conscience before.) Otherwise he was deliberately lying for the purpose of pulling the occult carpet from under Westcott's feet. Whichever, it was certainly not cricket, and it can come as no big surprise that this killed the original GD.

Florence Farr meditated on the situation for a week or so. Then she summoned some members, among them Yeats, Percy Bullock, and M. W. Blackden. They formed a committee. It never occurred to them to ask themselves the important question: What have I learned as a member of the Second Order? Have I found the time I have spent in it worthwhile?

If the answer to question one had been: "A lot!" or words to that effect, and the answer to the second was in the affirmative, then good. One would have expected them to keep on doing it and be blessed. If, however, the answers turned out negative, then they should have scrapped the project and resigned. It's as easy as that. There's really nothing more to it, but they couldn't let it go at that. They had to form a committee and, back stage, they all got busy sharpening their elbows. They wrote Mathers and challenged him to prove his allegation. Of course Mathers ignored it, but the hint was too subtle. They tried again two weeks later on March 18,

1900. In the meantime Mathers had written Florence Farr and bawled her out. He told her that he did not care to have his private letter to her dissected by an unauthorized committee, and that was that. Anyone who wanted to resign was welcome to do so. Then the committee tried Westcott instead. He refused to explain himself, referring to his lawyer's advice. He justly pointed out all the occult wisdom they had obtained through the Order, but that had apparently been lost in the heat of the argument.

One would have imagined that this was the end of it: the two lead players refusing to join the band, so no concert. But not so. They invited Mathers to meet them, but he wasn't interested. He didn't recognize the committee, who decided to suspend all activities of the Order until their report had been finished.* It tried to obtain the Anna Sprengel letters from Westcott, who couldn't or wouldn't oblige. Then they tried for the original cipher manuscript but, before they could get organized, Mathers decided to strike back. On April 17, Aleister Crowley, deputized by Mathers, arrived at the Vault of the Adepti at 36 Blythe Road with the purpose of taking over the Vault and the Order material.

With this incident, we pause in the history of the Golden Dawn. From here on, Aleister Crowley plays a central part in the Western tradition, and we will therefore have to go into this man's fascinating life. We will do that in the next chapter.

---

*A typical move for a committee. If it doesn't suspend all activity pending the investigation, one might be led to the fair assumption that the committee's work isn't really important enough to bother about.

Mister Crowley

Beginning with his first savaging in the notorious London tabloids, Aleister Crowley has consistently been an object of condemnation for everyone from hardened skeptics to white-light magi to radio evangelists. This often supercilious disapproval, parroted by almost every writer in the field since the 1951 biographical bash by John Symonds, seems to have been inspired primarily by the fact that Crowley was definitely anti-Christian and pro-sex, two items that have never gone down well with the general public, especially not in Victorian England.

This rather negative view of Crowley has even been accepted by many of his fans and followers, who say they are willing to accept the man "warts and all" (without making any effort to discover whether the warts are real). Even a few members of Crowleyish organizations seem to prefer to publicly dissociate themselves from some of the reputed antics of the Beast.

Be that as it may, the intent of this record is not to revise history by trying to defend the reputation of an often contradictory personality who has been dead for nearly 50 years. Therefore, what is related here merely reflects the traditional opinion held in magical and occult circles, the predominant picture of him that has been painted by various acquaintances and biographers. Was he truly a devil, or a saint? Don't ask me. I didn't know him. I am merely reporting what others have said, including the man himself in his *Confessions*.

Edward Alexander Crowley was born on October 12, 1875, about 10 minutes to midnight, at Leamington, Warwickshire. He never cared for his Christian names, and to most of the world he is best known by the Gaelic equivalent of his second personal name; i.e., Aleister.

His parents were bigoted religious fanatics of limited imagination, and his strong-willed ego bade him, from his very childhood, to explore and indulge in every taboo imposed upon him, first by his parents, later on by the establishment, and finally by anybody, including himself.

A lot of accounts of his early debauches have circulated, most of them probably apocryphal. It's hard to confirm them—not that Crowley himself denied them. On the contrary; he would admit to anything that would discredit his name and bring him to the attention of the public. Exhibitionism was an integrated part of his personality, and again and again he would act against his own interests.

One of these stories relates how he had sexual intercourse with the family housemaid on his mother's bed when he was 12 or 13 years old. The mother told him that he was the "Beast" of the Apocalypse, and after that time he called himself 666.

He was a bright young lad, witty and poetic,* a proficient mathematician, an accomplished chess player, and a skilled mountaineer.

He sought spiritual enlightenment along the left-hand path and desperately wanted instructions in the Black Arts. Near the end of the '90s, he met Julian Baker of the Golden Dawn while climbing mountains abroad during a vacation. Baker introduced him to another member of the order, George Cecil Jones, and they took the young man under their wings and initiated him in the first steps of the Art. But what was more important, Jones put Crowley's name up for admission into the GD, and on November 18, 1898, Crowley was initiated in the neophyte grade as Frater Perdurabo, which means "I shall endure until the end."

In the Order he was befriended by Iehi Aur (Allan Bennett), who accused him of having been meddling with the Goetia (evil spirits). When Crowley denied this, Bennett merely answered that the Goetia must have been meddling with him, then.

---

*He was a fair poet, but never anything like he thought himself. Either he had a great sense of wry humor, which he probably had, or he was a megalomaniac, which he probably was. To illustrate this point it is sufficient to relate that Crowley once, with stiff upper lip, made the observation that it was strange that the two greatest poets in the English language should both have been born in the same county, for one was not to forget Shakespeare, who was also born in Warwickshire.

The Beast 666—"I will deserve it if I can/It is the number of a man" (see Rev.
13:18: *"Let him that hath understanding count the number of the beast: for it is
the number of a man . . .").*

Crowley, *Ambergris*, 1910

He was possibly referring to another story about the young Crowley that is still going around. Dennis Wheatley, the novelist, writes:

> When an undergraduate at Cambridge he was brilliant and already deeply versed in the occult. He wanted the dramatic society to perform a play by Aristophanes which, in those days, was regarded as immoral, so the Master of John's refused to allow it. Greatly annoyed by this Crowley made a wax figure of the Master and, with a coven he had formed, took it out to a field on a night of bright moonlight. Crowley's companions formed a ring, while he stood in the centre, chanting a spell and with a large needle poised, intending to thrust it into the image in the place where its liver would have been. At the critical moment one of the undergraduates lost his nerve, broke the ring and grabbed Crowley's arm. In consequence his aim was deflected and the needle pierced the image's ankle. The following day the Master of John's fell down some steps and broke his ankle.*

Under the tuition of Allan Bennett, Crowley quickly excelled in the Arts. Crowley's parents had died and left him £30,000, a fortune in those days, more like £3 million in today's currency. Still he managed to waste it all in a few years.

First he settled in a flat at 67–69 Chancery Lane and invited Bennett to share it with him free of charge. It was turned into a veritable temple. They practiced magic around the clock. Crowley states:

> The demons connected with *Abra-Melin* do not wait to be evoked; they come unsought. One night [George Cecil] Jones and I went out to dinner. I noticed on leaving the white temple that the latch of its Yale lock had not caught. Accordingly, I pulled the door to and tested it. As we went out, we noticed semi-solid shadows on the stairs; the whole atmosphere was vibrating with the forces which we had been using. (We were trying to condense them into sensible images.) When we came back,

---

The Time Has Come by Dennis Wheatley. Arrow Books Limited, 1981, pp. 606–7.

nothing had been disturbed in the flat; but the temple door was wide open, the furniture disarranged and some of the symbols flung about in the room. We restored order and then observed that semi-materialized beings were marching around the main room in almost unending procession.*

Samuel Mathers had finally completed the translation of the manuscripts in the Bibliotheque l'Arsenal that I mentioned in the last chapter, and they had been published under the title of *The Book of the Sacred Magic of Abra-Melin the Mage*. This constitutes a magical system which is absolutely unique in the sense that it is the only system known to dispense with the magic circle. Since there is no circle, the magician's security lies in his purity. Therefore it is a long ritual, and one that taxes the magician heavily. He's required to possess a house of his own and means for the duration of a six-month period of purification, after which he will receive the enlightenment and conversation of his Holy Guardian Angel (his true self). The H.G.A. will then show him how to in- and evoke the hierarchy of entities at will.

It's a difficult process, as it opens up areas of the magician's mind that lie very deep and of which he may not even be aware. It has proved so dangerous that a karmic safety valve has been built into the infrastructure of the system. It so happens that people beginning the Abra-Melin ritual in an unprepared state of mind automatically become ill at the beginning of the period or are otherwise prevented from continuing the process. After a certain point one must endure to the end lest one lose one's mind.* It's a very powerful and dangerous grimoire.

This was the kind of thing that the young Crowley wanted to tackle. For that purpose, he bought the manor of Boleskine on the banks of Loch Ness in Scotland. He was now calling himself Aleis-

---

The Confessions of Aleister Crowley, ed. John Symonds and Kenneth Grant. Arkana, 1989, p. 182.

**For interested readers I recommend *The Sacred Magician* by Georges Chevalier, Hart-Davies, MacGibbon, 1976. The book is a day-to- day ceremonial diary kept by E. C. (a pseudonym) covering a period of six months, from March 20 to September 20, 1973, during which the author performed and completed the ritual of Abra-Melin.

ter MacGregor, Laird of Boleskine. The MacGregor part of it was probably a homage to Mathers, who stood for him as an idol.

This thing about the alias was nothing new. In Chancery Lane, he was known as Count Vladimir Svareff, but as George Cecil Jones later remarked: "A wiser man would have called himself Smith." Crowley claims that he invested himself with the Russian title in order to study people's reactions, but this is doubtful. Like Mathers, he had a weakness for fancy and pompous-sounding titles.

Crowley soon progressed to the grade of Adeptus Minor, which he took in Paris under Mathers. Back in London, he called at the Isis-Urania temple to obtain some Order material from what he describes as " . . . an ancient Sapphic [i.e., lesbian] Crack, unlikely to be filled." This "Crack," a Miss Maude Cracknell, conferred with the lodge, which felt repelled by Crowley; perhaps they were even jealous. No one can deny his magical gifts, whatever else can be said against him. In the end, they refused to acknowledge his claim and, consequently, Mathers' authority. When Crowley heard about the insurrection and the committee, he cheerfully broke off his Abra-Melin ritual* and hurried to Paris to offer Mathers all his physical, magical, and financial support, and that accounts for his turning up at the temple in Blythe Road as described in the last chapter.

After a siege of some days, he made arrangements with the landlord to enter the premises and occupy the temple, which he did Tuesday, April 17, assisted by a bouncer from a pub in Leicester Square.

Florence Farr arrived to a *fait accompli* and fetched a constable on the beat. Crowley had changed the locks and, as the landlord was absent, Farr couldn't prove her right of possession. Crowley held the fort for two days; then the Isis-Urania members broke open the doors and again changed the locks in Crowley's absence. The same day the committee assembled and suspended Mathers and the farce had been completed. Even Dr. Berridge and Mrs and

---

*One may have noticed that it was about this time, 1900, that the modern craze about the Loch Ness Monster began. This was at the very same time that Crowley banished the spirits of Abra-Melin. Other strange things happened. Some employee of Crowley's committed suicide and some dogs died. I'm not saying that there is any connection, but there may be what Jung calls synchronicity involved.

Miss Simpson were suspended. (They had sensibly taken sides with Mathers.)

On April 21, a general meeting of the Second Order was called; even Annie Horniman was there. It was what one would have come to expect: a lot of nonsense. Only one relevant remark was made by Colonel Webber Smith, who asked why, under such circumstances, the Secret Chiefs did not manifest themselves among them. Needless to say, this question was not included in the official minutes of the meeting.

The meeting resulted in a total break between Mathers and the Isis-Urania membership by an overwhelming majority. Only half a dozen members refused to acknowledge this new state of affairs. It constituted the end of the original Golden Dawn, although the order survived in other forms, as we shall see. Crowley had a writ issued against Florence Farr, but dropped the charges before it came to court.

The other temples remained loyal to Mathers, and Dr. Berridge was authorized to erect a new London temple, which was to become the new Isis-Urania. It was called Alpha et Omega and it was to be the first of many temples of that name. It was really inspired by Mathers, and heavily into the Isis rite. From about 1907, it was known as the Egyptian Lodge. It has been suggested that the famous Egyptologist Sir E. A. Wallis Budge was Praemonstrator and that the lodge used to meet in the Egyptian wing of the British Museum. Some atmosphere they must have had for their rituals! The mere thought should bring tears of envy to the eyes of any living magician.

Crowley went on an odyssey: mountain climbing, chess playing, practicing and studying magic as he went along. In June 1900, he left Europe for the Americas.

Upon his arrival in New York, he went straight on to Mexico City where, in the brief time he stayed, he succeeded in becoming a Freemason, somehow even being awarded the highest honorary degree of the Scottish Rite, 33°, without ever having gone through any of the previous 32 degrees. (We don't know whether he was told that Lucifer is God or not.) But that's not all. Authorized by Mathers, he erected a temple in Mexico of his own device. "A whole new Order," he claimed. It was called L.I.L., the Lamp of the Invisible Light. One Don Jesus Medina was installed as imperator or high priest.

Crowley left Mexico for San Francisco, where he spent most of his time in Chinatown. Eventually he went by boat to Hawaii, where he seduced the wife of an American lawyer before he continued to Japan. From Yokohama he went to Ceylon via Shanghai, Hong Kong, and Singapore to meet Allan Bennett who, due to chronic asthma, had settled here as a Buddhist monk. The journey had been paid for by Crowley.

After staying and meditating with Iehi Aur for some time, Crowley went north to India to climb Chogo Ri, otherwise known as K2, the second highest mountain in the world. (Or perhaps the highest. Experts disagree about it.) Crowley had arranged to meet his old teacher from the mountains of Switzerland, Oscar Eckenstein. He went to Calcutta via Madras in order to prepare the project. However, while waiting, he decided to visit Bennett again. Iehi Aur had moved to Burma in his search for enlightenment and a healthier climate.

Crowley chose a difficult road to travel, and he was accompanied by another Englishman named Edward Thornton. The two men sailed for Rangoon on January 21, 1901. When they arrived, they decided to hire coolies and walk through the jungle and make it a sort of hunting trip. It turned out to be more difficult than they had anticipated. Crowley was plagued by malaria, and their coolies refused to continue. They were finally forced to turn around and go back to Rangoon. There Crowley booked a seat on a steamer bound for Akyab, where Iehi Aur had joined a Buddhist monastery. Crowley recalled that the long, tall Bennett looked like a giant among the other Burmese monks. After a week or so, Crowley went back to Calcutta to continue his preparations for the conquest of K2. He had arranged to meet Eckenstein in Rawalpindi, and so he left for Benares on March 7. In Pindi, Eckenstein had gathered a small group of people who wanted to join them in their endeavors: two Austrians, two Englishmen (Knowles and Wessely), and a French doctor, Guillarmod, who would participate in a later expedition with Crowley.

The expedition to K2 failed. They had to turn back because of bad weather and illness among them. Crowley got a touch of his old malaria. On the 31st of September, Crowley reached Bombay and, after a few days rest, he left on board the *Egypt* bound for Europe. The boat called at Cairo, which it reached on October 14.

After a week at Shepherds Hotel, he went on to Paris, where he stayed with a friend from the GD, Gerald Kelly.* For a while, Crowley worked at setting poems to some of Rodin's sketches. They aren't bad, but they certainly can't be compared to the work of any of the masters, in spite of Crowley's own opinion. He also encountered people such as Arnold Bennet and W. Somerset Maugham, the latter of whom wrote a book with Crowley as its central character.** From November 18, 1902, until the next spring, he went back and forth between London and Paris, but after that he finally went back to Boleskine.

In August, Crowley went to Edinburgh to stay with the Kellys. Gerald was home on vacation. There Crowley met his sister Rose, who was to marry an American in a few weeks. Somehow Crowley managed to persuade her to elope with him instead. Her family was furious. But the new couple ignored them and moved to Boleskine for their honeymoon. After about a week of this, he solemnly and conscientiously spanked her for the purpose of asserting himself as the master, for, as he said: "Women, like all moral inferiors, behave well only when treated with firmness, kindness and justice." She proved to be the first of a long line of masochistic women that suited the "Beast's" sadistic urges.

Crowley was soon again attacked by wanderlust and planned another round-the-world trip, and after some weeks entertaining friends in London, they set out.

Their first stop was Paris, where they met Moina Mathers in the street. Crowley had fallen out with Mathers or vice versa. Both of them were inflated egos, demanding a tremendous amount of attention, respect, and admiration. As long as the young Crowley admired Mathers, their relationship had been most successful. Both recognized the magical potentials in the other; but, of course, sooner or later Crowley's ego would become blown up to a degree where only narcissism was left—just as in the case of Mathers. This was now. The crisis had been coming for a long time. Crowley's previous odyssey had ostensibly been for the purpose of establishing whether Mathers was still in favor with the Secret Chiefs. A long and subjective conversation with Allan Bennett proved to

---

*Later knighted and made president of the Royal Academy.

**The Magician, 1908.

Crowley's satisfaction that this was no longer so and that Mathers was no longer in a state of grace with the astral forces. Naturally, it would. Until this, Crowley's attitude towards Mathers had been one of indifference but, as a result of this meeting with Moina, the seeds of hostility burst forth from the occult soil. Until now he had regarded Mathers, at worst, with benevolent contempt, no doubt because he couldn't disregard his deep and profound skill and knowledge (even though he would have liked to). Crowley's later, often hateful attacks on Mathers suggest irritation at not being able to liberate himself from the influence of the master.

For instance, this was a very prolific period in Crowley's literary career, and he published a lot of poems, short stories, essays, and articles on magic. He excelled, sort of, or at least he had an original touch in everything except occultism. He published one of his most famous works in those days: his translation of the Goetia from the Lemegeton[*]—but, as everyone knows today, it was actually Mathers who had translated it at Crowley's expense. He had been commissioned to undertake the work of translating the full set of five parts but, when they fell out with each other, Mathers had only had time to translate the first book. Crowley admits as much in his *Confessions*, and that may be all right, but still he didn't hesitate to put his own name on the title page, and he only mentions Mathers in the preface. This was not the only time that he acted in a devious manner in such matters. An even bigger masterpiece of Crowley's turns out to be unadulterated pilfering: *Liber 777*,[**] which is a table of correspondences of great ingenuity and immense scholarship, is today sold as one of Crowley's most important works. It is indispensable to any serious student of the Qabalah. It began as a simple list of deities connected with the hierarchy of the GD. It was vastly expanded by Mathers up through the formative years of the '90s, by way of hard work and meditative research in the big libraries. It circulated among the members of the Order as an ordinary flying roll. It was meant entirely for internal use. Crowley, however, got settled with Allan

---

[*]*The Lesser Key of Solomon—Goetia: The Book of Evil Spirits*, currently in print by Magickal Childe, New York, 1989.

[**]Now published by Samuel Weiser, York Beach, Maine (their edition © 1973).

Bennett's copy, and as he was busy with his own order (a few years later than the time we are dealing with now), he added to it and published it under his own name, again without giving Mathers due credit.

As I said, Crowley met Moina Mathers in some Paris street, and the way he describes her in his *Confessions* shows that he had broken with whatever soft sentiment he may have had for Mathers. He describes her as looking like a common, unwashed whore. He even says that he later learned that she had been forced by her husband to pose as a model in the nude for various degenerate painters to keep Mathers supplied with alcohol. There is nothing to suggest this in any investigation into the lives of the Matherses, but Crowley had a verbal way of dealing severely with people whom he disliked. Like Adolf Hitler, he never forgot or forgave anyone who dared to disturb his circles. Heaven knows what Crowley would have done given the same opportunities as "Der Führer."

After Paris, the couple went by way of Marseilles to Cairo, where they spent a night in the "king's chamber" of the Great Pyramid, boosting magic to new heights. After that, Crowley decided to go big game hunting in Ceylon, after which he planned to visit Bennett in Burma. But, alas, Rose discovered that she was pregnant, so they returned to Cairo with the purpose of going on to Europe. This was at the end of January 1904. They decided to stay for a while in Egypt. They called themselves Chioa Khan and Ouarda (meaning "the Beast" and "Rose" in Arabic), for the purpose of studying Sufi and other Islamic lore. Crowley walked about the bazaar dressed as an Egyptian, turban and all. He loved this kind of thing.*

It was here in Cairo, at the equinox of March 20, 1904, near midnight, that he evoked the Egyptian god Horus according to an

---

*He once went to the Cafe Royal in Regent Street in his oriental attire. No one paid any attention to him, and he took it to prove that the GD ritual of invisibility was valid. Some of Crowley's critics have quoted this incident to prove that Crowley was stupid and therefore a fake, but "invisibility," as it was understood in terms of this particular ritual, merely means "the ability to pass unnoticed," and that was actually what Crowley did achieve within the meaning of the act. Whether the people in his surroundings failed to notice him or just ignored him out of embarrassment is perhaps relevant, but impossible to ascertain.

unorthodox ritual "channeled" by Rose. A couple of weeks later, on April 8th, 9th, and 10th, between noon and one o'clock each day, *Liber Legis*, or *The Book of the Law*, was dictated to Crowley by a disnarnate entity that identified itself as "Aiwass." *The Book of the Law* was nothing less than the Bible of the New Age, "The Aeon of Horus," or as it is known today, the "Age of Aquarius." Crowley was informed that the Secret Chiefs had appointed him herald and high priest of the new "gospel," and *The Book of the Law* was a sort of "Third Testament," hailing the New Age with the motto: "Do what thou wilt shall be the whole of the Law." He immediately went back to Europe to claim leadership of the Order after having dethroned Mathers in a letter. Mathers didn't bother to answer the letter, so the big magical battle commenced.

Mathers killed Crowley's bloodhounds by remote control. He also caused one of Crowley's farm hands to run amuck and try to kill Rose. However, he was apprehended and the local police dismissed the case, claiming that Crowley had misunderstood the whole thing. In answer, Crowley summoned Beelzebub and 49 of his minions, and they were finally left alone.

Rose gave birth to a daughter, Lilith, whom they eventually left in care of the in-laws and left for St. Moritz for their winter holiday. After a few weeks they were back at Boleskine, where they entertained. Among the guests was the French doctor J. Jacot Guillarmod, who had been with Crowley in his attempt to climb Chogo Ri. Now he was back with plans for an attack on Kangchenjunga. This was right up Crowley's alley. He went to India by way of the Suez Canal. After some weeks, the expedition set out from Darjeeling on August 8, 1905.

It proved to be an unmitigated disaster. One member of the expedition and three coolies were killed, and accusations flew back and forth between Crowley and Guillarmod. The latter claimed that Crowley had refused to come to the aid of four men who had been buried in the snow after a fall. Crowley's answer was that he had had enough of the rest of the expedition after they had deposed him as leader. They could have obeyed the orders he gave them. If they chose not to listen to him, they could go to hell for all he cared. He couldn't be bothered with stupid amateurs. He washed his hands of the whole affair and went to Calcutta.

The night before his wife and child were to arrive, he again made use of the GD technique of "invisibility"; i.e., to pass unnoticed. He was exploring an old part of the city when he was followed by a gang of native punks. He led them into a dark alley where he drew a gun on them and fired. They ran for their lives and, as the mob assembled, Crowley used the practice of the Order and walked unchallenged straight through the crowd.

After Rose's arrival they went on immediately to China, where Crowley experimented with opium.

He and his wife went back to England. She and the child went westward through India while he went east by way of Yokohama, San Francisco, and New York. It was about this time that Crowley considered himself to have been admitted by the Secret Chiefs into the Third Order as a result of his repeated invocations of Aiwass. Meanwhile, Lilith contracted typhoid fever in Rangoon and died. Once back in England, a new baby was soon born, Lola Zaza. This event once again offered Crowley an opportunity to show his spirit of bonhomie, which he demonstrated by savagely kicking his mother-in-law down the stairs from her daughter's bedroom. (She had refused to obey the doctor's orders about there being too many people in the sick room. It did not occur to Crowley, who claimed that he alone had saved the child from dying of bronchitis by sending for oxygen, that he himself might have been the excess party rather than Rose's mother.)

He was getting tired of Rose and from now on he left her to get along as best she could. Crowley never took his obligations to his ex-wives very seriously. They were left for karma to provide for. Any attempt at legal redress was by now an absurdity. He had no money left and he had had no formal training at anything, so he had to live by his wits, which he was to do for the rest of his life.

He had been wasting time, but now he started working on magic again. He found a rich pupil, Lord Tankerville, who paid the way for himself and the guru. Together they went to Spain and Morocco. The pupil soon got tired of Crowley's arrogant ways and skipped out, but the Beast soon found a new disciple. The new neophyte, Victor Neuburg, assisted the master by performing "Holy Magic"; i.e., sodomy.

It was also about this time, 1907, that Crowley officially founded the A∴A∴, or Argenteum Astrum; i.e., the "Silver Star" (not the "Atlantean Adepts," as one rather inept guess would have it). He started publishing his biannual Order paper, *The Equinox*. He had learned from his experiences in the GD that the members must be kept busy at all times and, above all, prevented from social intercourse—which inevitably leads to insurrection out of boredom. He therefore designed the AA along new and ingenious lines. For example, none of the members were to know each other. Only the big cheese, Crowley himself, knew everybody, and the members were referred to by their magical names only. The rules were strictly adhered to and it seemed to work. At meetings, they were dressed in hooded robes so they couldn't see each other's faces, and in the few instances that they did, they didn't know the member's real name. All this, despite its immediate success, of course had its drawbacks, of which the lack of a sense of fraternity was the most devastating for the Order in the long run.

In 1910, Crowley hired Caxton Hall in London and presented public performances of what he called the Rites of Eleusis on five or seven Wednesdays in a row. Mescaline is supposed to have been included in the admission fee of five guineas, which was an outrageous price for a thing like that in those days. The drug was handed out at the entrance. Not that it was illegal; mescaline wasn't classified as a dangerous drug until the 1960s. Around the turn of the century, it was considered smart to contribute personally to the advancement of culture, and it certainly helped to bring Crowley the fame and notoriety that he so desperately craved.

He also got involved in a lawsuit with Mathers. In his third volume of *The Equinox*, he had published some GD rituals and promised that he would continue to do so in the forthcoming issues. Mathers got a writ issued against him. The authorities impounded the entire edition pending the trial. Mathers won the case, but Crowley appealed and the higher court reversed the ruling. Mathers couldn't afford another appeal, so Crowley was free to publish, which he did. He had found a new source of income: litigation. He started to sue people for slander, libel, and defamation of character, sometimes even successfully (it must have been magic).

In 1912 he found the shoe on the other foot again. A German by the name of Theodor Reuss accused him of having published secret order material belonging to a German order called the OTO, or Ordo Templi Orientis, in one of his books, *Liber 333*, also known as *The Book of Lies*. Crowley emphatically denied even having heard of the order before, and for once he may have been telling the truth. He claimed it to be all his own work and, everything taken into consideration, it's more than likely. Reuss, realizing that a trial would bring the activities of the OTO before the public, a thing that wouldn't bother Crowley much, decided on what he believed to be the lesser of two evils. He appointed Crowley leader of the British branch of the order, newly established for the purpose.

During the World War, Crowley settled in New York, devoting himself to the writing of anti-British propaganda. After the war he excused himself by explaining that he deliberately exaggerated his efforts so that any idiot (except the German ones, of course) would get the message wrong; i.e., right.

He met and married Leah Hirsig, and after he had inherited £3000, they settled at Cefalu in Sicily. After a few years, his Abbey of Theleme, as he called it, had acquired such an unsavory reputation that he received a very dubious honor. His activities were evidently too much for such a connoisseur of abominations as Benito Mussolini. Il Duce himself thought Crowley too hot to handle and evicted him as *persona non grata*.

This eviction was a pity, really, as Crowley himself considered Cefalu the only real home he ever had, and the time he spent there the happiest time of his life. Small wonder. He entertained a lot of mistresses, and cocaine and heroin were virtually floating about the premises. At least two deaths occurred which hit the front page of the British newspapers in 1923, and when (unfounded) rumors began to circulate to the effect that local children were being murdered by Crowley and his guests in sadistic orgies and Satanic rituals, the Italian government for some reason found it embarrassing and incompatible with its fascistic principles, and he was asked to leave. Of course, like all dictators, Mussolini methodically suppressed anything that looked like a secret society, whether it be Thelemites, Freemasons, or the P.T.A.

Crowley, his family, and a disciple, Norman Mudd, went to Tunisia, where the master left them to go to Paris. In Nice, broke and destitute, he managed to obtain 500 francs with the assistance of the novelist Frank Harris. The rest of his household starved in order to scrape together the fare to Paris, only to find, upon their arrival, that he had met a rich American lady who had become his new mistress and with whom he was currently touring North

Africa. His wife Leah and Mudd had become lovers. She supported them both in Paris for a while as a part-time prostitute when things finally took a turn for the better.

Theodor Reuss, the leader of the OTO, died in 1922, and the only logical successor was Crowley. One must not forget that whatever can be said about Crowley as a human being, he was an outstanding magical adept and the Order recognized that. They sent for him in Africa and paid his fare to Germany, which was just as well, as he had spent all his mistress's money and was broke again. They even paid the fare for Leah and Norman, but Crowley didn't care for them anymore. As far as he was concerned, they were history. Like most of Crowley's girl friends, she became an alcoholic (if she hadn't been before, which might explain why she was attracted to Crowley in the first place).

Mudd committed suicide in 1934 by filling his pockets with rocks and walking out into the ocean to drown.

A lot of the members had second thoughts about Crowley after having met him personally, but as the majority still wanted to elect him top dog of the order, some of them broke loose and founded the Fraternitas Saturni under the leadership of Heinrich Tränker.

In 1927 or '28, Crowley acquired a new pupil and unpaid secretary, a young man, Israel Regardie, of whom we will hear more later. That same year, he also found a new girl friend, or "Scarlet Woman," as he called his female magical and sexual partners. The following year, they were all evicted from France, ostensibly because of an exotic coffee machine that the French police in their abysmal ignorance mistook for dope manufacturing equipment. But maybe the actual reason for eviction had something to do with his attempt to evoke the Great God Pan to visible appearance.

In a hotel belonging to one of his disciples (the guests having been evicted), it is said, another disciple died during a ritual. At midnight, the Chief Adept (Crowley) and his most advanced pupil went into the room which had been consecrated as a temple to evoke Pan. The rest of the circle was to wait outside chanting and meditating, with strict orders not to enter the room on any account. About two o'clock, goes the story, screams and the noise of furniture being thrown about were heard, but no one dared to go in until the next morning. When they did, they found the disciple dead and Crowley a gibbering idiot. It took four months treatment in an insane asylum to bring him around again. Whatever, he was asked to leave France.

Unfortunately for lovers of sensational stories, this one appears to have been made up for the express purpose of adding fuel to the anti-Crowley bonfire. In all likelihood, this is also the case with the tale previously quoted from Dennis Wheatley, who seems to have taken as gospel truth any tale told him about Crowley—as long as it was bad. In Wheatley's version, the doomed disciple was Crowley's otherwise undocumented magical son, "MacAleister." However, the one detail of the story which throws it all into grave doubt is the bit about the insane asylum. If Crowley had ever actually been committed to such a place, he would never have gotten out.

New apocryphal tales about Crowley continue to circulate even to this day. For example, in the 1970s, a friend told me that Crowley had defecated in the corner at a fancy dinner party and proclaimed the result a holy substance not to be defiled. The esoteric magazine *Gnosis* recently carried a piece containing a highly improbable tale about a visit by Crowley to George Gurdjieff's institute at Fontainebleau. Since the writer was a Gurdjieff fan, the disreputable old double-talking Russian came off the hero and sent Crowley crawling away in a state of abject humilitation. As the English might say, "not bloody likely."

In England, Crowley's current mistress Maria Teresa de Miramar was denied entry, so Crowley married her to get her on board, as it were.

In 1930, Crowley was to have lectured at Oxford, but his reputation preceded him, and the lecture was banned—a truly scientific and scholarly approach. His marriage was already getting strained because of jealousy between his wife and his current mistress, a German girl, Hanni, both of whom went insane after Crowley ditched them.

Again without funds, he took up an old practice: litigation. He sued a bookseller for some trifle and obtained £50. This helped to whet his appetite and he tried it again. This time he went after the bohemian poetess Nina Hamnett who, in her autobiography, had referred to Crowley as a black magician. The counsel for the defense naturally laid bare Crowley's whole life and quoted heavily from his works—especially the pornographic and homosexual works. One must say that it offered Crowley an opportunity to verbally horsewhip the hypocrisy and bigotry of British public morals. Of course he lost the case, and he was once again in the headlines of the tabloids as "the wickedest man in the world." On April 14, 1934, the court ruled against him and he was declared bankrupt, which under the circumstances didn't make any difference; he was broke as usual anyway.

He continued in the same fashion during the next ten years, and at the end of World War II, in 1944, he accomplished his last big feat. He finished *The Book of Thoth,* his version of the Tarot. It was illustrated by Lady Frieda Harris, who made the paintings after Crowley's directions. They were exhibited that year in a private gallery and didn't receive much notice, and it wasn't until the end of the 1970s that a pack of these cards was made commercially.

Crowley spent his final years at a modest boarding house in the seaside resort of Hastings, where he died December 5, 1947. He managed to shock the public one last time. At his funeral, his "Hymn to Pan" was read aloud by a friend. Afterwards, it dawned upon the congregation that this poem was an unadulterated phallic hymn. After the event, the local authorities examined every subsequent funeral arrangement to make sure that such a thing would never happen again.

Spawn of the Golden Dawn

After the expulsion of Mathers, the Golden Dawn's special committee called another meeting the following week, 27 April 1900, at which the poet W. B. Yeats was elected imperator and our old friend Annie Horniman was appointed the new scribe of the Order—another fatal step, as she now became aware of some internal groups that had been working within the Order without her knowledge. Since Florence Farr had been an important member of the most outstanding of these groups, the Sphere, Fortiter et Recte's jealousy broke out in virulent attacks on the group, and Yeats hurried to her assistance with his own axe to grind.

Yeats was afraid that the essential (i.e., magical) foundation of the Order was being gradually eliminated. With the dethronement of Mathers, there were some members who thought that the time had come for a thorough reorganization of the Order. Among other things, they wished to dispense with what to many members seemed tedious and annoying obstacles to promotion in the grades; namely, the examinations. Yeats, who was an accomplished magician, immediately realized the danger to the credibility of the Order should such a scheme be introduced. Without examinations, the GD would soon be filled with Adepti Minor, and those with even higher grades, who had no knowledge of magic whatsoever. With many Order members, even to this day, the grade they hold is inversely proportional to their spiritual or magical abilities. The GD would be dead if these examinations were banned.

To preserve the magical elements at any price, Yeats felt himself compelled to oppose any kind of change on principle. His arguments in favor of magic didn't go down well with most of the newer members, who thought of the GD as a social organization along the lines of the Freemasons rather than any semi-religious school of thought and practice.

It came to the vote on February 26, 1901, when the majority came out against Yeats and Annie Horniman, which caused them both to resign—at first from their offices, but eventually from the Order. Yeats had had enough, but Soror Fortiter et Recte continued her personal crusade against anything that she disapproved of for another few years.

The next setback was perhaps the most severe. It caused a scandal in the press, and a lot of members were suddenly anxious not to be associated with the Order. They jumped like fleas from a dead dog. It was the Horos scandal.

On September 26, 1901, the Horoses were arrested by the police, Mr. Horos for the rape of a young girl, Daisy Pollex Adams, Mrs. Horos for aiding and abetting. As I have mentioned in a previous chapter, the Horoses had managed to obtain some Order papers from Mathers; among others, the Neophyte ritual. This needn't have been so serious had it not been for the fact that the Horoses had a long record of bogus occultism behind them. For years, they had been scourging the world with religious and occult movements resembling those described by Mark Twain and O. Henry. They reappeared in Europe after a brief sojourn in South Africa, where they established an occult academy.

They left Capetown a few hours before a warrant for their arrests was to be issued, so it may be gathered that when Madame Horos got hold of the GD material, it was not entirely for reasons of idle curiosity. The lady had plans. First of all, after their arrival in London, they tried to infiltrate the Isis-Urania temple.

One may be disposed to imagine that, with the general decadence in the Order, it would be a pushover for a hardened con-artist who had successfully deceived Mathers himself, but things proved out differently. Mathers had been fooled by the fact that he recognized Madame Horos's undoubted occult faculties and knowledge, whereas the people in the reorganized Isis-Urania had no magicians of any standing after the resignation of Yeats; even Florence Farr was a minority in the Order by now. Mathers did write a letter of warning to Yeats, but it had no impact on the committee. They were more concerned with the proper passwords and signs, which, for once, proved fortunate: Theo Horos was unable to answer some formal questions concerning the grades of the Order satisfactorily. In consequence, the Horos couple decided to erect their own lodge, which they did and which they called the Order of Theocratic Unity.

In late Victorian times (as now), there was a multitude of weird religions, metaphysical, mystical, and psycho- and parapsychological activities, covering any field of investigation neglected by the official science of the day. Naturally, these activities attracted a fair number of cranks, but, more importantly, they also attracted the curiosity of the truly creative people with original minds, both within and without the establishment. Needless to say, they also attracted swindlers and charlatans.

The Horoses had tried their hands at this sort of thing for years, for the profits. They were eager advocates of the causes of abstinence and vegetarianism while they themselves both ate meat and heartily drank alcoholic beverages. They were also in the matrimonial racket, and this is among other things wherein the GD papers came in handy.

Theo had an ad in various papers and magazines—the usual stuff in those days, along the lines of:

> Middle-aged man of substance seeking acquaintance with lady of similar circumstances, with a view to matrimony.

A lot of swindlers used this device at that time. One need only think of the notorious case of George Joseph Smith, who married a lot of women whom he contacted under similar circumstances, and whom he disposed of by drowning them in their bathtubs.

To avoid this drastic step, and to actually avoid having to marry the women (Horos was actually married to Madame Horos), the couple devised a new routine. They made use of the GD Neophyte ritual, around which they had built the Theocratic Unity. Horos told his prospective wives that, as he was a member of this venerable organization, a special marriage ceremony was called for. They then went through the Neophyte ritual together and afterwards consummated the union in bed. But after a few days of wedded bliss, he and Madame Horos took the victim to the cleaners; i.e., secured the victim's assets and vanished.*

Of course, even this elaborate scheme could not work every time. Sooner or later a "wife" would be bound to become suspicious about the "wedding" ceremony. However, before this happened, the Horoses had dug their own grave to the infinitely worse detriment of the noble Order of the Golden Dawn.

On a lecture tour through England, on the "higher life," they had picked up a couple of children as apprentices (they taught typing and clerking as well), a young girl of 16, Daisy Pollex Adams, and her little brother. Their parents were a gullible couple completely ensnared by the Swami Vive Ananda, as Madame Horos now called herself.** The young girl, Daisy, was "initiated" into the

---

*These women were not merely stupid. They were victims of circumstances and Victorian morals. In those days, it was a social disgrace for a woman not to marry. She was considered a burden to the family (which had begotten her in lust). Her parents spared no effort or expense to provide her with a husband. They planned vacations that resembled medieval pilgrimages, except that the shrine was an eligible bachelor instead of a holy relic, and any husband would do. The welfare of the daughter in the hands of an unsavory degenerate was rarely a matter of consideration.

The girls' only alternative was the barren role of old maid spinster aunt—to many a sort of living death. Morals being what they were, no other solution was possible within the family structure. Some girls, understandably enough, dropped out. Most of these eventually became prostitutes, for which they really can't be blamed, but as most of the troubles of these unhappy creatures arose from, among other things, plain looks, they didn't really excel in the oldest profession either. Only a very few managed to secure a satisfying, independent life for themselves.

**This fad for posh-sounding foreign titles has continued to this day. Just visit your local spiritual center and attend their weekly event when some Oriental or pseudo-Oriental religion, philosophy, or meditation technique is being elaborated on or demonstrated. Most of the Caucasian teachers will have names like Swami Bramah Gupta, Mahatmah Goering Peshuawar, or something simple but dramatic, such as "Photon" (i.e., John Smith, George Jones, and Jim Brown, respectively).

If these birds know their business, they don't need to masquerade under various aliases. If they don't, they can't profit from it indefinitely anyway. There is always something suspicious about these bogus, self-ordained exotic masters—such as the Horoses.

GD by Theo Horos, who had sexual intercourse with her while the Swami was present in the bed watching the procedure. The first time was with the girl's consent, as she was ignorant of the world and thought that her guardians must be right. The second time, however, she had misgivings about the whole thing, whereupon they resorted to force. It leaked out, and they were both arrested. After a trial, amply covered by the press, in which all the juicy details of the GD ritual (which was read aloud in court) and the sexual perversions of the Swami and her husband were displayed before the public, Horos received 15 years penal servitude for rape and Madame Horos 7 years for aiding and abetting.

Needless to say, this unfortunate incident didn't improve the image of the GD. On the contrary, as mentioned before, a lot of members finally found the time appropriate to leave the organization. No doubt this was to the betterment of the Order, even though its internal problems were far from over.

Another attempt at reorganizing the sodality was made. A committee consisting of Percy W. Bullock. M. W. Blackden, and J. W. Brodie-Innes was invested with the authority to draw up a new constitution for the Order. This took more time than originally anticipated, partly because the problems were of a greater magnitude than they'd thought. It turned out that, in addition to a new constitution, a new name for the Order was needed—the notoriety of the Horos case still worried the majority of members. Another reason for the delay besides a new name was the resignation of Percy Bullock from the committee. He was replaced by Dr. R. W. Felkin, a distinguished medical scholar specializing in tropical medicine and an accomplished magician. The delay in the committee's work paved the way for the takeover of the Order by A. E. Waite, who produced his own constitutional draft at the annual meeting. The committee, however, claimed that it would soon have its own outline ready, and Waite's efforts were rejected by a majority, the committee's mandate being extended for another year.

When the committee's report was brought before the assembly the following year, Waite did all he could to discredit it and, as usual in dissident groups, any agreement was impossible.

The Second Order eventually split up. Waite became leader of a faction that kept the old lodge name of Isis-Urania. He revised or rewrote all the rituals and discarded everything connected with magic. It became a Christian mystical order.

The rest of the London members kept the original rituals and tried instead to make contact with the Secret Chiefs of the Third Order. These members constituted another two factions: those who were in contact with Mathers in Paris and owed allegiance to him, and those who were not. The first group was led by Brodie-Innes, who had moved to the metropolis, and the second was under the leadership of Dr. Felkin. They changed the name of the Order to Stella Matutina, and the name of the London lodge was Amoun. Brodie-Innes's temple was called the Alpha and Omega, not to be mistaken for the temple of the same name erected by Dr. Berridge in 1900. Brodie-Innes's lodge was the only apostolic one in the sense that it derived from the Amon Ra temple in Edinburgh, with the official sanction of Mathers. However, it wasn't known as the AO until 1913, when it merged with Dr. Berridge's order.

These three lodges (led by Waite, Brodie-Innes, and Felkin) now tried to come to an agreement about coexistence, because it was obvious that they had all come to stay, at least for a while.

First, Waite sabotaged an attempt by Brodie-Innes to keep the Order together with the three of them as joint chiefs, as in the original Order. Waite desperately wanted his own order to play with and would certainly not share the leadership with anyone. He would have happily preferred not to have any further associations with other lodges, but unfortunately for him it was not to be so. When Brodie-Innes suggested a concordat between the Orders so that members of a certain grade in one lodge would be accepted in another without question, Waite had to accept because of pressure from his own members. In the end, Waite's people demanded the restoration of magical practices, a thing that he refused with vehemence. The result was that his lodge discontinued operations in 1914, most members being absorbed by other lodges.

As regards Brodie-Innes's AO temple: after his death in 1923, it fell into the hands of Maiya Tranchell-Hayes, who closed it down in 1937. In 1966, her robes and regalia, which had been ceremonially buried on a cliff, broke loose and fell into the channel and were washed ashore on some beach. As a consequence, the press indulged in wild speculations about black magic cults. A so-called expert identified the regalia as belonging to a witch. As always, the

Arthur Edward Waite attempted to turn the Golden Dawn into an organization of Christian mystics. Crowley called him "Edward Arthwaite."

The Occult Review, January 1916

press was ready to print a good story without being hampered by things like facts.

It seems that, at this time, 1904–5, the gods (or at least the Secret Chiefs) had decided to favor Dr. Felkin. He first encountered some discarnate entities that he called the "Sun Masters." Later, he contacted some that he believed to be the Secret Chiefs of the Third Order. There may have been something to this claim, for he also received a communication from a German professor who wished to consult him about a patient of his by the name of Anna Sprengel.

Needless to say, Felkin got all steamed up and, on the advice of the Sun Masters, went to Germany. He didn't meet Fräulein Sprengel, but he was introduced to German Rosicrucian adepts, among others Rudolf Steiner, who was involved with several organizations: the Theosophists, the fringe Masonic rite of Memphis and Mizraim, the sex-magical OTO, and probably a lot of others. In addition to all this, he must have been busy working on his own brainchild, the Anthroposophical movement.

Through Steiner, Felkin succeeded in being initiated into several Rosicrucian societies and, after his return to Britain, he enthusiastically wrote to Brodie-Innes about it. Sub Spe (Brodie-Innes) was reluctant to accept anything that didn't originate from Mathers, so Felkin suggested that they ought to get a charter from Anna Sprengel or, failing that, from other continental adepts.

In consequence, he sent Neville Meakin, a representative of his own lodge, to Germany for the purpose of exchanging Order material. But before any deals had been concluded, Meakin flipped out and decided to follow the pilgrimage of Christian Rosenkreutz himself to the Orient, and he suddenly died at Constantinople in 1912.

After this, Felkin and his wife went to the continent themselves, where they were both initiated into more German Rosicrucian temples—he, by his own admission, to a grade equivalent to 8°=3° Magister Templi, and his wife to 7°=4°, Adeptus Exemptus. All this doesn't sound very likely, as Magister Templi is a grade that no one except Crowley had theretofore had the audacity to claim.

The Felkins were joined by Sapere Aude (Wynn Westcott) in their pursuit of Anna Sprengel. Several meetings between them were arranged, but the German lady failed to show up. However, they persevered till the very end. As a matter of fact, they were so busy in their pursuit that they were caught totally unprepared by the Great War, and it was only thanks to some high-ranking German Masons that they managed to get out of the country one or two days after the actual official declaration of war between Germany and Great Britain.

In 1916, Felkin opened a number of temples: the Hermes Lodge in Bristol, the Secret Lodge in London (a special lodge for Soc. Ros. members only), the Merlin Lodge also in London, and finally the Guild of St. Raphael. The Hermes Lodge may still be working for all I know. It changed its name to Hermanubis in 1930 and chartered a daughter temple in London about 1959. The occult writer Francis King is alleged to have been involved with it at some time.

In 1919, Felkin opened the Cromlech Temple, the members of which were mostly clergymen from the Church of England. Its teachings leaned more towards druidism and Christian mysticism than magic. Finally, in 1922, he opened the Smaragdum Thalasses in the most unlikely of all places, New Zealand.

After the war, Felkin settled in New Zealand, after which the usual struggle began about which of the lodges was the true one; i.e., really had contact with the Secret Chiefs. It seems to have been an easy match. Mathers died in 1918, and the following year Moina went back to London and erected the *third* lodge with the name of Alpha and Omega. Felkin died in 1922, Brodie-Innes in 1923, and Westcott in 1925. All the old giants were gone except Yeats, who had resigned and was busy getting the Nobel Price for literature, and Waite, who had founded another lodge, the Fellowship of the True Rosy Cross, in 1916. Moina Mathers seemed the only natural leader left.

Waite's order was not a magical order within the meaning of the act, of course. However, he should not be altogether discarded as an occultist. In 1910, he published his version of the Tarot, which is probably his greatest claim to immortality. The deck has been the most successful in history. But even here, criticism sticks up its ugly head, because the success was not due to Waite's design. In fact, as a symbolic representation of the Qabalistic universe according to the Golden Dawn, it is utterly corrupt. Waite never really understood the true nature of magic. The success of the deck is due partly to the fact that, for many years, it was the *only* Tarot deck that was widely available, and partly to the extraordinarily superb and suggestive quality with which the artist, Pamela Colman

Smith, managed to imbue the cards. As a tool for the mystic, they stand alone. Whether you are an adept or are totally ignorant of the existence of a spiritual world, a mere glance at any of the cards will captivate you completely. Even the pip cards, which in any other deck are represented merely with graphic designs relevant to the numbers symbolized, hold archetypal designs that give you infinite material for meditation and astral projection.

There are other decks with designs truer to the correspondences of the magical orders, but they lack the grace and artistry of Smith's deck. Ironically, she has never been properly credited. Even today, her name is not generally associated with her work. Waite's is, of course, as he was responsible for the overall design. For some obscure reason, so is the name of the publisher that first undertook the task of manufacturing the cards; viz., Rider and Company. Today, the cards are famous as the Rider-Waite pack, with no mention of Smith—a blatant display of a lack of any sense of proportion.

When Moina Mathers took over the Order, things changed. Her changes could be said to be equivocal. In a way it was bad because her policy ruined the Order. She started issuing charters to all and sundry for money. The worst example was an American lodge that obtained permission to issue Order material as a correspondence course and, finally, the right to initiate people into the various grades for $10 per initiation.

The positive aspect of this policy was the fact that the Order material was widely disseminated instead of disappearing into oblivion, as it would have if it had been preserved only by a few incompetent lodges with a penchant for secrecy. The chance of encountering able magicians is proportional to the geographical area covered. It's a thing that I have proved only to my own satisfaction, but the number of magicians within an area seems to have less to do with the number of people than the geographic spread. I'm not quite sure what I mean by this, but I think it's true. You work it out.

Another contributing factor to the winds of change was that a new generation of magicians was slowly taking over—a generation that had not known the old giants and that was accordingly not adverse to things that would most certainly have been considered sacrilegious by the older generation—except Aleister Crowley, who is considered a hot potato even today. The Beast was to be the inspiration of several future magicians, but very few would care to admit as much.

The spirit of rebellion seems to have been evoked with the Great War. The first incident involving the new generation was the sad case of Christine Mary Stoddard. She was a member of Felkin's lodge and had been with him in Germany in search of enlightenment and Anna Sprengel. She'd had enough sense to go home before war was actually declared; she left the day before.

When the Felkins went to New Zealand in 1916, the doctor left Miss Stoddard in charge of the lodge. She and her two fellow officers-in-charge, a couple of Church of England priests, indulged so much in scrying in the spirit vision that they went insane. In seven years, they developed schizophrenia and delusions of grandeur. The two clergymen had to be committed, and one of them actually died in the asylum. Stoddard developed an *idée fixe* to the effect that the members of the GD all were Jews, or Jewish dupes, and that the purpose of the Order was to establish Jewish supremacy in the world. From 1923 onwards, she wrote articles in the occult press under the pseudonym "Inquire Within." Her articles were later published as a book entitled *Lightbearers of Darkness*.

In the U.S., Paul Foster Case revised the Order teachings to suit his own ideas. He has been mentioned in a previous chapter so I'm not going to elaborate on him here, but some other American orders should also be considered.

Most of the magical orders of the Western tradition in America have been inspired by Crowley. A lot of them consist of cranks and freaks, but a few of them gave birth to reputable teachers.

C. F. Russell founded the Great Brotherhood of God, also known as the GBG, about 1925. He was a pupil of Crowley from his days in Sicily. Crowley mentions him in his *Confessions* under the pseudonym "Godwin."

One chapter of the GBG was later run by Louis T. Culling. As it is, or was (I believe that it has been extinct for about 20 years), inspired by the Beast, its teachings are not pure GD. As a matter of fact, most of the teachings are OTO-inspired sex magic. While still dominated by Russell, a strange and original variety of magic was introduced. As I have already hinted, it was a mixture of GD and OTO, but there was more to it than that. Francis King cautiously suggests that it could be a sort of Satanism, since Russell turned the Golden Dawn pentagram upside down. An inverted pentagram is generally associated with the Left Hand path, but by no means without exceptions. Also, at the very beginning, the GBG had been called the Choronzon Club, named after the spirit Choronzon, the demon or element of chaos in Dee's mythology, representing a principle normally considered evil.

Another order that derived from Crowley was the Agapé Lodge of the OTO, founded by another disciple, Wilfred T. Smith. He was soon promoted to the status of god in order to make way for another brief supernova in the occult night sky. His name was Jack Parsons, a genius physical chemist, who practically founded the California Institute of Technology, otherwise known as Caltech, a world-famous institute of scientific applications. A model for scientific researchers copied in most civilized countries, Parsons was unique. He conformed in all details to the public concept of the "mad scientist." He was a gifted genius, one of the pioneers of space science, but in his spare time he engaged in "Black Magic."

I want the reader to fasten his seat belt, because the following story has a plot that surpasses even those ideas that Steven Spielberg and George Lucas have discarded as being too unrealistic. And yet it is the truth, history. It actually happened—an obvious subject for a TV docu-drama.

Of course, it all happened in California. Pasadena, L.A., the neighboring district to Hollywood, the Dream Factory. The home of the weird cults and religions. Americans always seem to have a, shall we say, picturesque way of representing European phenomena, but this is ridiculous.

Inspired by Crowley's novel *Moonchild*, Parsons decided to father a magical child himself. To help him with the incantations, he trusted a third-rate science-fiction writer by the name of L. Ron Hubbard, the future founder and leader of the Scientology Church. Parsons was a scientific genius, but totally ignorant where human relations are concerned. They set up a joint bank account; i.e., Parsons contributed his life's savings of approximately $17,000 and Hubbard put up a thousand. Crowley, who knew Parsons well, said that there could be no doubt at all that Hubbard had, one way or another, managed to persuade Parsons to do this. Hubbard skipped out, first with Parsons' wife or mistress and eventually with $10,000 lifted from the joint account. He squandered it on a yacht and went to Florida, where Parsons finally tracked him down and had an injunction issued against him.*

A few years later, in 1948, Parsons went over the hill. He changed his name to Belarion Armiluss All Dajjal Anti-Christ. He died when his laboratory exploded during an experiment with high-octane rocket fuel in 1952.

While we are in California, we may as well look at another of the Crowley-inspired orders, the Church of Satan, founded in 1966 in San Francisco by Anton LaVey, a showman and former circus lion-tamer. Its teachings are a pathetic display of unadulterated egotism, as laid down in its gospel, *The Satanic Bible*, which consists of LaVey's "own" version of the 30 Aethyrs of Enochian magic, the backbone of the GD's Second Order teachings derived from John Dee. LaVey has concocted 30 travesties. All in all, it serves as an excuse for the members of his church to indulge in their own hang-ups instead of working with them.

Also the OTO itself is run from California, or at least one version of it is. One other has its headquarters in Switzerland, not to mention the "Typhonian" OTO of Kenneth Grant in England and the largely (but not entirely) defunct Society Ordo Templi Orientis (SOTO) formerly run by the late Marcello Motta. This has caused a legal problem since the death of the Beast. He left the copyrights to some of his works to the OTO, and the several groups all claim to be the heirs in question. At the moment, the courts in the U.S. have decided in favor of the Californian OTO, also known as the "caliphate" OTO because, at Crowley's instigation, it is headed up by an individual with the title of "caliph," currently a fellow who calls himself "Hymenaeus Beta." His true identity is more or less

---

*Hubbard later excused himself with a story to the effect that he had been employed or commissioned by the F.B.I., C.I.A., Naval intelligence, or some such organization to sabotage Parsons' occult activities. The Government was worried that an expert like Parsons attracted so many strange people to his circle of scientists. Some of them were probably Russian spies. The reader must remember that these were the early days of McCarthyism. Communist spies were seen everywhere. It doesn't sound very likely, but neither does Watergate when you stop and think about it. Personally, I don't believe it. I know a con racket when I see one, but Hubbard did manage to hold up Parsons' occult plans for a while. If that was Hubbard's aim under the direction of some government agency, however, one wonders if a more efficient means could not have been found than buying a boat.

common knowledge, but many members of the order seem to cherish the illusion that it is a well-kept secret, so I won't divulge it here. His predecessor, however, Hymenaeus Alpha, was Grady McMurtry, an initiate of the Agapé Lodge.

Another Crowley disciple, Charles Stansfeld Jones (Frater Achad), founded a group which was working in Vancouver on the Canadian west coast the last time I heard of it; the Ma-Ion fellowship. Wilfred T. Smith was originally initiated in Jones's Vancouver OTO lodge, but Ma-Ion was based on new "revelations."

Needless to say, the U.S. in general and California in particular are overflowing with magical groups based to a greater or lesser extent on the teachings of Crowley, but I am concerned here only with the direct offshoots.

We will now go back to Britain and pick up the thread from where we left it; i.e., Moina Mathers, the Alpha and Omega, and the new generation.

In 1919, a Neophyte was initiated into Brodie-Innes's AO. It was a woman, Violet Mary Firth. She chose the magical name of Deo Non Fortuna, from which she derived the name under which she was to become the best-selling author in the world on the subject, namely Dion Fortune.

After a year, Violet transferred to the new AO under Moina Mathers. Because of Moina's erratic way of running the lodge, some serious reorganization was indicated. Dion Fortune quickly laid such a scheme before Vestigia (Moina). It was accepted, and a sublodge called the Christian Mystic Lodge of the Theosophical Society was formed.

Dion Fortune seems to have had the same flair for advertising as H. Spencer Lewis, the founder of AMORC, a Rosicrucian order derived from the OTO and Rudolf Steiner.* Spencer Lewis and

---

*Both Lewis and Steiner later tried to minimize their connections with the OTO. As a matter of fact, they never mentioned the Order by name in any subsequent writings. To strengthen AMORC's claim to Rosicrucian truths, in 1934 Lewis, together with the leaders of a lot of other self-ordained orders, signed a document for the purpose of mutual self-glorification and recognition; i.e., they issued charters to one another. The assembly became known to themselves (not many outside it are aware at all of its existence) under the name of FUDOSI. FIDUSO would have been more appropriate.

Dion Fortune both used the media to attract new followers. In the newspapers, you could soon find the "Secrets of the Spiritual Life and the Universe" offered at a bargain, amid advertisements for discount soap and dog food. In the eyes of many serious members, this was a rather vulgar, not to say nauseating, procedure. Spencer Lewis seems to have been an advertising agent before he devoted himself to the great mystery of life. It attracted a lot of people, of course. As far as Dion Fortune is concerned, as her influence in the AO grew, it was bound to come to a confrontation with Moina Mathers sooner or later, and so it did. Together with her boy friend or lover, Charles Loveday, Dion contacted entities whom she supposed to be the Secret Chiefs. Mrs. Mathers, of course, saw her position threatened, and she expelled them in 1922.

Charles Thomas Loveday (1874–1948), who was "Dion's Loveday," may or may not have been related to Frederick Charles "Raoul" Loveday (1900–1923), who married an actress, Betty May, and died at Crowley's temple in Sicily after drinking bad water he had been warned about and, perhaps coincidentally, after the ritual sacrifice of a cat. In any event, his death was a contributing factor in Crowley's expulsion from Italy.

Dion Fortune changed the name of her faction to the Fraternity (later Society) of the Inner Light, which became one of the most successful of the modern lodges as far as producing able occultists is concerned. It was the mother of at least three other lodges; viz., the Guild of the Master Jesus, the Helios Lodge, and the Enochian Lodge. From the ranks of the Fraternity of the Inner Light have come many eminent writers on the Western tradition in all its guises. Apart from Dion Fortune herself, these include W. E. Butler, William Gray, Francis King, and Basil Wilby (who writes under the pseudonym of "Gareth Knight"). Butler founded the Servants of Light, now headed by Dolores Ashcroft-Nowicki, one of his students.

During the '40s, two of Dion's disciples, Christine Hartley and Charles Seymour, joined the Merlin Lodge of what was left of the Stella Matutina. They seem to have spent a great deal of time going into trances and exploring their past lives. Adepts are bound to have been somebody important in some past life or other: Crowley had to settle for Edward Kelly, Cagliostro, and Eliphas Levi, but Seymour had been no less a personage than Ramses II, the most famous and most powerful pharaoh of Egypt. It must have seemed like quite a comedown to being a tutor in a British officers' school in India and then to retirement as an occultist occupying his time with past-life regression, but he never complained.

During World War II, it seems that Dion and her followers contrived to win the Battle of Britain by summoning up King Arthur and the Jewish/Christian archangels to defeat the Luftwaffe. Even at the present day, a few of her followers are still saving Britian from this or that threat by going out into the woods and waving swords in the air.

The Society of the Inner Light flourished and, after Moina Mathers's death in 1928, it had no serious competition on the European side of the Atlantic. Dion Fortune's only rival was a young man, a disciple of Crowley, who spent three years as the Beast's unpaid secretary and companion and also stayed with Dion for a while when he was down on his luck. He never founded an order himself and so he never really threatened Crowley. His name was Israel Regardie. Born in England in 1907, Regardie lived in the U.S. until 1928 when he went to Paris to work for the Beast. In 1932, after parting with the master, Regardie published the first of his many books on occultism, *The Tree of Life*. Reactions were mixed. Dion Fortune liked it and thought it a good idea that the concept of modern occultism should be laid out for anyone to see, and for the sake of reassessment. However, E. J. Langford-Garstin and Maiya Tranchell-Hayes, otherwise known as Mrs. Curtis Webb (whose regalia had washed ashore in 1966), the leaders of the Stella Matutina after the death of Moina Mathers, felt that too many secrets were inadvertently given away by the young man, and they decided on the same policy as had Reuss to save the OTO from Crowley's indiscretions. They made Regardie a member in 1934, and he quickly progressed to the Second Order of the AO. He found the level of attainment among the adepti so deplorable that he decided, perhaps a bit rashly and prematurely, that the only way to save the teachings of the Golden Dawn was to publish all the Order material and be damned, and so he did. During the late '30s and early '40s, he published all that he could lay his hands on, in four volumes.

This certainly killed the London temple of the Stella Matutina and the AO (3), probably the only apostolic temple in England at that time. It stopped its initiations and Mrs. Tranchall-Hayes buried her ritual regalia, which, as mentioned before, was to reappear in 1966.

Dion Fortune died suddenly in 1946, and this marked the beginning of the end for the Society of the Inner Light. During the '50s, it was infested by a lot of foreign junk—among other things, L. Ron Hubbard's pseudo-psychoanalysis from the Scientology movement.

Another temple was opened in London in 1959. It was a descendant of the Hermes Lodge in Bristol. Around 1930 its members decided to return to the original GD teachings and accordingly changed the name of the lodge to Hermanubis, the original No. 2 temple. When they chartered a daughter temple in London, they suitably named it after the original Isis-Urania No. 3. This temple can almost certainly boast of having had the occult writer Francis King as a member for a while.

This is about the last lodge of the second generation that I'm going to deal with here. A new generation emerged during the '60s but, before we leave this chapter, I want to look at a group of orders or phenomena that lie a bit outside the ordinary run of the mill magical order: the Zos Kia Cultus, the order of the Aurum Solis, and the phenomenon of modern withcraft, the Wicca movement.

The first of these originated with the artist Austin Osman Spare. At the turn of the century, he was a member of Crowley's AA, but his ego was as great as that of the Beast. Therefore, in 1910, he developed his own particular brand of magic known as the Zos Kia Cultus. It would have remained an isolated idiosyncrasy had it not been for the fact that it was taken up by the third generation of magicians around 1970, by a group calling themselves the Illuminates of Thanateros, or, for short, the IOT. They have abandoned all pretense of tradition, and they have made a point of taking their magical forms and symbols out of anything at hand. For that reason, their approach has very aptly been termed Chaos Magic, because the borderline between the magical and the everyday personality becomes more or less obliterated. This can be very dangerous, as the magician can no longer tell the difference between imagination and reality. However, it can be argued whether there really is a distinction between the two at all, and that *everything* is reality of one kind or another. It doesn't seem to matter much, and the failure to realize this is responsible for all the evils in the world. There is no hope that things will ever get better until everybody— or at least a majority—understands this and lives accordingly. This seems to be the most important aspect of Chaos Magic.

The foremost spokesman for Chaos at the present time appears to be Peter J. Carroll, who presented the theory and practice of the genre to the world in *Liber Null* and *Psychonaut* (Weiser, 1987).

Rather more traditional is the Aurum Solis, an English lodge at one time active in Minnesota, that, based on some published minor rituals, might seem to be based on the GD pattern. They say not. The one thing they lack that the GD has is an emphasis on the legend of Christian Rosenkreuz; their background is said to have more of a gnostic and Neoplatonic focus—the "Ogdoadic Tradition"—and they claim an origin independent of and unrelated to the GD. Outside the order, not much is known of the organization, but the teachings have been published in five volumes (now expanded and reprinted in trade paperback as three volumes) under the title of *The Magical Philosophy*. This material was written or compiled by two members, Melita Denning and Osborne Phillips. At various times, the lodge has also been known as the OSV, or Order of the Sacred Word. According to Denning and Phillips, it was founded in 1897 by two occultists, Charles Kingold and George Stanton, of whom nothing is otherwise known. Phillips himself, so the introduction to the work claims, was trained under a warden of the order named Ernest Page, of whom I also know nothing.

The final phenomenon to be scrutinized in this chapter is the modern witch movement.

Since the dawn of ages, exponents of folk magic have practiced things that people in general today associate with witchcraft, but it was not until the beginning of the 1950s that Gerald Brousseau Gardner popularized modern Wicca. According to one account, Gardner was one of Crowley's perennial students, a member of the OTO and a retired customs officer, who asked Crowley if he could produce some suitable rituals with which to revive and rejuvenate the traditional craft. The Master wrote a new Book of Shadows, and in 1954 Gardner published *Witchcraft Today*. According to another account, Gardner wrote the rituals himself with the aid of Doreen Valiente. Gardner borrowed heavily from Crowley's published writings, but Doreen persuaded him to tone it down a little bit.

Gardner may have run covens, as circles of witches are called, since before 1949, when he published his first book, a novel called *High Magic's Aid*, but it wasn't until after *Witchcraft Today* that the number of covens suddenly exploded like mushrooms in a crypt. Since witchcraft is closer to folk magic, it falls a bit outside of the framework of this survey. So do a couple of other lodges I have not mentioned, or which I have mentioned only briefly, such as the Cromlech Temple, controlled by the Brodie-Innes AO from about 1890 and after approximately 1919 by Dr. Felkin.

Judging the relative success of all these various orders is a very subjective business. As far as is known in a historical sense, through the media and official and private correspondence, lodge papers, books, articles, and other sources, success can be measured in quantity only. In order to get an idea of qualitative success, the historian must step aside and let the practicing magician step forward, and even he can only guess.

The true adept today is seldom conspicuous in the orders, and he is certainly never to be found among the leaders of any big order. To preserve a leading position within a lodge that exceeds the traditional 13 people is to be a politician. Ideals will sooner or later have to be sacrificed for the sake of administration, generally sooner. Besides, the degree of egotism necessary for an organized leader far exceeds the maximum that is cosmically allowed for spiritual advancement. This explains why the real masters never had any organized movement of more than about a dozen disciples.

I would like to stress the fact that what is important today is not the orders and lodges as such, but their traditional teachings. Due to modern advertising it is impossible to achieve the same homogeneity that used to be the *raison d'être* of the traditional orders, but the system still works in a mysterious way.

If we look at a typical modern lodge of, say, a hundred members, we will find that the average meeting is attended by perhaps half that amount—not always the same half; only about 20 show up every time. The other 30 change. The remaining 50 are those who live too far from the temple to attend more than a few times every now and again, and those who, for some reason or another, are listed as members but have tired of the thing and are at present pursuing some other ready-made answer to the Great Mystery and who have not yet been scratched from the roll because they are perhaps still paying their dues. These 50 must be considered dead weight to any order. They are totally superfluous. The value of the money they provide is more than offset by the disadvantages they bring. Their ignorance of the work of the order ruins every ritual gathering and, of course, the more of them an order has, the more unsuccessful meetings it will have.

It's among the other half that we may be lucky enough to find the true adept. A few of the members find deep profundity and wisdom in the order teachings not because of but in spite of the order's other members and leaders. These few eventually get together in an anonymous group and perform their valuable spiritual work outside the order while, at the same time, they dutifully attend the order meetings to lend a hand to new neophytes of any true talent or spirituality.

Another adept is the lone wolf. He is the one who receives enlightenment while studying in some lodge and then suddenly drops out, fully aware that from now on the ossifying organization will only serve to hamper his further progress. He may continue as a paying member, hoping that his contributions will furnish some other would-be adept with the chance of sudden enlightenment. Such adepts only take one or two pupils privately in a whole lifetime, and presumably never more than one at a time.

All over the world there is a small number of these true adepts. They may have nothing else in common but the fact that they will never be found among the leaders of any lodge because they are utterly incapable of compromising the living truth of every moment of time. To them, the present *now* is all that exists, and to change this by compromising any ideal—or rather, truth—for any convenience is unthinkable and impossible. It was by so doing that man fell from grace with God in the first place.

World War II was a setback to magic in general, at least to "White Magic." Various claims to the effect that the Nazis were black magicians trying to conquer the world are often heard. We will examine these claims in the next chapter, along with some of the orders on the continent.

Occult Nazis

It has often been said that Adolf Hitler was a black magician who tried to win World War II by means of dark forces. It has even been suggested that the whole Schützstaffel (SS) and the Nazi party were nothing but secret magical societies, and that Germany would indeed have won the war had Hitler only continued to listen to the advice of the sorcerers working behind him.

The names of these sorcerers has been a matter of pure conjecture on the part of different writers. Names like Martin Borman and other low-profile Nazis have been suggested, but most of these suggestions have been backed by very little evidence.

Sufficient evidence does exist, however, to ascertain that occultism did play a part in the Third Reich, although a much smaller part than some have claimed, or so it seems.

The trouble is that most of the writers who support the idea of occultism in Naziland do not mince their words, and some of their theories are, to say the least, a bit extravagant.

Another problem is Hitler himself. After all, he was the big cheese, and he was much too complex to be written off as merely an occult monomaniac. Once, when called upon to decide between the two occult cosmogonies, Hörbiger's *Welteislehre* or the Hollow Earth theory,* he explained that he, or the German people (which amounted to the same thing) didn't need any holistic view of the world. Both might be true.

Now this statement is a first-class example of what is known as doublethink, as defined by George Orwell, and it does tell us something about "der Führer." One, he was an unadulterated

---

*For an elaboration of these theories, see *The Morning of the Magicians* by Pauwels and Bergier.

opportunist. We knew that. Two, it also tells us that he, personally, wasn't wholeheartedly committed to any existing movement, at least not to the point of being hampered with any truths to defend.

What then were Hitler's ideals, his *raison d'être?* It's hard to say, but we do have a few clues. We know that he was a dreamer. Also, he considered himself an artist rather than a politician. From 1908 to 1913, he lived in Vienna, in dire poverty, in sordid lodgings and regular flophouses. Unshaved and unwashed, he preferred to use his mediocre artistic talents to produce postcard-paintings with motifs from old Vienna rather than get involved with regular work.

One reason for his inability to succeed in any field was his dispersed interests. He was vehemently against specializing. Therefore he never committed himself to any one thing. His talents were obviously of a supervising kind. No wonder that he was successful when he entered politics. It was a made-to-measure job for him. Politicians usually know nothing except the outlines of their party program, but they have their own ideas as to how this should be brought about. Hitler had a lot of ideas but no program until he met with Anton Drexler's group after the 1914–18 war. This chemical reaction really started Hitler realizing himself.

Since he was uncommitted, he was open-minded enough to see which things worked and why, thus giving him an advantage over his adversaries who were all committed to something or other. Some things that did work were various occult movements and ideas. We will try to look into some of them.

Racism and nationalism are two such ideas which apparently are not connected in any way, but it is not so. They are two sides of the same coin—at least, as far as the German variety is concerned.

After 1815, the end of the Napoleonic wars, Prussia and Austria became rivals. Who was to become the dominant German-speaking nation? There had never really been a Germany. What we know as Germany today was a multitude of small kingdoms, each ruled by its own king or prince. None of these rulers owed allegiance to each other or to any central power, and all attempts at uniting them had hitherto failed. After the Vienna Congress, however, the lines for the future struggle were drawn. Prussia and Austria were the only serious contenders. It ended on the battle-field in 1866, and after the gun smoke cleared away, the Prussian army under the Iron Chancellor Bismarck had completely subdued the Austrians.

Black magician, or simply an unprincipled opportunist?

Mein Kampf, Angriff Press

In the peace negotiations, it was declared that Austria had no claims whatsoever to German-speaking areas outside its own borders. It was also laid out that the Germans in Austria were in no way considered part of any pan-German movement or people.

No doubt this was a concession by Bismarck to alleviate the demands of the Austrians and please them, but he forgot to take into account the ethnic minorities of the country. The result was devastating. Austria was composed of at least ten different peoples of whom most were Germans, but, since they were only 35 per cent of the total population, they couldn't take themselves for granted.

After 1866, German-speaking Austrians were made up of three groups: those who were Austrians first and believed that Vienna should be the ruling capital of a pan-German Reich, those who were pro-German and believed that even the Austrian Germans should be included in a pan-German federation under Prussian rule, and, finally, those who didn't give a damn one way or the other, who were perfectly happy being Austrians among a lot of other Austrians of different tongues. This was by far the smallest group.

Obviously the first two groups had no reason to love the other minorities. They feared, not without reason, that the pan-German federation suspected their credibility because they shared their country with a lot of strange, undesirable foreigners.

Under these circumstances it must be considered slightly undiplomatic on the part of the central government to enforce a law about civil servants and other officials having to be bilingual in areas that had a German-speaking majority.

At the same time, theories of social Darwinism were becoming popular, and this, of course, explained the whole deplorable situation. Austria had lost the war because her people were unworthy, a dirty cocktail of undesirable primates, whereas the Prussian armies were made up of the cream of the Aryan inheritance.

Such ideas originated with people like Ernst Haeckel and George Wilheim Friedrich Hegel; were propagated by Joseph Arthur de Gobineau, Houston Stewart Chamberlain, and Friedrich Nietzsche; and were popularized by Hans Hörbiger, Franz Hartmann, and Madame Blavatsky. These people held the view that different races have different values according to how close they are to the elder races. For example, the Aryans (i.e., Germans, the blond and blue-eyed) are direct descendants from the Atlantean root-race, whereas the Jews, Negroes, Slavs, and anyone else for that matter, are unfortunate mutants, further away from Homo sapiens than the snottiest gorilla. The reason for all the troubles in this world is the presence of these unsavory species that the master race should mercifully do away with so that peace and quiet could be restored and life imbued with a bit of style.

No wonder that the credibility of the Austrian Germans was suffering with all these co-existing minorities: Hungarians, Czechs, Italians, Bohemians, Moravians, Romanians, etc.—creatures completely unworthy to partake of the glorious Germanic inheritance, whose inability to appreciate the grandeur of the historical heroes was appalling.

Apart from these theories about the master race, another strong contributing factor to German occultism was the Teutonic Knights. The Order of German Knights had been humiliatingly defeated near the beginning of the 15th century in what had been one of the worst historical and cultural setbacks for the German "völkisch" spirit. It had never been forgotten, and in the late 18th century, during the Gothic romantic period, it was revived. In the days of Goethe and Schiller, hundreds of societies and fraternities were formed, especially among students. The ancient Germanic mythology became one of the most important subjects of study. The Nibelungenlied was set to music by Richard Wagner. The mere idea that a few operas can set a people aflame is appalling, but there can be no doubt that Wagner's works had a tremendous impact, as they masterfully lifted the subject above the ordinary, everyday atmosphere.

Under these circumstances, it is not surprising that Madame Blavatsky's Theosophy should be popular. It was fuel to the racist fire, and it became very popular indeed. The actual fusion was due to two Austrian magi, Guido von List and Jörg Lanz von Liebenfels.

Guido von List (1848–1919) was born at Vienna of wealthy middle-class parents. At an early age, he fell in love with the rural landscape surrounding the Austrian metropolis. He also became infatuated with the early history of the Germanic peoples and their myths and legends. He published theories about the occult significance of the old Nordic and Germanic writing, the runes. He won a lot of proselytes, and around 1910 a List Society was formed. List buried eight wine bottles in a swastika pattern on the bank of the

Danube in a midsummer ritual in 1874. The swastika was being used by Blavatsky for its original Indian symbolism, but to Europeans who had never seen it before, it gradually became the symbol of pure Germanism, and later on worse.

The other great influence in pre-war Austria and Germany was Jörg Lanz von Liebenfels. He was born at Vienna in 1874 and lived until 1954. He went a step further than List. Where the latter was pro-German, Lanz von Liebenfels was downright against all other races, especially the Jews. As a young man, he joined the Cistercian monastic order, but left it after six years to pursue a career as a writer and publisher.

As a romantic monk, he had been strongly influenced by the Knights Templar, who had always had a close connection with the Cistercians. Formed in 1118 at Jerusalem, the Templars received their papal commission ten years later, and the rule of the order was laid down by the leader of the Cistercians, St. Bernard de Clairvaux, in 1128. In two centuries, the order managed to rise and fall. The order was suppressed and banned in 1312 and its leader, Jacques de Molay, was burned at the stake for heresy and practicing the black arts. The actual reason was to be found in local politics. Philip IV of France was the instigator of the trial. When the order was found guilty of the charges, its assets fell to the crown, and this improved the economy of the kingdom. In other countries, this policy was duly taken up, and the Order had to move underground. Perhaps it did or perhaps it was dissolved.

The Templars have proved to be a rich mine for the imaginative faculties of occultists, mystery mongers, conspiracy buffs, Masons (particulary French Masons), and others. The top degree in the York Rite of Freemasonry is still known as "Knight Templar"— which is a bit odd, if you think about it, because the preceding degree (or "order") is called "Knight of Malta." The Templars and the Hospitalers (Knights of Malta) were rivals and were at each other's throats most of the time.

There have been as many theories to explain who and what the Templars were as there were Templars—probably more. The truth probably is that they were just a bunch of good old boys who decided to buy penance and salvation by the simple approach of smashing Saracen heads (and, later, after the failure of the Crusades, by sitting around the commandery and scratching fleas).

When they became too rich and enterprising, the greed (and need) of Philip the Fair and his puppet pope Clement spelled their doom. They were accused of a standard list of heretical atrocities. Since all the inquisitors were briefed beforehand as to what leading questions to ask when subjecting a Templar to torture, it is no great surprise that their confessions tended to agree on certain points, such as defiling the cross, renouncing Christ, sodomy, and so on. One rather unusual feature that emerged, however, was the admission that they had all worshipped an idol, a head or the image of a head, called Baphomet—which sounds like some sort of corruption of "Mahomet," the prophet of Islam. Eliphas Levi included a portrait of Baphomet—not a head—in one of his books, a drawing that has become rather well known by this time.

Of course, many people believe the charges against the Templars were true. Others believe they may have had some basis in fact. Still others imagine the Templars as some sort of proto-Rosicrucian lodge of magicians and philosophers, privy to all the arcane secrets. Did they not amass a great treasure? And did not that treasure—no doubt much to Philip's disgust—vanish along with the Templar fleet before it could be confiscated by the authorities? There are rumors that the Templar treasure is hidden beneath a castle or chapel in Scotland. Otherwise, it forms the basis of several works of fiction. Some of them, such as *Foucault's Pendulum* by Umberto Eco, even admit to being fiction.

It was on this admirable Order that Lanz* modeled his new sodality. He even went so far as to name it Ordo Novi Templi (ONT); i.e., the Order of the New Templars. It was officially founded on Christmas Day 1907 in an old medieval castle situated on the river bank overlooking a bend of the Danube. He had bought it with financial support from his proselytes in Vienna, and in the December issue of his periodical *Ostara*, the whole outline of the ONT was published. The *Ostara* was a magazine that Lanz had started in 1905 to forward his racial theories. The Order became very popular and, before the war, a second castle had been purchased.

Although the young Adolf Hitler was well-read in the *Ostara*

---

*Lanz von Liebenfels, Guido von List, and, later on, Rudolf von Sebottendorff are all bogus titles. Their real names were Guido List, Adolf Lanz, and Rudolf Glauer.

in the pre-war period, one can hardly say that the List society or the ONT had any direct influence on him.

At the time, a whole lot of small pan-German movements existed. They were united in a so-called Hammerbund, which was, in effect, an umbrella organization for anti-Semitic circles of every kind. In 1912, the leader, Theodor Fritsch, demanded that the wheat be separated from the chaff. He wished for an inner order to take the cream of the Hammerbund, as it were, and sent out a call to this effect. From Hermann Pohl, leader of the Hammer group of Magdeburg, came the answer that such a thing already existed, practicing German pagan magic. It had been running since the autumn of 1910 and was led by a man named Heinnatz. It had been inaugurated as the Wotan Lodge on April 5, 1911, under the leadership of Master Herman Pohl. Ten days later, a Grand Lodge was formed with Theodor Fritsch as Grand Master, and in the following year on March 12, it changed its name to the Germanenorden.

This Order is a step closer to Adolf Hitler. Although he was never affiliated with the Germanenorden, it helped to pave the way for him. Apart from the pagan lore, its first and foremost *raison d'être* was the fight against Jews and other inferior races.

The Germanenorden split up in 1916. Some lodges were dissatisfied with Pohl as leader. After the schism, the attention and interest of the public seemed to wane, and a lot of people thought they had heard the last of it. But Pohl had admitted a young adventurer, Rudolf Glauer, otherwise known as Rudolf von Sebottendorff, who, on December 21, 1917, was appointed Master of Bavaria, with the duty of establishing a lodge there as soon as possible.

Together with a war veteran, Walter Nauhaus, he started immediately, and in the spring of 1918 they had collected about 200 members. The figure had risen to 1500 by the autumn of 1919. The meetings were held at The Four Seasons hotel in Munich and, in order not to provoke the minority groups that they were fighting, they called themselves the Thule Society, hoping for anonymity during meetings.

All this was in the aftermath of the war, the days of the communist uprising in Bavaria and, two days later, in Berlin. The Thule Society was active in crushing the Reds. As a matter of fact, the society was responsible for organizing the resistance, as soon as the legal government had fled to Barmberg. The socialists killed seven

Thule members that they held as hostages, and the Thulekampf-bund retaliated by killing a lot of socialist sympathizers. Other free-corps joined in, and chaos became, more or less, the order of the day. This is one of the reasons for the tolerance of public opinion and the leniency of the courts later on, when the Nazi stormtroopers terrorized the nation. They were not the only ones, after all; they had only taken up a practice already well established.

Sebottendorff persuaded Karl Harrer, a sports journalist, to form a worker's circle, Deutscher Arbeiterverein, also known as Politische Arbeiter-Zirkel, in October 1918. Among the members were Harrer himself and a blacksmith, Anton Drexler. The latter decided to turn it into a political party, and on January 5, 1919, the Deutsche Arbeiterpartei (German Worker's Party) was launched. This was the party that Hitler later joined that was to become the Nationalsozialistische Deutsche Arbeiterpartei, or NSDAP (National Socialist German Worker's Party; i.e., the Nazi party).

Sebottendorff also contributed another thing to the Nazi movement; namely, the *Völkischer Beobachter*, the Nazi press organ. It was owned by Sebottendorff, or to be exact, by his mistress Katie Bierbaumer, and he sold it to Anton Drexler, who transferred his shares to Hitler in November 1921.

In addition, the Thule Society set another example: that of assassinating political opponents, Mafia-style. Some members formed a court modeled after the medieval Vehmgericht. They assembled secretly and passed sentence on adversaries by secret ballot, and an executioner appointed in a similar way carried out the sentence. They got away with it for the simple reason that two of its members were the Home Secretary of Bavaria and the Chief of Police of Munich.

From this it is easy to see that the Thule Society had a lot of influence and a tremendous impact upon Adolf Hitler, but hardly in a strictly occult sense. It has been said that a Thule member, Dietrich Eckhart, initiated Hitler into the black arts. It's possible; I will even go as far as to say that it's very likely, but in that case it has certainly not involved any teachings of the Germanenorden itself. Anybody thinking that Hitler was the cat's paw for the Thule Society is mistaken. If possible, it was the other way around. The society was full of people that Hitler needed in his stormtroopers; i.e., people in important places, politically and financially speaking, and people who could stand up and hold their own in a street fight, who would not be embarrassed every now and again by doing away with a troublesome opponent or ally, as the case might be. This was what Hitler needed at the moment and so he obligingly adjusted his policy to suit his followers.

I do believe that Hitler was much more versatile than he is generally given credit for. Of course, he was an ardent anti-Semite, no question about that, but never to the point of ruining his personal plans. As soon as his need for this kind of people terminated, he immediately ditched them. After that, the extermination of the Jews continued much more discretely, and the reason that so many were killed in the holocaust is to a great extent due to Heinrich Himmler and a lot of perverted and sadistic SS initiates. After the elimination of his stormtroopers in 1934 (the Night of the Long Knives), Hitler was in the pocket of Himmler and his organization. He couldn't have stopped the killing of the Jews without depriving the SS of its reason to exist, and this he couldn't do because he badly needed the SS.

I'm not questioning the fact that Hitler was a callous cynic, nor the fact of his guilt in the Nazi war crimes. What I do question are his real motives. No single person knows the complex nature of der Führer. His book, *Mein Kampf,* is a diffuse statement. It says a lot about Hitler's thoughts on different subjects, but it seems to be aimed at almost any reader. It lacks coherence and an overall structure. It hops and skips from one subject to the next. Of course, he makes it clear that there is no place for the inferior races, and that they will eventually have to make way for the superman.

He claimed to be in contact with the coming race, and I'm sure that he thought of himself as a herald of the times to come, but I'm also certain that these forces had cautioned him never to let anyone know the true nature of the master plan. That explains why he always, in some way, seemed an enigma to his followers. He agreed with anybody who could forward his plans to a certain point—the point of departure. Therefore, he could always keep a distance from his projects. It also explains the dedication of his followers. Everybody thought that he agreed with their philosophy. Any discord between them and him was ascribed to his genius, and they were quickly convinced that he was miles ahead of them. I'm not sure what his cause was. Perhaps he didn't have any. Perhaps he was just suffering from delusions of grandeur, but whatever it was, it was much more complex than these racist cliches with which he has been associated by most of his critics.

I'm not trying to excuse Hitler in any way. On the contrary, I feel that his guilt is infinitely greater than most people think, because in my opinion he was not really into the same trip as Himmler and his sadistic hordes. He preferred to let them have their fun rather than enlighten them about his true philosophy, thus sacrificing six million people for the sake of convenience. Of course, the status of the "inferior races" in a Nazi millennium is certainly not to be envied whatever Hitler's plans were, and it's obvious that, from time to time, he was bothered by the racial problem. He did issue the decree for the Final Solution, but a lot of these things were prompted by his advisors, and, after all, as he was the big boss, his signature was needed on all official government documents. But after 1939, when most of the really sordid things happened, Hitler himself was mostly occupied with fighting a world war.

Hitler does provide an interesting example of the phenomenon of total vilification, a propaganda technique that has also been applied to Aleister Crowley. The big difference is that Hitler actually *was* "the wickedest man in the world," even if he never sacrificed any toads. Hitler (or Crowley) is identified with Satan, the personification of total evil. Therefore, everything he said, thought, did, or *was* must be totally evil. The Volkswagen, the Autobahn, and trains running on time were either accomplished by somebody else without his knowledge or else they are somehow inherently tainted with evil.

A result of this attitude is that such critics have to assume that Hitler was some sort of sexual freak and/or pervert as well as everything else. It's as if there is no commandment that he is allowed not to break. It's not enough that he caused the death of millions of people and sacrificed Europe on the altar of his own ego, he also had to have all manner of sexual peculiarities. We know about these perversions because of the reports made after the war by Hitler's private and exclusive physician. Or one of his several dozen private and exclusive physicians, since there seem to be about that many independent reports, all different. Most say things such as Hitler had only one testicle or was otherwise sexually deformed, that he could achieve climax only by getting worked up during a speech to the masses, or that, being impotent, he was in the habit of using a loaded revolver as an artificial penis. Perhaps some of these reports are true, but the probability is that they reveal more about the minds of their authors than they do about Hitler.

Affiliated to the Thule Society was a minor group which probably had a lot of influence on Hitler. One thing is certain; he got a lot of his ideas from it. It was known as the Luminous Lodge, or Die Loge der Brüder vom Licht, otherwise known as Die Vrielgesellschaft (Vril Society), and was based on an insane doctrine derived from a novel by Bulwer-Lytton, *The Coming Race.* In the story, the protagonist encounters an underground race of superior beings who have mastered a sort of energy called "vril." In some ways, vril is like atomic energy; in other ways it is like the theoretical universal magical force variously known as baraka, mana, the odic force, orgone energy, the astral light, etc. The members of the Vril Society were convinced that a subterranean people would one day surface and take control of the world. Just to what extent Hitler believed in this I don't know, but evidence suggests that he followed it at least a bit of the way. As we shall see in the next chapter, this is not the only time that a group of people have chosen to believe a fictional creation to be a true account.

Among the members of the Vril Society were Dietrich Eckhart and a professor of geopolitics at the University of Munich, Karl Haushofer.

Eckhart was a drunken journalist and playwright who had done some masterful translations of Ibsen plays. *Mein Kampf* is dedicated to him.

Haushofer, on the other hand, was a general in World War I. He later came to Munich, where he gained the professorship in geopolitics at the university, in consequence of which he became the teacher of Rudolf Hess.

In his youth, Haushofer had traveled all over the world, but particularly in the Orient, where he is supposed to have been initiated into the Green Dragon Society, rumored to be some sort of Buddhist secret organization. Who knows? It is more than likely that he possessed considerable occult experience; after all, no one can travel many years in the Orient without being affected by local customs. I think that this is the most promising field of investigation as to Hitler's occult life.

What's in a name? As an aside, it might be noted that the Boston Tea Party was plotted and carried out by members of a Masonic lodge that met at the *Green Dragon* Tavern.

Certainly occultism played a considerable part in Nazism, but this had more to do with Heinrich Himmler than with Hitler himself. The SS department of occultism, the Ahnenerbe, was all Himmler 's pet toy, and all the strange radar experiments on the Island of Rugen in 1942 to substantiate the "Hollow Earth" theory probably had very little to do with der Führer himself.

There is no evidence linking Hitler to the fringe rune-magic societies. Even the OTO, which had been founded sometime between 1895 and 1904, had no impact whatsoever on the top brass. As mentioned in a previous chapter, the OTO had been divided into two separate orders after the death of its leader, Theodor Reuss, in 1922. One faction followed Crowley, but the other, under the leadership of Heinrich Tränker, founded the Fraternitas Saturni the following year.

All these occult and semi-occult sodalities were banned and suppressed after 1933, when magic became a state secret. The two last mentioned organizations resumed their activities after 1945.

Some readers may feel that I have passed too lightly over German magic of the last century,* and to some extent it may be so, but I have my reasons. The subject falls slightly outside the scope of this book, as Aryan occultism has been mainly borrowed from the Theosophists. Rune and solar magical disciplines do not strictly belong to the Western Esoteric Tradition, but are rather a revival of pagan shamanism.

•For readers who are interested in further facts—and speculative details and theories—about this vast subject, I suggest the following books:

Arktos: The Polar Myth in Science, Symbolism, and Nazi Survival by Joscelyn Godwin. Phanes Press, 1993.

The Occult Roots of Nazism by Nicholas Goodrick-Clarke. Aquarian Press, 1985.

Urania's Children by Ellic Howe. William Kimber & Co. Ltd., 1967.

The Spear of Destiny by Trevor Ravenscroft. Samuel Weiser Inc., 1973.

The only real connection with the Western Tradition is the OTO, when one tactfully overlooks its oriental slant, but this sodality has been dealt with in the chapter devoted to Crowley.

The neo-Nazi movements that have emerged in recent years seem to be all political and more interested in terrorism than in occultism, but magic is a tough and seasoned phenomenon and is bound to stick its head up again sooner or later. With this remark I'll leave the subject of Nazi occultism.

Magic Today

Where is Western magic today? Under what guise does it manifest itself? To be frank, it's discernible in many of the '"New Age" phenomena. Stripped of its more exotic accountrements, it has even managed to sneak into the business world, as part of modern holistic "management courses." The breathing, meditation, and visualization techniques that are so popular among the business executives of today have all been lifted from the magical tradition, East or West. Of course, most of the teachers of these techniques go out of their way not to admit to any influence before Carl Gustav Jung, the eminent psychologist. They seldom, if ever, mention the fact that the very same Jung drew heavily on both Eastern and Western magical traditions. Even Freud was directly influenced by Hargrave Jennings, although he never admitted it.*

However, I'm not going into any of these hybrid things. I'll stick to magical orders and movements where magic plays a major part.

In later years, we have seen orders such as the IOK, or Interna-

---

*Psychology, in essence, deals with the same phenomena as magic; viz., altered states of consciousness. Psychology, in fact, is magic. It's only a matter of concept. It depends on the magician. The more personal hangups he has, the more he leans toward psychology. They would all use the techniques but, since the magicians were outdated by modern science from about the mid-1600s, some magicians, such as Mesmer, tried to present magic in the guise of science as science became more and more respectable.

As the psychological bone was rather slim, more meat was indicated. This was supplied in the 1940s in the form of statistics by people such as B. F. Skinner. He mixed magic with new mathematics into a brand-new psychology called behaviorism.

tional Order of Kabbalists, in London, run by James Sturzaker and his wife Doreen. They work ceremonial magic, although Sturzaker asserts that the IOK's Qabalistic rituals have nothing to do with the Golden Dawn or Crowley. The IOK has been around for 24 years as of this writing. There is also the Order of the Serpent, founded in 1979, with Duncan G. Bourne as leader—if it still exists (it appears to have been inactive for a while now). The Order of the Cubic Stone in Wolverhampton, mentioned by Francis King, also worked GD-based magic during its existence, but it fell apart 10 to 15 years ago when the head of the order retired, resulting in a classic magical battle for leadership between two remaining rivals.

Besides the GD offshoots already mentioned in previous chapters, some additional sodalities are working, mostly in England and the U.S., of which the orders of the latter are too transient to be of any real importance, not to say too elusive to capture on paper. They appear, disappear, and reappear again under different names too frequently to map. The Ra-Horakhty Temple of Seattle, associated with Peter Yorke and his wife, Laura Jennings-Yorke, has been around for a few years, as have variously named and located Golden Dawn-type organizations associated with Christopher Hyatt and the Israel Regardie Foundation.

One Anglo-American organization that has been growing since 1985 or so is AMOOKOS, but this falls outside the scope of this book, being based as it is on Hindu traditions. Once you go through a few degrees, you get to be a Nath.

Among the lesser survivors of Crowley-inspired organizations may be mentioned the Ordo Templi Baphe-Metis (based on futher channeled revelations subsequent to *The Book of the Law;* viz., *The Book of Ba Neb Tet),* which is the brainchild of James Martin in Corpus Christi, Texas. The executive director, however, is in Rochester, New Hampshire.

Somewhat less active than it once was in the U.S. is the Cincinnati group now known as Bate Cabal, which arose out of the Cincinnati Chapter of the Crowned and Conquering Child in the '70s and now publishes (at long intervals) *The Cincinnati Journal of Magick.* Bate Cabal leans heavily on the ideas of Crowley, Frater Achad, Austin Spare, and Kenneth Grant, but it is said to be "a coalition of Magickians with eclectic philosophies." Perhaps the best known personality connected with this group is that of "Soror

Nema," who channeled yet another Crowleyan document, *Liber Pennae Praenumbra,* heralding the Aeon of Maat, "which is coterminous with that of Horus."

A splinter group from Anton LaVey's Church of Satan is Michael Aquino's Temple of Set, begun in 1975. Aquino apparently quit the parent group because LaVey wasn't serious enough about the reality of Satan (or Set, his Egyptian prototype). Like so many groups these days which try to follow in Crowley's footsteps, the the Temple of Set is based on a new, channeled revelation, *The Book of Coming Forth by Night.* The creed remains one of worship of the individual psyche, of one's own conscious intelligence; i.e., selfishness.

As for groups working in traditions only marginally related to the Western Hermetic Tradition, there are Edred Thorsson's Rune-Gild, Tadhg MacCrossan's Druidactos, and Douglas Monroe's New Forest Centre. Thorsson and MacCrossan are headquartered in Texas, Monroe in a small town in New York state.

There are a few fraternities on the continent, mainly in Holland and West Germany, but they are more into Wicca and other pagan varieties of the craft.

In Scandinavia is the OI et LT, which has been working GD-inspired Enochian magic since 1984. It operates from Malmö, Sweden, and draws its members from Copenhagen and the rest of Scandinavia. Then there are the Chaos groups as I have mentioned before, and that is practically all there is today. Some minor groups, however, are practicing what is called Aquarian Magic, but this is hardly a novelty. It's rather more mystery than magic. It contains a lot of "Grail" ingredients, but the magical elements can easily be identified as a mixture of Wicca and the Western tradition. It is not an unpleasant variety if you are into the legends of the Holy Grail. There are some very nice people involved in this endeavor. That's more than can always be said for the traditional groups. Of course a lot of the older groups, mentioned in previous chapters, are still active.

All of this is not to mention the fact that there are hundreds of small groups with grand-sounding titles that have few members and that come and go like people through a revolving door at the bank on payday. Someone may decide one day to unilaterally announce the existence of the Glorious Hermetic Order of the Paisley Doodlebug with himself as Grand Exalted Poobah and Master of the World, and eventually, by means of correspondence and computer networking, he will work around to having as many as half a dozen members worldwide—if his dues are not too expensive. Having come that far, he may publish leaflets, pamphlets, even books outlining the philosophy and practices of the order. In spite of the fact that there has never been a meeting of the order, beyond informal gatherings of two or three friends at the local pizza parlor, one gets the impression of vast temples and tesselated pavements, with robed acolytes lining the cloisters like extras at the opera. Somewhere in a hidden enclave are the secret masters of the order, running the show—and perhaps the world—from their arcane hideaway. Then, two years later, everyone has lost interest and forgotten all about it, including the Poobah himself.

This scenario is not always true, however. Sometimes the group will survive for many years while maintaining this mysterious and impressive reputation—but with no members at all except for the founder and his wife!

However, one tried, true, and oft-used technique for building up the membership of an otherwise shaky group is to let people subscibe to a mildly interesting 8-page newsletter for a nominal fee and count everyody on the subscription list as an "associate member." If you are really desperate, you can waive all or part of the subscription fee for "incarcerated individuals" (jail birds), although you do end up that way with a disproportionate number of your members in prison.

Then there are the correspondence schools. These far outnumber the groups that actually meet and operate in some fashion. Sometimes there is a central lodge that meets somewhere, but the vast majority of the members are correspondence-course students—members by mail only. More frequently, there are only the lessons, issued by some nebulous and anonymous authority with no credentials beyond his own hype.

Many correspondence schools, with or without a central, operating lodge, are quite good and reputable and will grade written lessons for you. Some of them dole out unpublished scraps from the masters at high prices so that you end up paying something like $90 for an unpublished "book" that could just as well be printed in a decent, bound format rather than on photocopied sheets of typing paper. Ah, but that would be giving away the secrets to the "profane" (i.e., those without lots of ready cash).

Some correspondence shools, not so reputable, just photo-copy—or retype and then photocopy—material from other people's published books. Meanwhile, they charge stiff prices for membership and various *in absentia* grade initiations. One of these I know of even tacks on an extra fee for mailing the lessons to you. The key to the mysteries of the ages comes with shipping and handling charges.

Heads of orders will please not now contact the author or publisher to complain that their group has been unjustly defamed. How do you know it's your group we're talking about—unless you have an uneasy conscience? Maybe it's somebody on the opposite coast.

As for specific examples of various groups, both reputable and not so wonderful (none of these has been checked out), the following have recently advertised in American publications and *seem* to have a Golden Dawn and/or Crowleyish orientation (although I certainly wouldn't want to offend anyone by saying so): The Hermetic Society of the Golden Dawn, The Servants of Light, The Fraternity of the Hidden Light, Builders of the Adytum, The Brotherhood of Light, Karin Kabalah Center, The Hermetic Order of the Eternal Golden Dawn, Ordo Baphe-Metis, Ordo Mysterium Baphe-Metis, International Academy of Hermetic Knowledge, Star & Cross, The Hermetic Temple and Order of the Golden Dawn, Draconis Lodge, and the Society Ordo Templi Orientis (inquiries bring you an information sheet signed "Frater Superior of the Entire World"). I have no reason to suppose that most of these groups are not on the up and up, but, as with anything else, *caveat emptor*. Some say that a real group will not advertise but will contact you when you're ready. Others say that you have to ask the right questions of the right people. Most such statements, however, refer to groups that are no different from any other except that they *can't afford* to advetise—either that, or it's just typical occultist mystification.

So, all in all, it would appear that only two forms of Western magic are being worked today (the GD tradition and Chaos Magic), and I would personally have been disposed to concede that it was so, had it not been for some strange phenomena taking place in the 1970s.

When I dealt with the Renaissance scholar-magus John Dee, I promised the reader that he or she had not heard the last of him. I said that he would be resurrected, and now the time has come to renew the acquaintance with this fascinating individual. In 1662, a man named Jones found some of Dee's papers in a chest that he'd bought from a second-hand dealer in Adle Street, London. Some of them were burnt by an ignorant servant girl (curse her) when lighting the stove. Eventually the rest of the papers ended up in the hands of Elias Ashmole, the antiquarian and Mason, and later on in the British Museum Library.

So here we cross the trail of the magus again, but before he makes his entrance upon the magical stage, we must present a prologue starring one of the most original and eccentric characters in Western subculture, a pioneer of the literary genre called science-fiction—although, strictly speaking, his output wasn't really s.f., but rather what in modern terms is called "fantasy" or "horror" fiction. Dungeons and Dragons.

Howard Phillips Lovecraft was born in Providence, Rhode Island, August 20, 1890. When the boy was eight, his father, Winfield Lovecraft, died of paralysis from syphilis contracted in his youth. His last years were spent in and out of the lunatic asylum.

The boy was sickly and was brought up by his mother and two maiden aunts, relics of New England aristocracy. His education was disrupted because of his frailty, and as he was unable to leave the family mansion save at night, he became a recluse, not unlike the men that he would later depict in his tales. When he did leave the house in the daytime, it was to roam the hills of the rural landscape surrounding Providence.

Apart from that, he spent most of his time in his late grandfather's library, where he delved into works on New England history and lore—especially the witch trials of Salem, Massachusetts. Cotton Mather made an indelible impression on him. Witchcraft and black magic were to play a dominant part in many of his stories. not so much in themselves, but as vehicles for the extraterrestrial horror that he tried to convey to his readers.

He was a very strange man indeed. He had no real aptitude for writing, although he began at a very early age. His prose is overloaded with adjectives to the point of nausea. None of his stories ever gets even close to the vicinity of realism, and yet they are, in a

H. P. Lovecraft—mechanistic materialist or master magus?

R. H. Barlow/Arkham House

sense, more real than the works of Dickens or Tolstoy. You can't even talk about Lovecraft's stories. Story is more like it, for he only worked with one theme, and his total output, about 60 short stories, are that one theme varied over and over again. When faced with the impossibility of further variation, he gave up and developed cancer and died—according to a theory held by the writer Colin Wilson, which I think isn't far from true. He also suffered from Bright's disease. That and cancer of the colon killed him at the age of 46 on March 15, 1937.

In spite of his atrocious style of writing, he found a publisher. His first tale in print was "Dagon," which appeared in 1917 in the amateur press. Later on he was to write for the classical *Weird Tales* magazine. Situated in Chicago, it was what is now known as a "pulp" magazine; i.e., a "read 'em and toss 'em" magazine. In other words, a publication generally considered "not fit for human consumption" by the literary establishment.

It had a vast audience, though. Together with its sister-venture *Black Mask,* it was a true descendant of the so called "penny dreadful." Cheap publications like the Nick Carter and Sexton Blake stories had been extremely popular among the "lower classes" in the late Victorian era, and they had lost none of their popularity during the reign of Edward VII or the Great War. On the contrary, the demand for this kind of literature, if you'll pardon the expression, was increasing rapidly all the time.*

In the American Midwest, in places like Saginaw, Michigan; Toledo, Ohio; and Manhattan, Kansas, thousands and thousands of farmboys and girls in their respective cultural backwaters longed for adventure and action. It may seem strange to the modern reader that such comparatively sophisticated subjects as space and time travel should find devoted followers among the badly educated farmers' children of the Midwest rather than among the university or big city kids, but it was so. The farm kids often never had more than a first-grade education because they had to work like adults at home on the farm. Let this chapter be dedicated to

---

* It may not be literature in the strictest sense, but there is a lot to be said for the best of it. It can be captivating, stimulating, and thrilling, and I must say it has done more for the colloquial vernacular than a lot of the applicants for admission to the Athenaeum.

the memory of these sons and daughters of the Midwest farmers, who created a market for this kind of fiction in areas where the annual cultural apex was the latest issue of the Sears Roebuck mail-order catalog, before the introduction of radio and TV.

One could say that Lovecraft did the same for science-fiction and *Weird Tales* as Dashiell Hammett and, later on, Raymond Chandler did for *Black Mask*. They created cult material.

One is as good as the other. To this audience, Mars was no less distant nor less accessible than New York, Los Angeles, or San Francisco. Their idea of a metropolis was Chicago, St. Louis, or Kansas City. So when Lovecraft had his first story published in 1917, he was immediately recognized. Not for his style, which even these illiterate children winced at, but for his message.

His talent for the spooky was so great that he was offered the editorship of *Weird Tales* in 1923 on the strength of it. His self-image, however, would not permit this. He considered himself a gentleman and a scholar, an amateur antiquarian of aristocratic descent who wrote these tales for the mere esthetic enjoyment of it, certainly not for a living. He declined the offer, and the job went instead to Farnsworth Wright. However, Lovecraft continued to contribute to the magazine for the rest of his life, but he never corrected any rejected material and seldom submitted it again anywhere else.

In 1926 he wrote a story called "The Call of Cthulhu." It was a reworking of his very first published story, "Dagon," and it was the beginning of the build-up of the so-called Cthulhu Mythos, around which the Lovecraft cult has been built.

What, then, is the Cthulhu Mythos all about? As established by Lovecraft and later elaborated by other writers such as Lovecraft's friend and correspondent August Derleth, it is based on the assumption that evil forces, gods, entities, whatever, once ruled this world, but some other gods (the good guys), the Elder Gods, came down from the stars and evicted the Ancient Ones, as the bad lot was called. All this happened in primeval times, and ever since then, the Ancient Ones have been waiting just outside the Gate of the Silver Key to be let in again, at any time, to take over. They are sleeping, waiting for someone to wake them up. To quote Lovecraft, "in his house at R'lyeh dead Cthulhu waits dreaming."

Of course, this good vs. evil idea was just sort of tacked on to Lovecraft's creation. Derleth tended to see it all in pseudo-Christian terms, the Fall from Heaven and all that. As Lovecraft conceived his entities, they weren't necessarily evil. They just regarded humanity the same way we might regard an anthill. If they stepped on a few hundred people, it was not a matter of concern; they probably wouldn't even notice it. This was Lovecraft's metaphor for a senseless and uncaring universe, a necessary consequence of his avowed philosophy of atheistic "mechanistic materialism."

The typical Lovecraft story runs something like this: the narrator (Lovecraft himself) begins to relate his tale in the lunatic asylum where he has been interred. He is a recluse, a scholar and a gentleman, who has happened to get hold of some "forbidden" books in the course of his antiquarian rambles; or he has found an old volume in the library of Miskatonic (Brown) University. These books differ, but they are all old grimoires. The narrator, accidentally or deliberately, evokes the Ancient Ones with one of the spells from the book. He is then pursued for the rest of the tale by the evil forces he has evoked. He is slowly overtaken by them, and is committed to a mental home from where he relates his sad story before his final suicide. This is the quintessential Lovecraft.

The titles of these grimoires differ. At the beginning, he referred to books like *The Key of Solomon, Grimorium Verum,* and similar bona fide grimoires, but gradually works like Comte d'Erlette's *Cultes des Goules* and, above all, the *Necronomicon* (The book of dead names) by the "Mad Arab," Abdul Alhazred were introduced. These fictitious works evidently suited Lovecraft better, as he was free to invent their content. Like A. E. Waite, he found the contents of the real grimoires childish and stupid. As time went on, the *Necronomicon* became the vehicle of the Cthulhu Mythos, the work around which Lovecraft more and more centered his tales.

A lot of readers thought that the book really existed and wrote Lovecraft and *Weird Tales* making inquiries about how to obtain a copy, or suggested that the magazine should print it in full or, at least, excerpts from it. *Weird Tales* explained to its public that these works didn't actually exist. Comte d'Erlette, for example, was a play on words on the name of August Derleth. The two of them, and their friend the science-fiction writer Robert Bloch (of *Psycho* fame) used to use each other as characters in their books and brutally kill each other on the pages. Lovecraft loved these kinds of in-jokes.

In the 40s, about 10 years after Lovecraft's death, some of his tales were published in book form, and for the first time he reached a wider audience, including critics and scholars. By the '50s, he had become a cult figure for university students and teachers.

In spite of all this, everybody took it for granted that the *Necronomicon* was a figment of Lovecraft's imagination. Of course he had invested it with a history for the sake of verisimilitude.

> The NECRONOMICON is, according to Lovecraft's tales, a volume written in Damascus in the Eighth Century, A.D., by a person called the "Mad Arab," Abdul Alhazred. It must run roughly 800 pages in length, as there is a reference in one of the stories concerning some lacunae on a page in the 700's. It has been copied and reprinted in various languages—the story goes—among them Latin, Greek and English. Doctor Dee, the Magus of Elizabethan fame, was supposed to have possessed a copy and translated it. This book, according to the *mythos*, contains the formulae for evoking incredible things into visible appearance, beings and monsters which dwell in the Abyss, and Outer Space, of the human psyche.*

In the 70s, this suddenly changed. No less than three books purporting to be the one and only *Necronomicon* stepped out of the dark pages of history. Unfortunately, the contents of all three copies differed. This didn't do the credibility of the work any good, but when the critical gun smoke cleared away, most authorities on the Cthulhu Mythos realized that there was ample space for all three within the framework of the *Necronomicon*, as all three copies put together didn't come anywhere near 800 pages. So it was at least technically possible that they were all part of the longer work referred to by Lovecraft. Not many scholars believe that, though. Some maintain that it's all a big hoax, but it's not necessarily so. The magic in them actually works. At least in two of them. I don't know about the first one. But let's begin at the beginning.

---

*Simon (ed.), *The Necronomicon*. New York: Avon Books, [1977] 1980, p. xv.

L. Sprague de Camp has written a biography on Lovecraft (*Lovecraft: A Biography*, Doubleday, 1975). While he was working on it, he said, he visited the Near East in 1967. In Baghdad, he met a man who told him that he had a manuscript for sale that he, de Camp, perhaps would be interested in buying. It was written in an old Persian dialect and was entitled *Al Azif*, which was one of Lovecraft's alternative titles for the *Necronomicon*. The man who possessed the manuscript was a Baghdad official.

L. Sprague de Camp bought it and returned to America, where he tried to find someone to translate it. An expert scholar whom he contacted declared it to be a 19th-century forgery. Nevertheless, de Camp received a letter from the official, who offered to buy back the manuscript for more than he had paid for it originally. He decided to hang on to it, and later learned that the official had been jailed for embezzlement of government funds. The implication was that he also had been selling out of the national treasures, but had managed to avoid charges on that point. This in itself is not at all unlikely.

A facsimile edition was published in Philadelphia in 1973. It appeared under the title of *Al Azif* and was thus the first of the copies to be sprung on an unsuspecting public.

The second copy emerged from the crowd involved with the Magickal Childe bookshop in New York. The story is that a "wandering bishop" or monk appeared one day out of the blue with a robe full of manuscripts. After publication, he collected the papers and disappeared into limbo or oblivion; make your own choice. As I make it out, the people who were involved with the publication encountered cosmic setbacks of the kind usually associated with occult projects; i.e., papers disappearing, employees abandoning the project, trouble in the family, etc., but finally, on December 20, 1977, the book was published.

The people behind it claim that experiments with the magic have been carried out, and to the great surprise of those involved it has been found impossible to banish the forces evoked, and, accordingly, warnings to this effect have been inserted in the book.*

I agree that these two copies can easily be wishful thinking or hoaxes and not have anything to do with the *Necronomicon*—the first one because *any* book may be called *Al Azif*, the second because the story of the monk is a bit extravagant. Inaccessible sources should always be regarded with a certain amount of suspicion. The mere fact that the magic works doesn't prove that it is the *Necronomicon*.

The third and final copy is the most promising from a historical point of view. It was the joint effort of the writer Colin Wilson; a magician of the now-defunct Order of the Cubic Stone, Robert Turner; and a computer expert and cryptographer, David Langford.

Robert Turner had, after many years' study of Lovecraft's works, arrived at the conclusion that they were the real thing, inspired by grimoires such as *The Sword of Moses*. The problem was that Lovecraft, according to his own testimony, didn't believe in magic at all. But apart from this, how did Lovecraft, who was living in the cultural backwater of provincial Providence most of his life, obtain knowledge of such obscure works as medieval grimoires?

However strange it may sound, Lovecraft was actually married for two years, 1924–6. It was the bride, Sonia Greene, who proposed to him, and the couple went to live in New York. The experience proved too much for him. In 1926, the marriage broke up and he went back to Rhode Island.

He wouldn't have had time to get acquainted with the arcana of occult lore in those two years, especially as he only went out at night if he could help it. Besides he had been writing about these things literally since childhood. (The answer is that he consulted A. E. Waite's *Book of Black Magic and of Pacts*, Lewis Spence's *Encyclopædia of Occultism*, and other such works in an attempt to give his stories something approximating an authentic background.)

The break came when Wilson found out—or so he said—that Lovecraft's father had been an Egyptian Mason. He expounds the theory that Winfield Lovecraft in his final years of insanity, when

---

*It is of course possible that this is nothing more than a glib publicity stunt in dubious taste, especially as the foreword is written in a very flippant manner. However, flippancy should not be confused with lack of sincerity.

On the other hand, I have it on good authority, that the magic circle isn't effective here. Perhaps that is what they mean. It seems to be working on the same lines as the magic of Abra-Melin. After proper mental purification, it seems to run very smoothly indeed, but caution is indicated anyway. It is essential where all unknown workings are concerned. To underestimate obscure conjuration can be, at best, very hazardous.

Howard was from 3 to 8 years old, spent most of his time with the boy and unloaded everything he had on his rambling mind; among other things, his Masonic experiences. Wilson found out from an Austrian source, he said, that Winfield Lovecraft had had access to a copy of a real *Necronomicon*. A copy was known to exist in Boston. This would also explain why Howard claimed that he didn't believe in these things. It could be an act of psychological repression.

I can readily understand that some readers, at this point of the narrative, are wondering where Dee comes in. Well, when informed about the possible connection between Lovecraft's father and an actual *Necronomicon*, Wilson and Turner remembered that Lovecraft, in his stories, claimed that Dr. John Dee had translated that arcane tome in 1571. Wilson found that the book was listed in the library catalog of Rudolph II of Prague. Dee and Kelly had spent two years at the Emperor's court in the 1580s.

Inspired by this revelation, or so goes the tale, Turner renewed his efforts, and in the British Museum Library found some manuscripts written by Dee under the title of *Liber Logaeth*. It had been in the museum's collection for ages, but it was unintelligible. It was obviously a cipher, so nobody had bothered with it. Wilson and Turner enlisted the assistance of a young cryptographer and computer-wizard by the name of David Langford, who enthusiastically accepted the assignment of breaking it. After about a year and several thousand pounds worth of computer time on one of the best computers of the day, one of the most clever ciphers in the history of cryptography was finally broken. Although the Elizabethan era was the heyday of early cryptography, and men like Francis Bacon made a lot of ciphers based on the binary code, Dee's variety was so subtle that it took Langford, who is an expert on Elizabethan ciphers, that long to break it.

Finally, in 1978, it was published together with the fascinating, detailed accounts of Wilson, Turner, and Langford as to how their joint venture resulted in the final copy of the *Necronomicon*. There are also a couple of other essays on Lovecraft included that are not without interest.* It has not gone down without criticism, though. Michael-Albion Macdonald, in his *De Nigromancia of Roger Bacon* (Heptangle Books, 1988), in the so-called "Afterward," says:

At that time a rather spurious book called the "Necronomicon or Book of Dead Names" was enjoying a certain
popularity. The contributors to this book were famous
people, some of them science fiction writers, and others
notable occultists, yet the book itself was the most
appalling scheme to deceive the public I had seen in
years; a blatant attempt to capitalize on the "Lovecraft
phenominon" [sic]. Among the sources cited in the text
were Sloane MS. 3885 & Additional MS. 36,674. My
curiosity was naturally piqued, and I sidetracked my
original research. ... What I found was far from the
"Necronomicon" but instead a whole genere [sic] of
Catholic Magical tracts, of which one of the most notable
was "De Nigromancia."

In short, there seems to be a discrepancy of astronomical magnitude between what the parties read in the manuscripts, but in
my copy of the *Necronomicon*, the emphasis is on Sloane MSS. 3188,
3189, and Cotton Appendix XLVI (parts 1 and 2). These are mentioned rather ambiguously in the footnotes, but not in the bibliography, where some other manuscripts are mentioned; viz., Magical
treatises to Caius, Foreman, Dee and Kelly, Add. MS. 36,674, 16th
century; *Invocation of Spirits*, Sloane MS. 3702, 17th century; *Tracta-
tus magici et astrologici*, Sloane MS. 3821; *Schema Magicum*, Sloane
MS. 430, 14th century; *De Maleficiis*, Sloane MS. 3529, 16th century.
All these are in the British Museum.

As far as I can make out, the translation of the *Necronomicon* is
supposed to have been made from Sloane MS. 3189, *Liber Logaeth*,
also called *The Book of Enoch*, and not MS. 3885, which isn't referred
to at all in either the footnotes nor the bibliography, at least not in
my copy. The only grounds for dispute would thus be Add. 36,674,
but this is obviously an anthology of magical treatises which at the
most can be classified as a subject of translation (from Latin) but
not deciphering (from a secret cipher).

---

*This chapter is mostly based on material related in the following books:
The Necronomicon (London: Neville Spearman), which contains Colin Wil-
son's, Robert Turner's, and David Langford's accounts, and also *The
Necronomicon* (New York: Avon Books, ©1977) and *De Nigromancia of
Roger Bacon*, ed. and trans. Michael-Albion Macdonald (Gillette, NJ: Hep-
tangle Books, 1988).

As I have mentioned before, the magic in both the latter copies of the *Necronomicon* seems to work, but definitely not in the same way as GD or Chaos Magic. It opens up channels to areas that are perhaps different from the ones that are usually shared by mankind. It is difficult to say anything definitely, as it is comparatively new, but one hypothesis has been suggested to the effect that this magic releases forces that are not part of our usual collective subconscious.

So far, so good. There's just one problem about the whole thing. It seems that it's all lies. The writers of these works have been confronted with opposition and attacks to the point that their scholarship and ethics have been challenged.

This has caused Colin Wilson and L. Sprague de Camp to concede that at least *their* versions of the *Necronomicon* are forgeries. Wilson's story is that he was asked by an old friend to edit a "spoof" edition of, or volume about, the *Necronomicon*. So together with Robert Turner and David Langford et al., he concocted this book for Neville Spearman.

That they were able to fool people, Wilson apparently takes as appreciative admiration. He says, "An even greater compliment was an indignant article by Gerald Suster, himself a serious student of magic ... denouncing the book as a cynical piece of commercial opportunism. The fact that he found it necessary to denounce such an obvious spoof indicates that we succeeded beyond my original expectations."

He goes on to say that "anyone with the slightest knowledge of Latin will instantly recognise it for a fake—it is subtitled 'The book of dead names'—when the word 'Necronomicon' actually means the book of dead laws."

I personally failed to recognize it instantly as a fake. In fact, I didn't even recognize the title as Latin, but rather as Greek. But, even if my Greek were good enough to note this anomaly, I don't see that it proves anything beyond an error in translation. I do not really understand how it is supposed to tip everyone off that the entire book is a forgery—excuse me, a "spoof." If Wilson can't tell the difference between Latin and Greek, how are readers—eagerly clutching their butter-and-egg money and standing in line to purchase a copy of "the genuine article at last; Colin Wilson says so"—supposed to possess enough classical erudition to recognize the derivation from (according to Lovecraft) νεκρός + νόμος + εἰκών?

I must confess that personally I am at a loss to understand the purpose of presenting fiction as fact. I know it is sometimes considered witty by editors of college literary magazines. At least it was during the '20s.

As for L. Sprague de Camp's version: Even he seems to have had no objection to participating in forgery, on the pretext that, if no real *Necronomicon* existed, it was necessary to invent one.

It seems that he is "only" responsible for the preface. As with the other edition, this one seems to be a conspiracy as well—or a joint venture, at any rate.

When all this is said and done, some readers may ask themselves how these people get away with it.

Part of the answer is that the "magic" actually works. But, as I said before, the fact that it works doesn't prove that it's the *Necronomicon*. Anything "works." Even Dungeons and Dragons "magic" works if you put your mind to it. I'm not questioning the efficacy of these books, only the ethics and integrity of their authors.

These "confessions" appeared in an obscure American periodical: *Crypt of Cthulhu*, vol. 3, no. 7, St. John's Eve 1984. I suppose it would have been too much to expect a front-page statement in the international edition of *The Herald Tribune*, but I wonder how large a circulation this small-press Lovecraftian magazine has.

Different versions of the *Necronomicon* notwithstanding, various groups are active in the pursuit of Lovecraftian magic based largely on Kenneth Grant's theory that HPL was an adept who tried to cross the Abyss and baulked. The only such order I know of by name is the Esoteric Order of Dagon, not to be confused with the literary and artist's fan organization of the same name. A subsidiary group seems to be the Miskatonic Archaeological Expedition.

Anyway, it all goes to prove that, about magic, more than anything else, it can be said that it's the singer, not the song.

So we see that magic is at a crossroads. On one hand we have the traditional magic, as provided by the Golden Dawn and its offshoots, and on the other we have the existentialist Chaos Magic, which is also a sort of tradition as it is derived from Crowley, who in essence was a conveyor of the GD teachings. But we may have a whole new third and enigmatic variety, for all we know at the present time, and it would thus be obvious that magic is part of and dependent upon our culture. It has always been there, and will probably always be there. It renews itself again and again and changes its terminology to suit the majority of people at any time, but it also preserves its traditional lore and techniques by appealing to minor groups with Gothic archetypes.

That's the way it has always been, and I see no reason why this should not continue forever, for, as Howard Phillips Lovecraft observed, "That is not dead which can eternal lie, and with strange eons even death may die."

Appendix A

Pilgrims

Medieval

Roger Bacon	1190?–1289?
Albertus Magnus	1193?–1280?
Thomas Aquinas	1225?–1274
Raymond Lully	1225 –1315?
Arnold of Villanova	1235?–1313?
Peter d'Abano	1250?–1316?
Nicolas Flamel	1330?–1418?
Basil Valentine	1355?–1420?

Renaissance

Bernardo de Trevisano	1406–1490
Marcilio Ficino	1433–1499
Johann Reuchlin	1455–1522
Johann Trithemius	1462–1516
Giovanni Pico della Mirandola	1463–1494
Johann Faustus	1480–1540
Heinrich Cornelius Agrippa von Nettesheim	1486–1535
Paracelsus	1493–1541
Nostradamus	1503–1566
Denis Zachaire	1510–1556
Guillaume Postel	1510–1581
John Dee	1527–1608
Giordano Bruno	1548–1600
Simon Forman	1552–1611
Edward Kelly	1555–1597

Francis Bacon	1561–1626
Robert Fludd	1564–1637
The Cosmopolitan	1560?–1610/1640/1666?
Michael Maier	1566–1622
Tommaso Campanella	1570?–1639
Johann Valentin Andreae	1577–1638
Michael Sendivogius	1580?–1646

The Reformation

Athanasius Kircher	1602–1680
(Egyptian cabalist)	
William Lilly	1602–1681
Kenelm Digby	1603–1665
Eyrénée Philaléthe F.R.C.	1612?–1666?
Fama Fraternitatis (at Kassel)	1614
Confessio Fraternitatis (at Kassel)	1615
Chymische Hochzeit (at Strassbourg)	1616
Elias Ashmole	1617–1692
The Paris Manifesto	1620 or 1622
Thomas Vaughan	1622–1666
Christian Knorr von Rosenroth	1636–1689
Lascaris	1660?–1730/40?
Johann Friedrich Böttger	1682–1719/20?

The Revival

Comte de St. Germain	1700?–1790?
The Freemasons	1717
Giacomo Casanova	1725–1798
Sehfeld	1725?–1780?
Martinez de Pasqually	1727–1779
Franz Anton Mesmer	1734–1815
Giuseppe Balsamo Cagliostro	1743–1795
Louis Claude de St. Martin	1743–1803
Iolo Morganwg/Ed. Williams	1747–1826
Francis Barrett	1774?–?
J. M. Höene–Wronski	1776–1853

| James Morrison | 1795–1874 |
| Robert Cross Smith | 1795–1832 |

The Moderns

Cyliani	1800?–1890?
Bulwer Lytton	1803–1873
Frederick Hockley	1809–1885
Eliphas Levi/A. L. Constant	1810–1875
Hargrave Jennings	1817–1890
E. V. H. Kenealy	1819–1890
Paschal Beverly Randolph	1825–1871/75?
H. P. Blavatsky	1831–1891
Kenneth MacKenzie	1833–1886
Franz Hartmann	1838–1912
William Stainton Moses	1839–1892
Spiritualism	1848
Guido von List	1848–1918
William Wynn Westcott	1848–1925
Karl Kellner	1850?–1905
John Yarker	1850?–1913
Samuel Liddell MacGregor Mathers	1854–1918
Josephin Peladan	1858–1915
Stanislas de Guaita	1860–1898
Alan Leo/W. F. Allen	1860–1917
Rudolf Steiner	1861–1925
Max Heindel	1864–1919
Gérard Encausse/Papus	1865–1916
Adolf Lanz/Jörg Lanz von Liebenfels	1874–1954
The Theosophical Society	1875
Aleister Crowley	1875–1947
Pamela Colman Smith	1878–1951
Fulcanelli	1880?–1960?
Harvey Spencer Lewis	1882–1939
Paul Foster Case	1884–1954
Gerald Gardner	1884–1964
Charles Stansfeld Jones	1886–1950
Austin Osman Spare	1886–1956
W. E. Butler	1898–1978

H. P. Lovecraft	1890–1937
V. M. Firth/Dion Fortune	1891–1946

After 1900

Karl Ernst Krafft	1900–1945
Israel Regardie	1907–1985
L. Ron Hubbard	1911–1986
William G. Gray	1913–1992
Jack Parsons	1914–1952
Anton LaVey	1930–
Peter J. Carroll	1953–

This list is long but by no means exhaustive. We have not studied every item in detail, but we have plucked here and there to see what emerged. The actual purpose of the list is to furnish the reader with some material for his own edification and further studies, if he so desires.

Appendix B

The Magical Curriculum of the Golden Dawn

Modern magic is eclectic. It consists of bits and pieces from a vast variety of sources.

The first great modern compiler was Agrippa, who, in his *De Occulta Philosophia* (1531), merged all previous western magical disciplines: astrology, numerology (gematria Pythagorea), folk magic from the Celts, Latins, Germans, Arabs, etc.

The magical philosophy derived from these sources is very closely connected with pantheistic religion in the sense that both claim the presence of God in all things. The difference is that the former tends to isolate phenomena in order to manipulate Cosmos, somewhat analogous to a doctor who isolates and removes the appendix in order to heal the whole patient. These isolated aspects of the Cosmos have different labels, names, and numbers according to system and age. They are referred to as gods, angels, archetypes, etc., and are arranged in hierarchies, to be approached according to very strict rules, and that's what practical magic is all about.

From the beginning, these phenomena were divided into 7 or 12 categories symbolizing the 7 original planets or the 12 signs of the Zodiac, but from the mid-1600s, the 10-fold division of the Qabalah became more and more popular. It was a favorite with the Rosicrucians and has remained popular until the present day, although the Zodiacal system has had a comeback in the last few decades, thanks to an increasing popularity of astrology with the general public. But as the masses on the whole are unaware of the occult applications of the horoscope, it has had no proportional influence on the modern craft.

The symbols are numerical, geometrical, and archetypal. Abstract or concrete. Actually, in magic, all things are both.

The Qabalastic division consists of 10 *sephiroth* (singular, *sephirah)*, with one of which every conceivable phenomenon can be associated. But as nothing in life is altogether black or white, the sephiroth are connected with each other by means of 22 paths, illustrated by the 22 trumps of the Tarot cards.

The Magical Art consists of working with these symbols until they yield the results that the magician desires.

Thus today, a typical magical curriculum could be one resembling that of the Golden Dawn. In fact, it is almost impossible to escape the influence of the GD in any occult or magical working.

Such being the case, and it undoubtedly is, it is amazing to observe how many groups vehemently deny any connection with or influence from the Golden Dawn (much less Crowley). One such group in California even uses the GD rose-cross lamen as one of its own emblems and apparently tries to create the impression that they have it under copyright. Other groups take some of the GD's simpler rituals, such as the Lesser Banishing Ritual of the Pentagram, change the names and perhaps some of the gestures, and claim that it was independently invented, or "derived from a common source." Sorry, but it wouldn't hold up in court if the ritual were patented.

It seems to be some sort of frantic attempt to appear totally original, or perhaps the reputation of the GD is so shady in some circles that to be associated with it in any way is anathema. That doesn't keep people from borrowing from it, though. Even some Witches use the Lesser Banishing Ritual of the Pentagram, complete with the Judaeo-Christian archangel names.

To get back to the GD's magical curriculum: to become a Theoricus Adeptus Minor in the GD you had to pass examinations in, among other things, the following subjects, and to become a Practicus A.M. you had to excel in them.

The Ritual of the Pentagram
The Ritual of the Hexagram
The 5=6 Adeptus Minor ritual
Rituals of consecrating the elemental weapons.
The art of divination; i.e., astrology, numerology, geomancy, Tarot, pendulum techniques, *I Ching*, etc.
Travelling in the spirit vision; i.e., astral projection
The making of talismans, sigils, etc.
The Enochian system of magic (the *pièce de résistance*)

That represents about a fifth of the syllabus.

The knowledge would be theoretical until you had consecrated your elemental weapons (pentacle, dagger, cup, and fire wand). After that, as a Zelator Adeptus Minor, you would actually practice magic, which has been defined by Aleister Crowley as "The Science and Art of causing Change to occur in conformity with Will." This is followed by a postulate decreeing that: "ANY required Change may be effected by the application of the proper kind and degree of Force in the proper manner through the proper medium to the proper object." Apropos of which Crowley's theorem no. 3 states that "Every failure proves that one or more requirements of the postulate have not been fulfilled."

An example: You travel in the spirit vision (i.e., project your astral body) anywhere in the universe, and if you encounter any conditions that you, for one reason or another, wish to change, you employ the order's divinatory techniques to find the best cosmic conditions for interfering with the karmic flow.

When the time has been satisfactorily established, the time has come to design the ritual suitable for attracting the forces ruling the moment in question.

Then comes the execution of the ritual, moving the hierarchy or forces to alter conditions on the astral levels and eventually manifest the karmic changes in the physical world.

When you can do all this and grasp the philosophical implications as well, you will attain to the degree of Practicus Adeptus Minor.

This is in practice the highest degree that you can attain to in this life. The rest are for dwellers in the astral world or higher. But in theory one can reach any degree, the only limitation being lack of audacity.

From the very beginning, Mathers, Westcott, and Woodman had reserved the degree of 7=4 for their astral bodies. It seems all right under the circumstances, but in practice it is very difficult to keep two magical personalities apart. Sooner or later, generally sooner, the two become integrated, which sometimes leads to mental troubles. On the other hand, Crowley's claim of having attained to the degree of Ipsissimus can be disregarded as megalomania or, at best, overconfidence.

Appendix C

How Does Magic Actually Work?

Sometimes people have asked me: How does one become a magician?

It's a good question, and I'm not sure that the reader will be entirely satisfied with my attempt to answer it. My opinion is simple in a way: You must be called! One doesn't wake up some morning and spontaneously exclaim, "I've got nothing to do today. Seems like a good day to study magic!" If you do not still have the time, inclination, or opportunity to go on studying magic tomorrow and the day after, you had better give up the whole enterprise.

Some acquaintances tell me now and again, and some others perhaps don't say so in so many words, that they believe that magic "is something to do with" that once in a while when you've got a problem (e.g., your spouse has left you, you have no more money, and the bailiff is due tomorrow), then you dress up like a mountebank and depart for the forest at dawn, draw a circle on the ground, and wave a sword above your head while yelling a number of curses and blasphemies into the air. After that you go home and wait, and hocus pocus and alakazam, the bailiff drops dead as he is ascending the staircase and the IOU blows out through the window. That same night you win $10,000,000 in the lottery, and before the authorities have time to reorganize you have paid your debts and the spouse is back and all is joy and happy ending. A couple of months later they hit you for six again. Then it's time to get the fancy dress out once more and take to the woods to meet your deadline.

Superficially perhaps, you can't blame the uninitiated for getting such ideas about magic, because magic sometimes actually works in a way that resembles what I have just described. It is precisely this acausal element that causes the skeptic to exclaim: "Why, this is not magic. It would probably have happened anyway!" Perhaps this is the point at which I should attempt to render my interpretation of what happens in a case like the one with the bailiff.

An outsider perhaps only observes the magician once in a while when he goes out to perform his rituals, but you should know that, before he reaches that stage, he has been through enormous preparation. It's no use just standing there reading a conjuration (spell) from an old grimoire (book of spells). That will result in nothing. There's a misconception to the effect that some innocent bugger with no knowledge of magic can get hold of a "dangerous" grimoire by chance and unfortunately tip the lid off Pandora's box and consequently cause earthquakes and epidemics. It simply can't be done that way.

Results in magic are not achieved without long and arduous training, and even then the "miracles" of magic are neither so striking nor so spectacular as one might be disposed to imagine. It's the rarest of masters who causes the sun to stand still or the earth to stop in its orbit, which amounts to the same thing. However, he enlists the aid of inertia. This, the mightiest force of the universe, is his most important ally.

When the magician wishes to accomplish something which cannot be achieved more easily without occult forces, he designs a special ritual or uses one already in existence that will attract the forces he wishes to utilize in order to achieve the required result. (It must be said that the magician makes no distinction between one force and another in this respect. The force that will most easily help him achieve his ultimate end is the force he will employ.)

Thereafter, he chooses a cosmically suited time for the performance of the ritual, and, if it is performed properly, these forces will be put into action.

As I said, this won't cause the sun to stand still if the result can be achieved with less drastic means, for, like any other natural force, the magical force is a natural law, of which it can be said that it works with the least possible energy and over the shortest possible distance.

That is why its manifestations always seem to be accidental ("It would probably have happened anyway"), because the force moves through the nearest but often most acausal and apparently irrelevant canals or channels of the same kind that brought the Admiral to stardom in *Pinafore.*

It's always bound to look that way to an outsider. Only the magician himself knows just how much he has invested and how much he will achieve, and this is where the concept of Will enters the picture, because without it, magic is a hopeless enterprise.

I'm not referring here to what is ordinarily meant by "will," when someone says that this or that would be nice if it happened, but to the real, conscious Will. Magical will is when your whole total consciousness is concentrated in one direction and you really "will" this or that; e.g., you don't get a new job by sitting down and wishing for it to come along by itself, but if your whole organism is concentrated on the thought, things will happen. Then you get up early, look in the classified ads, go to the employment agency, and so on, and if you really want *any* job, you'll get it. If you want a special job, it'll be a bit more complicated, but here a good efficient magic ritual can help you obtain it.

When the forces once have been set in motion, the job will be vacant one way or another. The one who possesses it at present will be tired of it, promoted, fall ill, be dismissed, etc., depending on which forces have been employed, and this is where serious moral, karmic determinations enter the picture. It's the magician who sovereignly decides when, where, why, how, and what he requires, and he knows that nothing is free.

As opposed to the laws of society, the karmic laws pay most attention to the intention and means employed, and it is here that the perennial problem of man's free will enters the picture.

Personally I'm inclined to believe that we do have free will, but I am also of the opinion that very few people ever go to the trouble of actually using it. It is obvious that no man is an island, and that we cannot help but affect our environment from the second we are born. In that respect, we have no free will. From the moment of our birth to the instant of our death we perform certain actions and think certain thoughts which all have various consequences. We cannot alter that fact. We may here throw ourselves into a futile philosophical discussion as to whether free will really makes any difference, seeing that if we don't do one thing we'll certainly do something else, and whether we ultimately do what we have been predestined for, no matter how hard it may have been for us to make up our minds about it.

The important matter is not the concept of free will or determinism. The crucial point is the element of uncertainty, which at least creates an illusion of possible free will. It is of very little practical significance which alternative is the right one, since we haven't any way of finding out which is actually the truth. At least, philosophy hasn't yet come up with a concise answer to the question. In the final analysis, it remains a matter of taste.

But what is of the utmost importance is the individual's motive for his actions. An action or a thought is, like a force, always neutral, and cosmic and karmic effect is proportional to the intention in a straightforward manner.

Furthermore, karma never remains undone. Somebody or other needs must do the things that have to be done; e.g., if Hitler hadn't done what he did, somebody else would have, but then, of course, things would not have come out exactly as they did. Who knows? After all, perhaps we may consider ourselves comparatively fortunate with Adolf and the Nazis. One can attempt to contemplate what the world would be like today with Stalin as world ruler with a monopoly on nuclear weapons. Fortunately, some of us will say, it was decided otherwise way back in the '30s and '40s, and that bears thinking about once in a while.

Thus we can choose ourselves whether we wish to look at existence as something chaotic, which just happens to flicker past our field of vision, or if we prefer a life where every little thing that happens has a deep and profound symbolic meaning. Then you can call the symbols whatever you like. As the eminent magician Brodie-Innes said around the turn of the century, "It's comparatively unimportant whether gods and archangels really exist or not; the important thing is that the Universe acts as if they do!"

So, even if you cannot take the old gods seriously, then at least feel free to use the powers they represent and regard them as a convenient working hypothesis. But that demands staying power and diligence.

A modern magician, David Edwards, who is a cofounder of the now legendary magical fraternity, the Order of the Cubic Stone, writes, in his highly commendable book *Dare to Make Magic*, as follows:

"I got up early and worked a ritual at dawn," you tell your neighbours. They are not interested; they doubt your sanity. Say it to me and I will reply; "Good, now do it again on each day for the remainder of the week."

"Horror, horror, he is asking me to put myself out!" Yes this is magical discipline. When you can get up each day before dawn and greet the Rising Sun, you will be able to work Sun Magic and make it Work.

Today, then, is important, but so is tomorrow and the day after. It is by realizing this, accepting it, and in the last instance adjusting your life accordingly, that you become a magician, and, of course, it follows that it's nothing that you "become." It's something that you *are*. It's a vocation, and a lot of people don't know for a long time that they are called, and even *if* they're called. It's but a few who are chosen, and you never know that until you have left the "Abyss" behind.*

---

*The Abyss is the point of no return, or "the lifting of the Veil." It's associated with the degree of Adeptus Minor, insofar as you have to face your so-called Holy Guardian Angel before you can attain to the degree of A.M. Its not as frightening as it sounds. It is merely a way of describing the magician's new awareness of the universe and the cosmic plan, which is so strikingly beautiful that for the first time all doubts about life disappear and a better balance between mind and spirit is achieved.

Appendix D

Astrological Charts

In this appendix, I have supplied the reader with some astrological charts relevant to persons and events described in the book, for his or her edification.

Since the subject of astrology in this century, and particularly after World War II, has become the victim of "expert" analyses ranging from the sublime to the absurd, but unfortunately all more or less missing the point completely, I think it might be appropriate to explain my own philosophy concerning the Celestial Art.

I am aware that what I am about to say may upset and disturb some people, but I do feel that I have the right to express my opinion. No one says that you have to agree with me, and Lord knows no one ever worries about offending *me* when they spout off about something!

I am also not speaking as an outsider who has formed some half-baked opinions about astrology while sitting in his armchair and reading Martin Gardner. I was a professional astrologer for about 20 years, and no better than others of that ilk, when it gradually began to dawn upon me that the whole damn picture was wrong. Looking around me, I saw the mercenary "alternative society" squeezing hard-earned cash out of the "seekers"; i.e., people who had come to a crossroads in their lives. They were tiring of the material rat race and looking for something better and more meaningful, but what were they finding? A multitude of strange offers of "magical" talismans; stones; wooden pieces; Buddhas; herbs; oils; Indian shaman beads; and spells of ancient lore that would cure any disease or win a fortune for you on football, horses, and the numbers racket or make you sexually irresistible to the opposite sex.

In addition to this, there were countless crystal gazers, dowsers, Tarot readers, and astrologers masquerading as "Cosmo-

Biologists," "Cosmo-Psychologists," "Celestial-Cycle-Counselors," and so on. All of them denounced each other as quacks, and I realized that I was taking part in this conspiracy myself.

Could this really be the "Dawn of the New Age," the Aquarian Age for which mankind had been waiting for centuries, the New Jerusalem, the Second Coming of Christ (if not in fact, then at least in spirit)? I'm afraid I'm a bit of a doubting Thomas, and I couldn't quite square prophecy with actual fact. So I retired to my sanctuary and emerged again with a new bit of philosophy:

One, astrology is for the elect few. That has been stated often enough throughout history. Looking at most of today's practitioners, it makes sense.

Two, casting horoscopes for others is essentially worthless and I'll almost go as far as to say unethical, at least the way it's done these days.

I'll explain:

Astrology is for the elect few who take the trouble to learn the subject properly. Only this way is it possible to know how and possibly why it works the way it does and to learn its limitations. The only way to get motivated to pay attention to celestial indications and act in accordance with them is to know what it's all about, and that's impossible without first-hand experience, with yourself.

Realizing that, it seems to me downright dishonest to charge people money for astrological counseling *unless* you make it abundantly clear that it's next to worthless. People who consult astrologers generally act on the pleasant parts of any advice and on things they've made up their minds to do anyway; they disregard the rest. Nobody is going to go to a lot of trouble merely on the say-so of an astrologer, even if he dresses in a white coat (as some of them probably do). No! When you have worked out a chart for yourself and have interpreted it as well as you can, you may discover a thing or two about yourself that might entice you to go on.

Which brings me to another thing. There seems to be a connection between esotericism and computer science. Most astrologers I know who have given up their practices (if one may be so bold) in recent years have all drifted into something involving computers. I'm not sure what the connection is, but it's definitely there. And it helps, perhaps, to explain the fixation of a lot of serious (or so-called serious) astrologers on the mechanical features of the art. I seem to have noticed a predominance of articles lately on various obscure methods of direction and exotic house systems and determining the Midheaven to the nearest microsecond of exactness.

Don't these people realize that if astrology were dependent on this kind of nit-picking exactitude for success, it would never have existed at all? The Art has existed for millennia, but accurate observation as such didn't exist prior to Tycho Brahe. The first consistent ephemerides that I know of are those of Johann Müller of Nuremberg (1436–1476). He called himself Regiomontanus, so he probably came from Königsberg. It was not uncommon in those days to call oneself by the name of one's birthplace.

So what did astrologers do before that? They had to rely much more on direct observation and had to be deft hands at practical astronomy. How many modern astrologers can calculate the Midheaven and the Ascendant directly from the sidereal time and the geographical latitude, I wonder?

So, with their primitive astrolabes and other crude instruments, these early astrologers were out (weather permitting) making records of celestial phenomena. It was they, not the guy with the billion-dollar computer, who kept this ancient Art alive during the Dark Ages. Surely, in spite of instruments such as the brittle, impractical hourglass, they must have achieved some measure of success or the Art would not have survived.

So what did they do when they were asked to cast a horoscope for a client?

Answer: They didn't. How could they?

Picture a medieval astrologer suddenly confronted with a customer wanting his chart done. Odds are that he didn't even know how old he was. Only learned people, or people who could read and write, which amounted to the same thing, could be expected to know what year it was, and only people of a certain degree of distinction could expect their births to have been recorded for posterity.

So our hypothetical astrologer would have been obliged to estimate his client's age from his features and general looks and then rely on what we today know as horary astrology; i.e., astrology based on the position of the celestial bodies at the moment of consultation, and whether the client looked like a Leo or an Aquarius. Sometimes the astrologer would be lucky. He might perhaps be informed that the native was born in the year of the great famine or perhaps in the year of a big battle or church reform or some other auspicious occasion for which a previous chart had been erected. And if in addition to this the astrologer had such staggeringly precise details as knowing it was summertime, or just after the harvest, or the Tuesday after the third Sunday in Lent, it was a piece of cake and merely a matter of interpolation.

This procedure may not sound very convincing to the modern computer-buff variety of astrologer, but it should. It might perhaps persuade him that a chart calculated to the 16th decimal of exactness is not the be-all and end-all of the Art. Nor of course is all the psychological claptrap that the rest of them put into it: "... Venus in Libra: 10 points; square to Jupiter in the second house, that's minus four points. Moon void-of-course: another five points. That means the native has something to do with shoes. Perhaps a shoemaker. Not sexy enough. Another three points and he would have been an estate agent. We'll call him an orthopedic shelter supplier."

And that's if it's really good. Otherwise, you get long rehashes of the more obscure works of Jung.

Where's the divine inspiration? Missing? Could it be because it doesn't work that way? It wasn't meant to! Today's "astrologers" don't seem to realize that with people like Alexander, Caesar, and Wallenstein who were ipso facto great men (i.e., commanded a lot of power), it was a safe bet that they would win a few battles and lose a few. If the aspects were good, they'd probably win. If not, they'd probably get their arses kicked. Modern astrologers don't appreciate that what may be a safe bet in the case of Alexander far from guarantees anything similar for the fate of Jones the shopsteward at British Rail. Poor Jones has not been born great; nor is he likely to have greatness thrust upon him.

I think this argument is conclusive for my thesis that astrology is basically a personal tool for personal use.

With that said, I'd like to stress that, under this provision, the ancient Art can be employed in a variety of subtle ways. As an aid to the imagination, it is unsurpassed—hence the reason for including this appendix. I feel that the charts provide the student of astrology with valuable clues to the characters and subtle undercurrents of influences at crucial moments in history.

Even though the horoscopes have been calculated with the aid of the most accurate and modern algorithms of spherical geometry and celestial mechanics on an IBM-compatible personal computer, the positions shouldn't be taken all that seriously. The position of Mercury is very difficult to establish with any certainty before 1900, and Pluto, which of course was unknown to the medievals, as were Uranus and Neptune for the most part, is completely hopeless. For all practical purposes, the outer planets can be regarded as nonexistent in charts before 1781. Of course, with the benefit of hindsight, all sort of enlightening things can be deduced from the charts, which may add depth to the often very complex characters who for one reason or another devoted their lives to the pursuit of magic.

The first chart is that of Heinrich Cornelius Agrippa von Nettesheim. As for accuracy, it was obtained from a biographical sketch in some encyclopedia. I won't vouch for it, as these short sketches are generally compiled from earlier sketches of the same kind, and minor details such as the correct birthday and year are not usually subject to such rigid scrutiny as the year in which the subject is supposed to have written or said such and such. However, if true, I consider it very likely that he was born about 11:30 AM GMT, because having Saturn on or near his Ascendant would not be irreconcilable with the general pattern of his life. Its semi-square to Pluto would also explain the frequent and abrupt changes in his physical environment all through his life. The Sun square with Uranus and Jupiter, conjunct with the Midheaven, and in opposition to the Moon would further correspond to Agrippa's constant dissatisfaction with things in general. The Moon makes him sell himself short karmically, but the Sun indicates that his fate was fulfilled in the end

John Dee is represented by two different charts because I have two different times on the same day for his birth. The chart for 4:40 AM is from *Fowler's Compendium of Nativities*, supposedly from a horoscope erected by Dee himself and salvaged from Alan Leo's *Modern Astrology* files from about the beginning of this century—which unfortunately, frequently does not give the source. The 16:11 chart is based on information from the historical foreword of the *Heptarchia Mystica of John Dee*, published at Edinburgh by McClean in 1983. This information is quoted from a biography of Dee by a

Dr. Thomas Smith, of whom I know nothing. I have presented both choices so the reader can decide for himself.

Kelly's data is from Dee's diaries. I'm not going to comment on the various charts in detail, but I will suggest that, in view of the partnership of Dee and Kelly. I find 4:40 AM the more likely of Dee's times because it's likely that the two had major bodies and angles in common; viz., both Suns close and Dee's ASC conjunct Kelly's MC. It was probably Kelly who was responsible for the major decisions in the partnership, and that would be consistent with the aspects in this case. However, it's for the reader to decide.

I included Francis Bacon's chart even though he wasn't a magician because he's been determined by later researchers and oddballs as having been associated with the Rosicrucians. Mainly, however, I include him for readers who are interested in the "Bacon wrote all of Shakespeare's plays" theory. The reason that I don't include the horoscope of the Bard himself is that I don't know which one to choose. There are many different suggestions. Most people, however, agree that he was born on April 23, 1654, at Stratford-on-Avon. If any reader should come upon a truly authoritative time of birth and feel like sharing it with me, it will be received with thanks—but I fear that such a prospect is too much to hope for.

Cagliostro—well, what can I say? (Source: A.B.C.)

Mathers—well, no! I think there may be stuff enough for a book about the astrological implications of the people involved, and I would like to be able to write such a book myself in the future, so I'll leave the readers to make up their own minds first. Then I'll throw in my two cents' worth later. (Source: *The Wizz of Swordom* ... sorry, *The Sword of Wisdom* by Ithell Colquhoun.)

Crowley's horoscope (source: A.B.C.) is based on data from *A Guide to Qabalistic Astrology* by "Horus" and is corrected, as it were, to fit important dates in Crowley's life. I must, in all honesty, point out that there are so many events that any degree of certainty is virtually impossible to establish, and the suggestions as to the native's time of birth are legion. Any chart will be highly subjective and not necessarily correlated with any given established fact. You just can't cover them all.

The Aiwass/*Liber vel Legis* chart is of course also related to Crowley. The master claimed that he received this revelation during a sojourn at Cairo in 1904, beginning at the Equinox and continuing over the next three weeks, culminating on April 8, 9, and 10 and resulting in *The Book of the Law,* the new gospel for the Aquarian Age or, as Crowley and his disciples put it, the Aeon of Horus, which, one would be disposed to imagine, would, in correspondence with esoteric tradition, commence at the Equinox, the map of which I present here.

I have included three possible charts for the foundation of the Golden Dawn. The reason for this is that there seems to be a wide range of disagreement in the field of mundane astrology as to when a horoscope should be erected; i.e., when is a thing or event actually founded? When someone gets the idea? The first time he shares it with someone? When he takes the first practical step in the matter? As you can see, opinions differ. Therefore, I submit three possible dates and times for the foundation of the Golden Dawn.

I haven't been able to ascertain exactly when—if ever—Woodman found the papers in the book, and anyway no one could have foreseen at that time what it would develop into.

The chart entitled "G.D. Pledge" is cast for February 11, 1888, simply because it's the first date quoted on the membership list. (Actually, Soror Sprengel's date of entry is the day before, but as she is listed after the three chiefs, it must have been set down later. Since evidence as to her actual existence is scarce and widely disputed, I have chosen to disregard her in this context.) The time of day is highly speculative. I have chosen this time because, with the benefit of hindsight, I find it very likely that Saturn played a dominant part in the secret intrigues and conspiracies that in the end caused the original Order to collapse, and the position in the 12th house is more likely than any other, in my opinion. Add to this the fact that the membership list was signed by all three chiefs; since Woodman was an old man, Westcott and Mathers probably visited him at his home in Clapham. Thus it would probably have been in the afternoon so that they could be back in town before darkness. Although it was a Saturday, I would imagine that Westcott had professional duties to perform (he was Coroner of North London). and although Jack the Ripper didn't start his campaign until the autumn of that year, it was customary to work until 1 o'clock on Saturday in those days.

Some writers and experts on the subject claim that the charter was signed March 1, 1888, so I have also furnished a map for that day. Again, the time is conjectural, but the nature of the growing Order seems to me unique enough to warrant the position of Uranus in the first house. A meeting at 8 o'clock at night would probably not be far amiss.

Finally, the "inauguration" map is cast for the Vernal Equinox that year, and we know that on this occasion a meeting was held with actual members. This is the first ritual of this kind that we know of, and for lack of better material it can certainly be said that at this occasion all the prerequisites of a normal, working esoteric order were fulfilled. I doubt very much that they assembled at 4 o'clock in the morning; very few fraternities are that dedicated. But whatever the actual time, the purpose of the ritual enacted was to celebrate the equinox, which did take place at that time. Even if the ritual were performed at another time, it symbolized the celestial moment at 4 AM and should probably be regarded in that light. Of course, you might disagree with that, in which case you'll have to somehow establish when the ritual really took place. I wish you all the luck in the world.

Lovecraft's data are from the inside jacket of a pocket book and represent his official date of birth, I suppose. As to the time of day, I confess that I'm all at sea. I don't know enough about him to attempt a correction. With the comparatively few facts at hand, there are several obvious possibilities, but to decide upon one of them would demand access to more research material than I have available at this time.

I have recently come into possession of some more birth times, among other's Galileo's. I'll submit them chronologically without comment so you can work them up any way you like and we'll compare notes afterwards. How's that? I do not vouch for the accuracy of these data.

Galileo Galilei, February 16, 1564, Pisa, Italy. (All dates before 1582 are according to the Julian calendar unless otherwise indicated.) (Source: *The American Book of Charts* by Lois M. Rodden.)

H. P. Blavatsky: July 31, 1831 (Julian), 3:02 AM, Ekaterinoslav, Ukraine.

W. B. Yeats: June 13, 1865, 10:45 AM (local time), Sandymount (near Dublin), Ireland.

Adolf Hitler: April 20, 1889, 6:30 PM, Braunau am Inn, Austria.
Israel Regardie: November 17, 1907, 6:10 AM GMT, London, England.

That's about it.

Heinrich Cornelius Agrippa

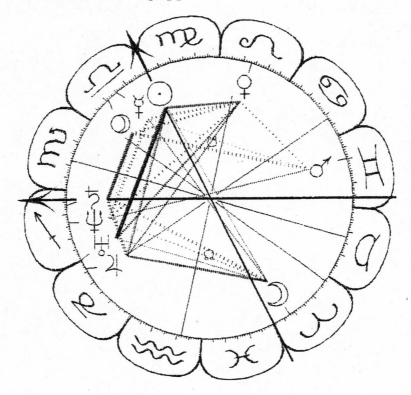

Date of Birth: Sept. 14, 1486	**Planet**	**Degree**	**House**
UT: 11:24:02	Sun	0 ♎ 11	10th
Latitude: 50°53′ N	Moon	7 ♈ 48	4th
Longitude: 7°3′ E	Mercury	14 ♎ 48	10th
	Venus	16 ♌ 49	8th
ASC 4 ♐ 0	Mars	20 ♊ 28	7th
MC 0 ♎ 11	Jupiter	3 ♑ 38	1st
	Saturn	6 ♐ 26	1st
Placidean House Cusps:	Uranus	28 ♐ 55	1st
11—27 ♎ 41	Neptune	13 ♐ 23	1st
12—17 ♏ 45	Pluto	19 ♐ 6	10th
2—8 ♑ 10	Asc. Node	2 ♓ 18	3rd
3—21 ♒ 41	Part of		
	Fortune	11 ♊ 36	7th

N.B. No birth time is known. Disregard houses and axes.

John Dee (1)

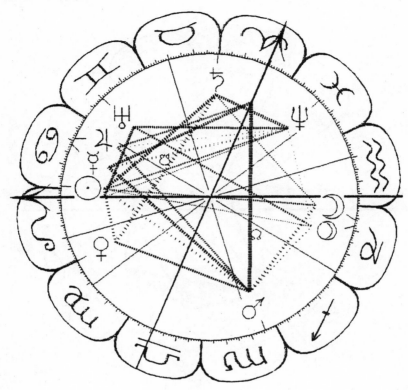

Date of Birth: July 13, 1527	Planet	Degree	House
UT: 04:40:23	Sun	29 ♋ 01	12th
Latitude: 51°31′ N	Moon	24 ♑ 01	6th
Longitude: 0°6′ W	Mercury	11 ♋ 28	12th
	Venus	0 ♍ 09	2nd
ASC 3 ♌ 43	Mars	25 ♏ 35	5th
MC 10 ♈ 40	Jupiter	9 ♋ 03	12th
	Saturn	0 ♉ 33	10th
Placidean House Cusps:	Uranus	19 ♊ 51	11th
11—20 ♉ 13	Neptune	16 ♓ 05$_R$	9th
12—1 ♋ 44	Pluto	21 ♑ 48$_R$	6th
2—20 ♌ 17	Asc. Node	22 ♐ 39	5th
3—11 ♍ 27	Part of		
	Fortune	28 ♑ 43	6th

John Dee (1)

John Dee (2)

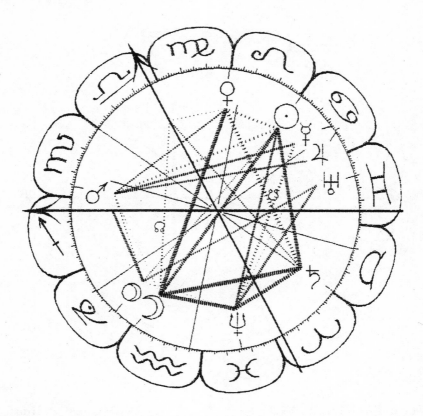

Date of Birth: July 13, 1527
UT: 16:11:00
Latitude: 51°31′ N
Longitude: 0°6′ W

ASC 5 ♐ 31
MC 3 ♎ 11

Placidean House Cusps:
11—0 ♏ 05
12—19 ♏ 38
 2—10 ♑ 23
 3—24 ♒ 53

Planet	Degree	House
Sun	29 ♋ 29	8th
Moon	1 ♒ 20	2nd
Mercury	12 ♋ 14	8th
Venus	0 ♍ 43	9th
Mars	25 ♏ 44	12th
Jupiter	9 ♋ 10	2nd
Saturn	0 ♉ 34	5th
Uranus	19 ♊ 52	7th
Neptune	16 ♓ 04ᴿ	3rd
Pluto	21 ♑ 48ᴿ	2nd
Asc. Node	22 ♐ 38	1st
Part of Fortune	7 ♊ 22	7th

Edward Kelly

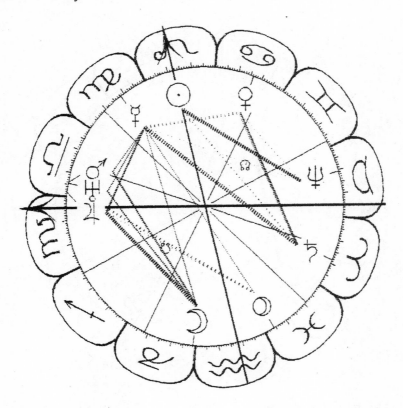

Date of Birth: August 1, 1555
UT: 12:13:23
Latitude: 52°12′ N
Longitude: 2°12′ W

ASC 4 ♏ 55
MC 17 ♌ 45

Placidean House Cusps:
11—21 ♍ 0
12—16 ♎ 0
 2—2 ♐ 46
 3—8 ♑ 16

Planet	Degree	House
Sun	17 ♌ 45	10th
Moon	29 ♑ 12	3rd
Mercury	11 ♍ 40	10th
Venus	13 ♋ 36	9th
Mars	24 ♎ 10	12th
Jupiter	28 ♎ 26	12th
Saturn	11 ♈ 39$_R$	5th
Uranus	24 ♎ 20	12th
Neptune	19 ♉ 16	7th
Pluto	4 ♓ 03$_R$	4th
Asc. Node	20 ♊ 04	8th
Part of Fortune	16 ♈ 22	6th

Francis Bacon

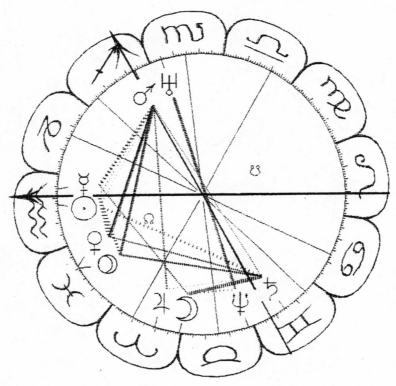

Date of Birth: January 22, 1561	**Planet**	**Degree**	**House**
UT: 07:38:23	Sun	12 ≈ 19	1st
Latitude: 51°31′ N	Moon	29 ♈ 19	3rd
Longitude: 0°6′ W	Mercury	6 ≈ 02ᴿ	12th
	Venus	9 ♓ 14	1st
ASC 9 ≈ 0	Mars	6 ♐ 30	9th
MC 7 ♐ 27	Jupiter	19 ♈ 23	2nd
	Saturn	14 ♊ 10ᴿ	4th
Placidean House Cusps:	Uranus	25 ♏ 05	9th
11—25 ♐ 5	Neptune	27 ♉ 45ᴿ	3rd
12—13 ♑ 10	Pluto	9 ♓ 52	1st
2—9 ♈ 40	Asc. Node	4 ♓ 07	1st
3—15 ♉ 25	Part of		
	Fortune	26 ♈ 0	2nd

Cagliostro

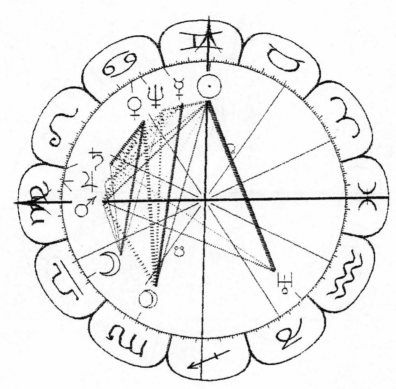

Date of Birth: June 2, 1743
UT: 11:07:58
Latitude: 38°7′ N
Longitude: 13°23′ E

ASC 14 ♍ 27
MC 12 ♊ 20

Placidean House Cusps:
11—15 ♋ 50
12—16 ♌ 56
 2—9 ♎ 38
 3—9 ♏ 19

Planet	Degree	House
Sun	11 ♊ 22	9th
Moon	18 ♎ 00	2nd
Mercury	0 ♋ 34	10th
Venus	14 ♓ 28	10th
Mars	5 ♍ 52	12th
Jupiter	5 ♍ 37	12th
Saturn	0 ♍ 11	12th
Uranus	27 ♑ 15ᴿ	5th
Neptune	10 ♋ 21	10th
Pluto	14 ♏ 37ᴿ	3rd
Asc. Node	17 ♉ 38	9th
Part of Fortune	21 ♑ 05	5th

S. L. MacGregor Mathers

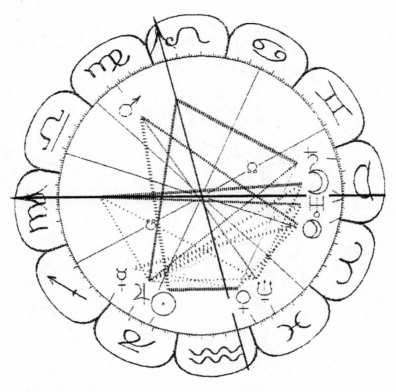

Date of Birth: January 8, 1854
UT: 02:39:45
Latitude: 51°31' N
Longitude: 0°6' W

ASC 10 ♏ 5
MC 24 ♌ 53

Placidean House Cusps:
11—27 ♍ 23
12—21 ♎ 38
2—8 ♐ 46
3—15 ♑ 21

Planet	Degree	House
Sun	17 ♑ 34	3rd
Moon	9 ♉ 33	6th
Mercury	29 ♐ 19	2nd
Venus	3 ♓ 03	4th
Mars	16 ♍ 52	10th
Jupiter	8 ♑ 32	2nd
Saturn	25 ♉ 11ᴿ	7th
Uranus	8 ♉ 37ᴿ	6th
Neptune	11 ♓ 33	4th
Pluto	0 ♉ 46ᴿ	6th
Asc. Node	8 ♊ 28	7th
Part of Fortune	2 ♓ 04	4th

Aleister Crowley

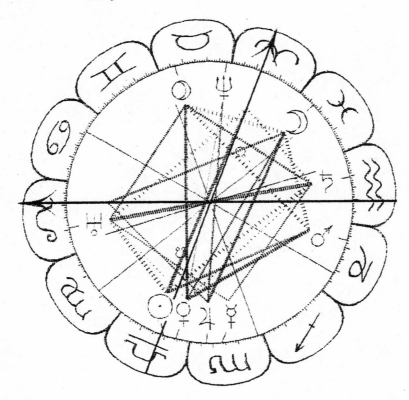

Date of Birth: October 12, 1875	Planet	Degree	House
UT: 23:48:10	Sun	19 ♎ 15	4th
Latitude: 52°18′ N	Moon	22 ♓ 52	9th
Longitude: 1°32′ W	Mercury	13 ♏ 22	4th
	Venus	21 ♎ 26	4th
ASC 9 ♌ 4	Mars	22 ♑ 54	6th
MC 18 ♈ 3	Jupiter	7 ♏ 08	4th
	Saturn	19 ♒ 31$_R$	7th
Placidean House Cusps:	Uranus	19 ♌ 08	1st
11—28 ♉ 8	Neptune	2 ♉ 00$_R$	10th
12—8 ♋ 21	Pluto	23 ♉ 14$_R$	10th
2—25 ♌ 53	Asc. Node	7 ♈ 35	9th
3—17 ♍ 45	Part of Fortune	12 ♑ 41	6th

The Golden Dawn

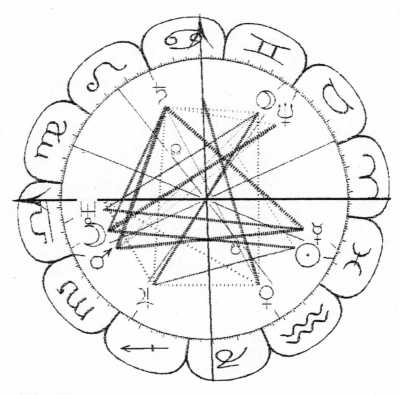

Date of Birth: March 1, 1888
UT: 20:00:00
Latitude: 51°31′ N
Longitude: 0°6′ W

ASC 7 ♎ 1
MC 9 ♋ 8

Placidean House Cusps:
11—14 ♌ 44
12—14 ♍ 0
2—1 ♏ 42
3—2 ♐ 34

Planet	Degree	House
Sun	11 ♓ 43	5th
Moon	27 ♎ 30	1st
Mercury	15 ♓ 35ᴿ	6th
Venus	8 ♓ 13	4th
Mars	0 ♏ 10	1st
Jupiter	5 ♐ 43	3rd
Saturn	0 ♌ 21ᴿ	10th
Uranus	16 ♎ 33ᴿ	1st
Neptune	27 ♉ 26	8th
Pluto	3 ♊ 05	9th
Asc. Node	8 ♌ 02	10th
Part of Fortune	22 ♉ 48	8th

G.D. Pledge

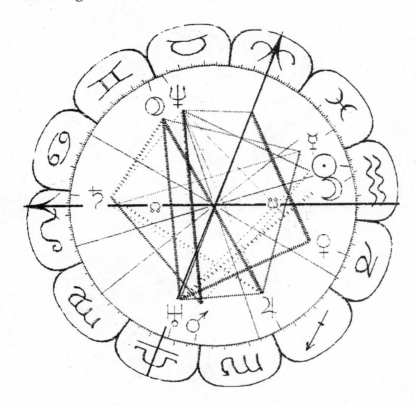

Date of Birth: February 11, 1888
UT: 15:30:00
Latitude: 51°31′ N
Longitude: 0°6′ W

ASC 6 ♌ 21
MC 14 ♈ 42

Placidean House Cusps:
11—24 ♉ 24
12—5 ♋ 1
 2—23 ♌ 11
 3—14 ♍ 51

Planet	Degree	House
Sun	22 ♒ 24	7th
Moon	18 ♒ 16	7th
Mercury	9 ♓ 03	8th
Venus	14 ♑ 55	6th
Mars	27 ♎ 36	4th
Jupiter	4 ♐ 01	5th
Saturn	1 ♌ 34$_R$	12th
Uranus	17 ♎ 03$_R$	4th
Neptune	27 ♉ 17	11th
Pluto	3 ♊ 03$_R$	11th
Asc. Node	9 ♌ 03	1st
Part of Fortune	2 ♌ 13	12th

G.D. Inauguration

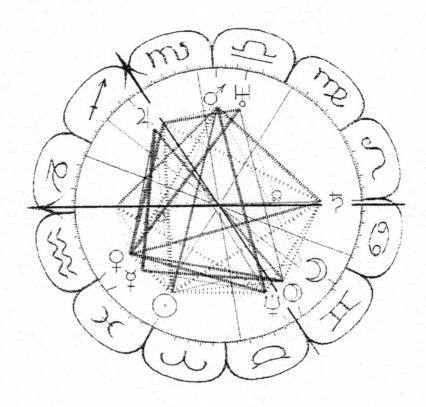

Date of Birth: March 20, 1888	**Planet**	**Degree**	**House**
UT: 04:00:00	Sun	0 ♈ 00	2nd
Latitude: 51°31′ N	Moon	22 ♊ 10	5th
Longitude: 0°6′ W	Mercury	5 ♓ 41	1st
	Venus	0 ♓ 36	1st
ASC 27 ♑ 39	Mars	28 ♎ 38ᴿ	8th
MC 0 ♐ 12	Jupiter	6 ♐ 21	10th
	Saturn	29 ♋ 42ᴿ	7th
Placidean House Cusps:	Uranus	15 ♎ 52ᴿ	8th
11—18 ♐ 19	Neptune	27 ♉ 47	3rd
12—5 ♑ 37	Pluto	3 ♊ 14	4th
2—26 ♓ 36	Asc. Node	7 ♌ 04	7th
3—6 ♉ 15	Part of		
	Fortune	19 ♈ 49	2nd

Aiwass/AL Vel Legis

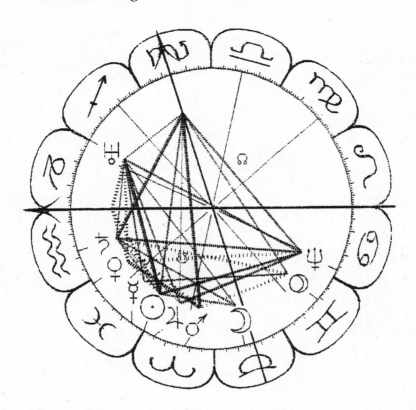

Date of Birth: March 21, 1904	**Planet**	**Degree**	**House**
UT: 01:00:00	Sun	0 ♈ 00	2nd
Latitude: 30°3′ N	Moon	12 ♉ 59	3rd
Longitude: 31°15′ E	Mercury	24 ♓ 19	2nd
	Venus	1 ♓ 42	1st
ASC 29 ♑ 55	Mars	17 ♈ 30	3rd
MC 16 ♏ 50	Jupiter	4 ♈ 47	2nd
	Saturn	17 ♒ 08	1st
Placidean House Cusps:	Uranus	29 ♐ 52	11th
11—11 ♐ 22	Neptune	3 ♋ 09	5th
12—4 ♑ 19	Pluto	18 ♊ 4ᴿ	5th
2—9 ♓ 44	Asc. Node	27 ♍ 36	8th
3—17 ♈ 0	Part of Fortune	16 ♐ 56	11th

H. P. Lovecraft

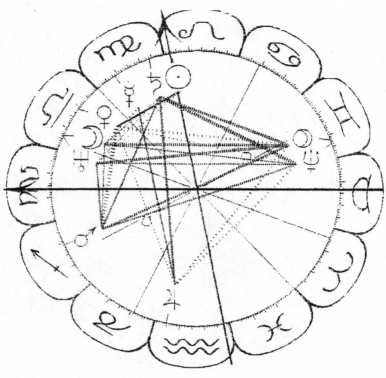

Date of Birth: August 20, 1890	**Planet**	**Degree**	**House**
UT: 16:48:42	Sun	27 ♌ 34	10th
Latitude: 41°48′ N	Moon	23 ♎ 34	11th
Longitude: 71°23′ W	Mercury	21 ♍ 11	10th
	Venus	11 ♎ 02	11th
ASC 16 ♏ 34	Mars	10 ♐ 46	1st
MC 27 ♌ 34	Jupiter	4 ♒ 38ᵣ	3rd
	Saturn	6 ♍ 02	10th
Placidean House Cusps:	Uranus	23 ♎ 42	11th
11—29 ♍ 46	Neptune	6 ♊ 43	7th
12—25 ♎ 39	Pluto	7 ♊ 51	7th
2—16 ♐ 16	Asc. Node	20 ♊ 17	8th
3—21 ♑ 4	Part of		
	Fortune	12 ♑ 34	2nd

Appendix E

The Tarot
or
The 78 Steps to Enlightenment

Anybody who has gone through the preliminaries of occultism knows what the Tarot is—or at least has a misconception of it. It's the first thing the novice encounters after he thinks he has successfully mastered astrology.

The general reader, on the other hand, may be excused for not knowing the abstruse teachings of this, by now, rather overworked subject. But even he is not totally ignorant of it. At least he knows of its existence. Who hasn't seen the displays of this multitude of illustrated pieces of cardboard in occult shop windows, even if merely thinking that they're just another pack of playing cards of obscure, exotic, and Oriental origin and, therefore, not fit for any decent Wednesday-night poker player?

In a way, the general reader is perfectly right. These Tarot cards, as they are called, were originally used for playing and not for magic, i.e., no magical connections can actually be established until the late 18th century. The greasy, beer-stained, and nicotine-reeking Ace of Spades on which he sometimes ill advisedly bets his entire bankroll is most likely part of a corrupted version of this ancient pack of picture cards. The minor part.

The Tarot cards are divided into two parts: the Major Arcana and the Minor Arcana. They are called thus probably because the first contains the minor and the latter the major number of cards. This is a perfect example of occult logic; sort of the Western equivalent to the Zen Buddhist koan—you know: the celebrated one-hand clap and like that.*

Just how old the Tarot cards are is anybody's guess, but the

---

*For the benefit of the total beginner, I should perhaps explain that I'm not referring to any venereal disease connected with masturbation.

playing cards as such can be traced back in the West at least to late 14th-century Italy. Theories to the effect that they originated in the Orient are many and varied. According to some, they were modeled after the game of chess, the major pieces being equivalent to the trumps (Major Arcana) and court cards and the pip cards representing the pawns. From India, the Gypsies are supposed to have introduced them to the Western world.

It has been also suggested that they were the remnants of the secrets of the Egyptian pyramids, the hidden lore of the ancient priesthood, copied from the walls of the holy temples and hidden away when they were destroyed and the ancient empire declined and fell.

Most of these theories can probably be explained as wishful thinking on the part of ever-romantic amateur occultists, but one must not be blind to the fact that the Tarot cards, regardless of age, fulfill the same basic function for the modern magician as the cave paintings of Altamira did to his Neolithic colleague: they serve as points of departure for journeys to the depths of the universe within and without.

The magical properties of the Tarot cannot be historically traced back any farther than the late 1700s when Antoine Court de Gebelin (1719–84) suggested that the compilation of wisdom by the Egyptian priesthood, "The Book of Thoth," was the actual origin of the Tarot. In his book *Le Monde Primitif Analyse et Compare avec le Monde Moderne* (1781), he expounded this theory and even pointed out the correspondence between the Major Arcana and the 22 letters of the Hebrew alphabet.

Le Monde Primitif was a scholarly work, if not scientific—Gebelin wildly denounced anyone suggesting the need of evidence to support theories. However, it would probably have gone unnoticed if it hadn't been for low magic's aid—the prime function of low magic seems to be to thwart science's conspiratorial attempts to suppress inconvenient facts—in the guise of Etteilla (or Alliette, to give him his real name).

In his book *Meniére de se Récréer avec le Jeu de Cartes Nommées Tarots,* he expounded Gebelin's work and enlarged its scope by introducing the reader to a system of fortunetelling by means of the cards.

Other fortunetellers took up this practice and kept the thing going in the usual degenerate way: amusing the nobility—and, after the Revolution, the new nobility—in the boring hours between the often even more boring sessions of French erotic pastimes. "Which partner will I get tonight? Oh. The King of Cups. That must surely be that good-looking Marquis de Bladderskide ... And tomorrow? Le Diable (the Devil) ... Ugh, that's Count Merde de Taureau. What a bore ..." and so on.

Not until the 1850s, with the publication of Eliphas Levi's two major works, *Le Dogme de la Haute Magie* and *Le Rituel de la Haute Magie*, printed together in English as *Transcendental Magic*, did the magical properties of the Tarot extend beyond mere fortunetelling. In these works, Levi claimed that, apart from this trivial pursuit, the cards also symbolized the progress of the soul and spirit, and that the way to command the Universe lies hidden in the proper understanding of this Divine Book of Pictures.

From then on, every dabbler in the occult has gone more or less nuts over the Tarot—and indeed not without reason. They are a unique means with which to explore various archetypal states of consciousness.

The most successful pack of all time is without doubt the so-called Rider-Waite pack. Executed by Pamela Colman Smith after A. E. Waite's designs, they remain even today, in spite of being continually confronted with desperate competition, the Tarot pack *par excellence*. Even though they leave a lot to be desired as far as occult symbolism goes, and they do indeed, they nevertheless have a captivating quality that draws most of the die-hard magi back to them time and time again, somehow laying bare the barren results of their own efforts at self-improvement. At least I've found it so, and I'm not, if I do say so myself, totally without experience.

There are of course minorities so wholeheartedly dedicated to special doctrines that anything other than Countess Asenath's Secret and Arcane Pnakotic Tarot Deck or what have you amounts to no less than betrayal of the Spiritual Truth.

Likewise, a so-called Rosicrucian lodge with which I am familiar, and with some quantitative standing, if not qualitative, has done something similar. Its problem is ignorance of esoteric matters in general. Its leaders have, probably because of popular demand by the members, and contrary to the official teachings of the order (which denies any correspondence between the Qabalah and the Tarot), adopted the B.O.T.A. pack of Paul Foster Case and the Builders of the Adytum.

Why they didn't choose the Rider-Waite deck is beyond my comprehension, but I suppose it's because the leaders believe that choosing an odd pack demonstrates the abstruseness of the order's teachings. After all, the B.O.T.A. pack comes with a ready-made philosophy that can be "borrowed," as almost all the rest of the important order material already has been. Meanwhile, choosing a pack so nearly identical with the Rider-Waite pack will assure members of any "depth" that the order has no iconoclastic pretensions, thus preventing any serious drops in membership fees. Finally, because the pack is black and white, and because this is a very materialistic order,* actually coloring the cards themselves will give the model members a priceless experience of having carried out an act of profound wisdom, or so it is hoped.

Then how does one use the cards? Well, there are basically two ways of doing it: for fortunetelling, and for spiritual attainment/meditation/magic. You name it, they've got it. I'll try to explain how and perhaps kill a few myths while I'm about it, because, as with astrology, it's been bogged down in mystery by people who have a vested pecuniary interest in the subject.

There are two ways of telling fortunes. One is to express yourself noncommittally and in such general terms that it can be interpreted either way; e.g., "You will meet a tall and handsome stranger, if nothing of a contrary nature interferes." Obviously it does in many cases, or you meet the stranger and it's a case of "hello, goodbye." The other way is to be really talented and, together with the cards, act as a medium for the cosmic forces—the genuine article.

Most practitioners claim to be of the last category, either from financial design or megalomania, but the fact is that to become a reader of this variety not only takes years but also probably demands karmic disposition, whereas anybody can buy a pack of cards and set himself up as a swami within half an hour. I daresay most of them do. So a conservative guess would be that approximately 50 people (if that many) out of the multitude of "learned"

---

*Although it calls itself differently. We are in the world as well as of it, and it's not shameful to pray to the Cosmic Forces for money as long as you spend it wisely, etc.

counselors with Gypsy, shamanic, Celtic, or any other exotic back-ground are actually the real McCoy. Fifty in a country like the U.S. The rest of them are get-rich-quick merchants or poor deluded fools who think that the gods have singled them out for the salvation of mankind.

Again, as with astrology, you can use the cards successfully when dealing with your own life. As a Tarot consultant, in addition to the usual layout and show, I have made it my personal habit to ask the querent (if such a word exists) what associations he gets from meditating on the various cards of the spread. This brings up his or her subconscious response. After all, it's the client's problems that matter, so I think it appropriate to let the client come forward while I merely act the part of guide and syn-thesizer. I have found this procedure very satisfactory. After all, who is closer to the client's problems than the client?

About the cards themselves? First of all, there is a great diver-sity of Tarot packs. I don't know exactly how many different ones there are, but my guess is at least a thousand. And what's more, it's my impression that each new sunrise brings another one along with it. So the searcher for profound wisdom is to some degree excused for not wanting to jump in at the deep end.

But forget all the claptrap and just buy a pack of Rider-Waite cards. They are the ideal beginner's cards. They're the most sold, so they're cheap and easy to come by. Most other amateurs and students will be familiar with this particular pack, and in addition to that most books on the Tarot are illustrated with them.

Many people believe that it takes years to master the art of for-tunetelling with the Tarot. Of course they are right if it is the true master you have in mind; i.e., one of the celebrated 50. But if you just want to reach the level of those advertising in the occult mag-azines, then you can achieve that level in about five minutes. In fact, I can state positively that if you are not able to do it immedi-ately after having read this appendix, it can only be due to lack of a Tarot deck.

Of course you won't be an "adept" right away—that is, some-one with such histrionic qualities that you can make people believe you actually know something about the future, or a *real* adept, either—but you will know what it's all about, and that is the begin-ning of all true adeptship.

The cards, drawn at random, serve to focus the mind on some basic situations common to us all and to bring up from the subconscious thought associations relevant to the query at hand.

The easiest way to do it is to sit down at a table and concentrate on a question while shuffling the cards. Ancient tradition—i.e., books from the early 1970s and a few earlier ones—outlines special esoteric ways of shuffling, cutting, and spreading the cards, but these are optional extras.

You can lay out the cards according to various ingenious patterns; e.g., the ancient Celtic Cross spread, which distinguishes itself by being neither ancient nor Celtic. However, it does to some extent resemble a cross, so one out of three isn't too bad. The spread itself generally generates a higher score in actual practice. This particular spread and the meaning of the cards are to be found in the small booklet accompanying every deck of cards sold, so I won't repeat it here.

The basic idea, no matter how vast the amount of incense, candles, robes, wooden boxes, and esoteric platitudes that some practitioners use to conceal the fact, is that you look at the cards in turn until a consistent thought, applicable to the query, presents itself. When it does, you go on to the next card, and so on. When you've gone through the whole spread in this fashion, you try to synthesize the whole set of impressions into a simple intelligible statement relevant to the original question. And that's it!

Of course, with a ready-made spread such as the Celtic Cross, you are operating within a framework already set up by someone else. But don't panic. If it seems too esoteric for you, dispense with the whole thing and make up a layout of your own. For example, you can lay the cards out in three positions only, representing Past, Present, and Future, and apply this framework instead. One of the very simplest of spreads is the one-card query. You concentrate on a question—say, "Should I go out tonight?"—while you are shuffling the cards. Then you spread the pack out over the table and pick out one. Then you apply the meaning of the card in terms of yes or no. Simple?

One wouldn't think that this sort of thing would be capable of occupying people's minds for years on end, but there is actually a bit more to it than that. If for instance the card called the Devil comes up in a spread, it may be interpreted to the effect that you'd better stay at home tonight watching TV. On the other hand, it could also mean that you'll have a hell of a time if you decide to go out. It rather depends on your attitude to life in general.

That's what takes time: learning to interpret the cards in terms of your own and/or your client's archetypes and karmic predilections.

This is also where the multitude of different packs come in. Decks like the Witches' Tarot, the Arthurian Tarot, the Egyptian Tarot, the Golden Dawn Tarot, the Rune Magic Deck, the Enochian Tarot, and those to come: The Butchers', the Bakers', and the Candlestick Makers' Tarot, and perhaps even the Ronald MacDonald Tarot or the Teenage Mutant Ninja Turtles Tarot. And so on and so forth. All of them have companion volumes desperately trying to make it appear that this deck is actually essentially different from the rest.

Although basically the same in function, the different styles, craftsmanship, and pantheons of the various packs appeal to different people. Some of us have Gothic archetypes, some of us are Pagans, and so on. After some initial experience, the beginner will naturally be attracted to some exotic deck or other and try his hand at it for a while. The more different packs he tries, the sooner he will discover that they are all alike in certain respects, and this is where the real occult properties of the Tarot come in.

Now's the time to deal a little more explicitly with the Tarot cards. I've mentioned before that they are divided into two categories: the so-called Major Arcana and Minor Arcana (arcana = "secrets").

The Major Arcana consists of the 22 trumps, as they are sometimes called. The Minor Arcana is the remaining 56 cards, which can again be subdivided into two: the court cards and the pip cards. We'll deal with the latter first.

The pips resemble ordinary playing cards in that they are also numbered from one to ten. They also consist of four suits, but instead of clubs, diamonds, hearts, and spades, they symbolize the four Elements of traditional natural philosophy: Air, Fire, Water, and Earth. Experts have written several papers to the effect that the one set of cards is derived from the other. Most of these "experts" agree that the Tarot came first and that it degenerated into ordinary playing cards, losing the trumps and one of the court cards in the process. But I have also heard theories propounding the point of view that it was the other way around: that they started out as playing cards such as we know them and then grew into the Tarot by inspired development. Frankly, I don't see why not, but as it doesn't add anything to the efficacy of the cards, I can afford to keep an open mind on the subject. In short, I don't give a damn one way or the other.

The court cards of the Tarot consist of king, queen, knight, and page, or, in feminist-inspired decks, a young girl with different titles according to the deck: Maiden, Shepherdess, Lady-in-waiting, and so on. This card later disappeared from the ordinary poker deck, perhaps due to the battle of the sexes. Who knows? I'm sure that the day is just around the corner when we will see an ordinary deck of poker cards with a Jill instead of a Jack.

Another explanation for having the fourth court card represent a female, such as a Princess, is that it is said to represent the fourth consonant of the Tetragrammaton and thus the bride of the Son (the third consonant) in the *Zohar*. However, this is probably far too abstruse for our purposes here.

In Tarot the court cards represent the four elements yet again, so a Knight may stand for Water, or Fire, according to the system used.

The allocation of cards to the elements, the Zodiac, and other occult systems is purely arbitrary. Everybody is totally free to make up his own set of correspondences. In fact, it can be argued that no orthodox system exists at all, since any of the modern "ancient" systems you encounter is different in some detail or another from any of its competitors. The criterion for being classified as a "system" is having at least the majority of correspondences in common with some other "system."

For the benefit of the reader, I'll elaborate a bit on astral travel and the Tree of Life of the Qabalah. This will give you an idea of how occultism works, along with its strengths and limitations, and hopefully remove your awe and respect for so-called authorities on these subjects, the present writer included. Verily, there are no authorities or experts on the practical side.

The only system that anyone can claim to be an expert about is his own personal system and, sad to say, they do. Some of these inflated egos do have the power to convince people without critical faculties that they (the egos) possess the One True Key to the Mysteries.

Don't believe them. It's true that a group of people sometimes can make a system work, but that's because they are in agreement about the symbolism, not because some leader tells the rest what to believe. Obviously, such a group can't be very big, human nature being taken into consideration. If you think you know such a group with more than about 12–13 members, or meet somebody who claims he does, you can safely discard it as nonsense. Almost any formal organization with a membership roll of more than a dozen or so is, at best, a money-grabbing big business. At worst, some charismatic psychopath is indulging his illusions of grandeur, exerting a terribly unwholesome influence on mentally crippled members of the Silent Majority. As if it weren't bad enough that these people are allowed to vote.

On reflection, I qualify and amend the above statement: I abstain from determining which of the two evils is actually "best" or "worst." Who can really tell?

Astral travel, or "Scrying in the Spirit Vision" as it is sometimes archaically called, is a very controversial subject. It's gullible lunacy or hypersensitivity to cosmic currents, depending on your point of view. The theory is that we are born with the faculty of being able to penetrate the borders of our universe, allowing us access to other dimensions, the so-called Astral World. Communion with the gods or neurotic self-indulgence? Opinion is divided, but again: don't bother to participate in the debate. It doesn't really matter. Try it! And if you can use it, do so. Then you call it whatever you like.

And if you can't use it, then don't, and you can still call it what you like. It always reminds me of the anecdote about the famous nuclear physicist Niels Bohr, who, when challenged by a reporter about a horseshoe over the door to his cottage, replied, "Oh, no, of course I don't believe in such superstitious nonsense, but I've been told that it works whether you believe in it or not."

When performing astral travel, you lie down on a bed or couch and relax. Then you imagine that you are in some other time and place: India in the 12th century, China in the 16th, Oceania in the 21st, or just about anywhere else than where you happen to be at the moment. After some practice at this, you find yourself, if not actually in one of these places, then at least somewhere from which you can actually influence and communicate with them. To guide you on these travels, you have certain aids, visual as well as through the other senses. Occult practices are nothing but practices for the purpose of controlling the powers of the Astral World, and any occult system can be regarded as a travel guide with astral highway numbers.

Of course it takes some practice before you can actually use the correspondences, just as it is too late for you to look up a traffic sign in the manual when it's 50 yards away and you're doing 100 mph. You must be well versed in theoretical occultism before you actually try it on. All systems fulfill the same basic function; which one to choose is a matter of individual taste. The Tarot is related to the Tree of Life.

To begin with the Qabalah then. Here we encounter our very first difficulty: How to spell it? Consider 10 different ways, the most common being Qabalah, Qabbala, Quabballa, Cabala, Kabala, Kabbala, QBL, etc. It's also up for grabs as to whether to capitalize it or not. If the novice feels like giving up occultism after this dire beginning, I don't blame him. How can he ever hope to understand anything when the very first concept offers such utter confusion?

Don't worry! The important things will sink in in spite of these attempts to corrupt the issue. Just read a few treatises on the subject and don't worry about not understanding a lot of things. The things you do remember after the ordeal are the salient points. Forget the rest until later or make it up yourself.

In case you're wondering which is the right way to spell "Qabalah," the answer is all or none, which amounts to the same thing. To avoid or increase confusion as the case may be, make up your own way of spelling it: kaplah, Qaabalaah—or if you're an anarchist, why not "food shortage"?

To demonstrate the futility of trying to master any subject 100 percent, and the reason why you had better forget anything that doesn't make sense to you, I can inform you that you don't need to know anything you wouldn't know without a working knowledge of the Hebrew language.

The variety of spellings is due to the sad incompatibility of the Latin and Hebrew alphabets, the latter of which seldom uses vowels. Therefore, any rendering into English will have to be phonetic; i.e., a feeble attempt to spell the sound of the spoken word—which, of course, differs with every listener. Therefore: forget it!

The Tree of Life consists of ten spheres called sephiroth (sing. sephirah). Forget what it means; just remember that there are ten of them. They have different names, of course, and, indeed, each name is spelled in as many different ways as "Qabalah," and for the same reason. Any primer on the subject will explain what the names mean and what they signify.

Basically the uppermost one (no. 1) can be regarded as Heaven, and the nethermost (no. 10) as Earth. All the rest are in between, including everything beyond the scope of poor Horatio's philosophy.

To each of these sephiroth is allocated a set of Minor Arcana, the pip cards corresponding to the number of the sephirah. Which card to use in what situation depends on which suit of cards rules the Tree in question. The suits of the Tarot are: Swords, Wands/Rods/Staves, Cups/Chalices, and Pentacles/Discs/Coins.

There is a major general agreement as to which element belongs to what suit. Most people tend to regard Swords as Air, Wands as Fire, Cups as Water, and Pentacles as Earth but, as with any other occult phenomenon, there is no absolute consensus in the matter. Francis King and Stephen Skinner have suggested the dagger for Fire and the wand for Air. The dagger and the sword are often interchanged in magical work involving the Tarot because it has no suit representing the dagger. This procedure is obvious, although it should be pointed out that the dagger and the sword are by no means identical—according to tradition, that is. They become identical the moment you say they do.

I'm not suggesting that you should discard all traditional teachings. The reason that tradition has survived to become tradition is obviously because it works. What I'm saying is: Don't worry about details that have become bones of contention among various "schools." They are not worth arguing about. By all means, read what they have to say for themselves—we can all do with a good laugh now and again—but think about it and meditate on it and then decide for yourself.

So, in a matter concerning, for instance, the concept of Revenge, you are referred to the Five of Wands and the fifth sephirah: Geburah, meaning strength or severity.

"White" magicians will protest against the use of the word "revenge," but remember that one man's revenge is another man's retribution—Buddhists excepted, of course. But such matters needn't be thought of in these terms at all. Feel free to consider them merely as karmic correctional measures.

However, if we stay in the language of the simple-minded and the world of Harry Callahan, we will decide on the Five of Wands. That the fifth sephirah, Geburah, is astrologically associated with the planet Mars will be sufficient explanation for most people. The Suit of Wands is indicated because we are going to do it *now* and not later. The Five of Cups would suggest slow poison instead.

Now you ask, "What's the point of it all?" Does all this have for its purpose the mere act, admittedly sophisticated, of presenting the victim with the Five of Wands as a kind of calling card in the style of Jack the Ripper? Not at all. The purpose of finding the relevant card is to meditate on the problem or to perform a ritual to achieve the desired end, either by occult forces or by mustering up enough courage and determination to carry it through. So in essence the card is an incentive to keep your nose to the ground, so to speak.

Needless to say, nobody should go out and kill someone just like that, and most people don't, but it would be less than the truth to say that these things don't happen. One has only to think of the Manson case. But at the same time I would like to dissolve the myth that "dabbling" in magic is evil and Satanic and leads young people to drug abuse and crime and should therefore be discouraged. This is putting the cart before the horse. It is true that some drug-addicted criminals use rituals in the process of murdering people, but that's hardly any reason to have misgivings about magic. Lots of religious maniacs and fanatics commit atrocious murders without anybody suggesting the abolition of organized religion. I have yet to hear the argument that, because a minority of cancer patients are criminals, doctors shouldn't try to cure people suffering from this disease because it puts the criminals back on the streets.

There are a number of organizations that exist for the purpose of suppressing various things of which their members disapprove. Their members should be regarded as mere hysterical cranks. They all use the same argument: i.e., that rock music (50 years ago it was jazz), short skirts, coeducation, Darwinism, sex before marriage, comic books, civil rights, pepperoni-salami sandwiches with garlic, or whatever lead to drug abuse, suicide, and/or murder. The members of these organizations are mostly suburban middle-class housewives with nothing to do all day and with whom the specter of menopausal terror is catching up. They desperately need to do something "important" in order to balance the Book of Life before it's too late. The traditional occupation for spinsters of the leisured classes, "the Worthy Cause," is in fact rather pathetic, but it's a sure winner on daytime television talk shows.

Of course, matters are seldom as simple as the semi-fascistic Hollywood cop makes them. Therefore you can't altogether trust the Minor Arcana and the sephiroth. Life is a balance of opposing forces, Yin and Yang and so on. And that's what the Major Arcana (the Trumps) and the Paths are all about.

Nothing in life is strictly black or white. Even the Yin and Yang symbol has each half containing the seed of its opposite, even when at its apex. That's how life is, and the Qabalah would be worthless indeed had it not allowed for this. It has. The sephiroth 3–5–8 and 2–4–7 are located opposite each other on the Tree of Life because they represent opposing forces. All ten sephiroth are connected, directly or indirectly, by means of 22 so-called Paths, to each of which a Trump is allocated. These paths are connecting links between the various sephiroth and symbolize actions, thoughts, and other phenomena related to the senses.

The occultist uses the Major Arcana as an aid to achieve perfect mental and spiritual balance whenever he detects traits in his character that he finds undesirable. By meditating and concentrating on a certain card, he can bring forth subconscious elements and eliminate them, much the same as with psychoanalysis. But of course the cards also help to create a special atmosphere. By means of a symbol, they help the magician focus his attention on mental and spiritual matters too elusive to be held in the mind for even the briefest of periods because of their ephemeral nature.

This is very important, because you can't produce magic without a force, and you can't have force without a form. Magic is much like electricity and water. It needs a medium to work through. Water is just water, but inside a suitable container it becomes the mattress in a waterbed.

When the magician, guided by any Tarot card (and of course by any other kind of visual, audible, or other aid relating to the senses: incense, perfumes, etc.), is in a state of total concentration, his mental picture is built up on the Astral Plane. There an astral force fills it, "creating havoc in Heaven," as the saying goes. The Astral Plane is a world or dimension reflecting the one we live in, a sort of shadow universe, but with its own laws different from those we know. The idea is that any changes achieved on the Astral Level will in due course manifest here. At least that's the story.

"How can anybody believe such crap? It's even worse than Russell and Wittgenstein." But the truth is that it's very simple and straightforward and neatly accounts for the facts. "Too simple!" some will say, but what's the point of making it more complicated than it has to be? Dressing up a plain subject in esoteric terminology, as is customary in occultism, medicine, psychology, and politics, serves only one purpose; namely to take it upon oneself to make decisions on other people's behalf, after persuading them that the issue at hand is much too complicated for them to make up their own minds about. Strangely enough, it seems as if the more complicated, inexplicable, and unlikely you make something out to be, the more likely you are to be believed by the hypercritical segment of modern humanity. This is indeed one of the great paradoxes in life.

But all right, you don't have to believe in this Astral Level stuff. It doesn't matter if you do. Like Niels Bohr's horseshoe, it works anyway. Besides, even if it isn't true, as Brodie-Innes said: "It works as if it were so." So for all practical purposes it *is* so. Of course, if the reader can find any other explanation, he's welcome to it; magic is very broadminded.

Just buy a pack and play with it, and you will have a lot of fun and excitement. You may even find a whole new use for the Tarot. I have. I use it by drawing random cards, and the sequence thus obtained serves as a plot outline when I write fiction. It's as good as any "Plots Unlimited" kind of computer aid for the budding author.

Like I say, you may come up with something entirely new yourself. Your imagination is the only limitation. The Tarot is exactly what anyone wants it to be.

STAY IN TOUCH

On the following pages you will find listed, with their current prices, some of the books now available on related subjects. Your book dealer stocks most of these and will stock new titles in the Llewellyn series as they become available. We urge your patronage.

To obtain our full catalog, to keep informed about new titles as they are released and to benefit from informative articles and helpful news, you are invited to write for our bi-monthly news magazine/catalog, *Llewellyn's New Worlds of Mind and Spirit*. A sample copy is free, and it will continue coming to you at no cost as long as you are an active mail customer. Or you may subscribe for just $10.00 in U.S.A. and Canada ($20.00 overseas, first class mail). Many bookstores also have *New Worlds* available to their customers. Ask for it.

Stay in touch! In *New Worlds'* pages you will find news and features about new books, tapes and services, announcements of meetings and seminars, articles helpful to our readers, news of authors, products and services, special money-making opportunities, and much more.

Llewellyn's New Worlds of Mind and Spirit
P.O. Box 64383-474, St. Paul, MN 55164-0383, U.S.A.
* * *

TO ORDER BOOKS AND TAPES

If your book dealer does not have the books described on the following pages readily available, you may order them direct from the publisher by sending full price in U.S. funds, plus $3.00 for postage and handling for orders *under* $10.00; $4.00 for orders *over* $10.00. There are no postage and handling charges for orders over $50.00. Postage and handling rates are subject to change. UPS Delivery: We ship UPS whenever possible. Delivery guaranteed. Provide your street address as UPS does not deliver to P.O. Boxes. UPS to Canada requires a $50.00 minimum order. Allow 4-6 weeks for delivery. Orders outside the U.S.A. and Canada: Airmail—add retail price of book; add $5.00 for each non-book item (tapes, etc.); add $1.00 per item for surface mail.

FOR GROUP STUDY AND PURCHASE

Because there is a great deal of interest in group discussion and study of the subject matter of this book, we feel that we should encourage the adoption and use of this particular book by such groups by offering a special quantity price to group leaders or agents.

Our Special Quantity Price for a minimum order of five copies of *Pilgrims of the Night* is $36.00 cash-with-order. This price includes postage and handling within the United States. Minnesota residents must add 6.5% sales tax. For additional quantities, please order in multiples of five. For Canadian and foreign orders, add postage and handling charges as above. Credit card (VISA, MasterCard, American Express) orders are accepted. Charge card orders only ($15.00 minimum order) may be phoned in free within the U.S.A. or Canada by dialing 1-800-THE-MOON. For customer service, call 1-612-291-1970. Mail orders to:

LLEWELLYN PUBLICATIONS
P.O. Box 64383-474, St. Paul, MN 55164-0383, U.S.A.

Prices subject to change without notice.

THE GOLDEN DAWN
The Original Account of the Teachings, Rites & Ceremonies of the Hermetic Order
As revealed by Israel Regardie

Complete in one volume with further revision, expansion, and additional notes by Regardie, Cris Monnastre, and others. Expanded with an index of more than 100 pages!

Originally published in four bulky volumes of some 1,200 pages, this 6th Revised and Enlarged Edition has been entirely reset in modern, less space-consuming type, in half the pages (while retaining the original pagination in marginal notation for reference) for greater ease and use.

Corrections of typographical errors perpetuated in the original and subsequent editions have been made, with further revision and additional text and notes by noted scholars and by actual practitioners of the Golden Dawn system of Magick, with an Introduction by the only student ever accepted for personal training by Regardie.

Also included are Initiation Ceremonies, important rituals for consecration and invocation, methods of meditation and magical working based on the Enochian Tablets, studies in the Tarot, and the system of Qabalistic Correspondences that unite the World's religions and magical traditions into a comprehensive and practical whole.

This volume is designed as a study and practice curriculum suited to both group and private practice. Meditation upon, and following with the Active Imagination, the Initiation Ceremonies are fully experiential without need of participation in group or lodge. A very complete reference encyclopedia of Western Magick.

0-87542-663-8, 840 pgs., 6 x 9, illus., softcover   **$19.95**

CRAFTING THE ART OF MAGIC, BOOK I
A History of Modern Witchcraft, 1939-1964
by Aidan A. Kelly

This is a history of the development of modern Witchcraft as a religion during the later lifetime of Gerald Gardner, the religion's most important founding figure, from 1939 to his death in 1964.

Modern Witchcraft is a vital religion in the process of being created by its members. Since the publication of Gardner's *Witchcraft Today* in 1954, Gardnerian Witchcraft has blossomed, carried by Gardnerian initiates and admirers throughout the Western world.

No other book before now has relied solely on the historical evidence to reconstruct the history of modern Witchcraft. *Crafting the Art of Magic* doesn't rely on unverifiable (and often simply false) statements from any individuals, but on the application of standard scholarly techniques of the available documentary evidence, which consists largely of drafts of materials for the Gardnerian *Book of Shadows* written by Gardner and/or Doreen Valiente.

0-87542-370-1, 224 pgs., 5-1/4 x 8, softcover   **$10.95**

THE ENOCHIAN WORKBOOK
The Enochian Magickal System Presented in 43 Easy Lessons
by Gerald J. and Betty Schueler

Enochian Magic is an extremely powerful and complex path to spiritual enlightenment. Here, at last, is the first book on the subject written specifically for the beginning student. Ideally suited for those who have tried other books on Enochia and found them to be too difficult, *The Enochian Workbook* presents the basic teachings of Enochian Magic in a clear, easy-to-use workbook.

The authors have employed the latest techniques in educational psychology to help students master the information in this book. The book is comprised of 11 sections, containing a total of 43 lessons, with test questions following each section so students can gauge their progress. You will learn how to conduct selected rituals, skry using a crystal, and use the Enochian Tarot as a focus for productive meditation. Also explore Enochian Chess, Enochian Physics (the laws and models behind how the magic works), and examine the dangers associated with Enochian Magic. Readers who complete the book will be ready to tackle the more complex concepts contained in the other books in the series.

One of the reasons why Enochian Magic is so hard to understand is that it has a special, complex vocabulary. To help beginning students, Enochian terms are explained in simple, everyday words, wherever possible.
0-87542-719-7, 360 pgs., 7 x 10, illus.,
16 color plates, softcover   **$14.95**

THE THREE BOOKS OF OCCULT PHILOSOPHY
Completely Annotated, with Modern Commentary—The Foundation Book of Western Occultism
by Henry Cornelius Agrippa, edited and annotated by Donald Tyson

Agrippa's *Three Books of Occult Philosophy* is the single most important text in the history of Western occultism. Occultists have drawn upon it for five centuries, although they rarely give it credit. First published in Latin in 1531 and translated into English in 1651, it has never been reprinted in its entirety since. Photocopies are hard to find and very expensive. Now, for the first time in 500 years, *Three Books of Occult Philosophy* will be presented as Agrippa intended. There were many errors in the original translation, but occult author Donald Tyson has made the corrections and has clarified the more obscure material with copious notes.

This is a necessary reference tool not only for all magicians, but also for scholars of the Renaissance, Neoplatonism, the Western Kabbalah, the history of ideas and sciences and the occult tradition. It is as practical today as it was 500 years ago.
0-87542-832-0, 1,080 pgs., 7 x 10, softcover   **$29.95**

LIGHT IN EXTENSION
Greek Magic from Homer to Modern Times
by David Godwin
Greek magic is the foundation of almost every form of ceremonial magic being practiced today. Elements of Greek philosophy summarize the bulk of modern esoteric thought and occult teachings. Even the cabala contains many features that appear to be Greek in origin. The systems formulated by the direct progenitors of Western culture speak to the modern soul of the Western world.

This book explains in plain, informal language the grand sweep of Greek magic and Greek philosophical and religious concepts from the archaic period of Homer's *Iliad* right down to the present. It begins with the magic and mythology of the days of classical Athens and its antecedent cultures, gives detailed considerations of Gnosticism, early Christianity and Neoplatonism—all phenomena with a Greek foundation—explains the manifestations of Greek thought in the Renaissance, and explores modern times with the Greek elements of the magic of the Golden Dawn, Aleister Crowley and others.

For the practicing magician, rituals are given that incorporate elements from each historical period that is discussed. These ceremonies may be easily adapted for Pagan or Wiccan practice or otherwise altered to suit the individual operator.

From the plains of Troy to the streets of Los Angeles, Greek magic is alive and well. No one who has any interest in magic, occultism, or hermetic thought and who is also a citizen of Western civilization can afford to ignore this heritage.
0-87542-285-3, 272 pgs., 6 x 9, illus., softcover   **$12.95**

MAGIC AND THE WESTERN MIND
Ancient Knowledge and the Transformation of Consciousness
by Gareth Knight
Magic and the Western Mind explains why intelligent and responsible people are turning to magic and the occult as a radical and important way to find meaning in modern life, as well as a means of survival for themselves and the planet.

First published in 1978 as *A History of White Magic*, this book illustrates, in a wide historical survey, how the higher imagination has been used to aid the evolution of consciousness—from the ancient mystery religions, through alchemy, Renaissance magic, the Rosicrucian Manifestoes, Freemasonry, 19th-century magic fraternities, up to psychoanalysis and the current occult revival. Plus it offers some surprising insights into the little-known interests of famous people. The Western mind developed magic originally as one of the noblest of arts and sciences. Now, with the help of this book, anyone can defend a belief in magic in convincing terms.
0-87542-374-4, 336 pgs., 6 x 9, illus., softcover   **$12.95**

PSYCHOLOGY, ASTROLOGY AND WESTERN MAGIC
Image and Myth in Self-Discovery
by Luis Alvarado

Self-development, self-discovery and self-awareness can all be found through the use of "God-images" or archetypes—for it is the stories, or myths, found in the God-images that shape our lives.

Images, the primary data of soul, allow us to know archetypal structures. Archetypes—pre-existent patterns of emotions, behaviors, perceptions, and responses common to all of humanity—are the primary forms that govern the psyche.

Psychology, Astrology and Western Magic is the first scholarly examination of the God-images as they apply to mythology, astrology, archetypal psychology, and Western magic. It explores their psychological implications as well as historical and theoretical applications. It discusses how God-images can also teach us about the non-human "others" who appear in our dreams, fantasies, creative works, and our unique obsessions.

This is a practical and pragmatic book that the reader can use for gaining self-knowledge or for the counseling of others. It explores a psychology based on soul and presents a therapeutic approach based on image. Above all, it is a how-to book that challenges the reader through word, image and a wealth of case materials.

0-87542-006-0, 240 pgs., 6 x 9, illus., softcover $12.95

RITUAL MAGIC
What It Is & How To Do It
by Donald Tyson

For thousands of years men and women have practiced it despite the severe repression of sovereigns and priests. Now, *Ritual Magic* takes you into the heart of that entrancing, astonishing and at times mystifying secret garden of *magic*.

What is this ancient power? Where does it come from? How does it work? Is it mere myth and delusion, or can it truly move mountains and make the dead speak. . . bring rains from a clear sky and calm the seas. . . turn the outcome of great battles and call down the Moon from Heaven? Which part of the claims made for magic are true in the most literal sense, and which are poetic exaggerations that must be interpreted symbolically? How can magic be used to improve *your* life?

This book answers these and many other questions in a clear and direct manner. Its purpose is to separate the wheat from the chaff and make sense of the non-sense. It explains what the occult revival is all about, reveals the foundations of practical ritual magic, showing how modern occultism grew from a single root into a number of clearly defined esoteric schools and pagan sects.

0-87542-835-5, 288 pgs., 6 x 9, illus., index, softcover $12.95

MAGICIAN'S COMPANION
A Practical and Encyclopedic Guide to Magical and Religious Symbolism
by Bill Whitcomb

The Magician's Companion is a "desk reference" overflowing with a wide range of occult and esoteric materials absolutely indispensable to anyone engaged in the magickal arts!

The magical knowledge of our ancestors comprises an intricate and elegant technology of the mind and imagination. This book attempts to make the ancient systems accessible, understandable and useful to modern magicians by categorizing and cross-referencing the major magical symbol-systems (i.e., world views on inner and outer levels). Students of religion, mysticism, mythology, symbolic art, literature, and even cryptography will find this work of value.

This comprehensive book discusses and compares over 35 magical models (e.g., the Trinities, the Taoist Psychic Centers, Enochian magic, the qabala, the Worlds of the Hopi Indians). Also included are discussions of the theory and practice of magic and ritual; sections on alchemy, magical alphabets, talismans, sigils, magical herbs and plants; suggested programs of study; an extensive glossary and bibliography; and much more.
0-87542-868-1, 522 pgs., 7 x 10, illus., softcover $19.95

GODWIN'S CABALISTIC ENCYCLOPEDIA
A Complete Guide to Cabalistic Magick
by David Godwin

This is the most complete correlation of Hebrew and English ideas ever offered. It is a dictionary of Cabalism arranged, with definitions, alphabetically in Hebrew and numerically. With this book, the practicing Cabalist or student no longer needs access to a large number of books on mysticism, magic and the occult in order to trace down the basic meanings, Hebrew spellings, and enumerations of the hundreds of terms, words, and names that are included in this book.

This book includes: all of the two-letter root words found in Biblical Hebrew, the many names of God, the Planets, the Astrological Signs, Numerous Angels, the Shem ha-Mephorash, the Spirits of the *Goetia*, the correspondences of the 32 Paths, a comparison of the Tarot and the Cabala, a guide to Hebrew Pronunciation, and a complete edition of Aleister Crowley's valuable book *Sepher Sephiroth*.

Here is a book that is a must for the shelf of all Magicians, Cabalists, Astrologers, Tarot students, Thelemites, and those with any interest at all in the spiritual aspects of our universe.
0-87542-292-6, 528 pgs., 6 x 9, softcover $15.00